Metamorphoses

CHARLES TOMLINSON was born in Stoke-on-Trent in 1927. He studied at Cambridge with Donald Davie and taught at the University of Bristol from 1957 until his retirement. He has published many collections, including his *Selected Poems*, available from Carcanet, and volumes of criticism and translation. He also edited the *Oxford Book of Verse in English Translation* (1980).

CHARLES TOMLINSON

Metamorphoses

Poetry and Translation

CARCANET

This collection first published in Great Britain in 2003 by
Carcanet Press Limited
Alliance House
Cross Street
Manchester M2 7AQ

A CIP catalogue record for this book
is available from the British Library.

ISBN 1 85754 586 9
The publisher acknowledges financial assistance
from the Arts Council of England.

Set in Monotype Garamond by XL Publishing Services, Tiverton
Printed and bound in England by SRP Ltd, Exeter

To Brenda

Acknowledgements

Acknowledgements are due to publishers and editors of journals who have previously printed some of the material in this book: *Arion*, Cambridge University Press, *The Independent*, *The New Criterion*, North Eastern University Press (Boston), Oxford University Press, *Times Literary Supplement*, *Translation and Literature*.

Contents

Foreword

The themes of this book arose from my experience as a practising poet and translator from Russian, Spanish, French and Italian. As editor of *The Oxford Book of Verse in English Translation*, I also became increasingly conscious of the way the translation of foreign poetries changes the history of our own, extending its range and making available a new kind of self-awareness on the part of the poet-translator, a theme on which I was to write a number of essays that appear in the present volume.

When in 1982 I was invited to give the Clark Lectures in the University of Cambridge, I entitled the series *Poetry and Metamorphosis*, and turned to the way certain fables of metamorphosis had laid hold on the imagination of the poet. Ovid, of course, was the prime example here. Eliot in *The Waste Land* and Pound in his *Cantos* supplied the other two major figures in my exploration. This circled back in the final lecture to translation itself and the way its metamorphic presence enriches literary possibilities. This book contains a reprint of *Poetry and Metamorphosis* which has been out of circulation for some years.

The Presence of Translation:
A View of English Poetry

I propose to discuss some of the preferences displayed in editing *The Oxford Book of Verse in English Translation*, and also to note regretfully one or two poems that got away and that I would have liked to include. My initial choice brought home to me how centrally the art of translation has mattered in the history of English poetry, though its history has never been fully written from that point of view. The presence of translation changes, or should change, our vision of the whole. Its presence in the *oeuvre* of a number of major poets should change our all-over view of *them* and of the riches they have to offer to present and future heirs. This is a long story, and I shall confine myself to a handful of protagonists in it, chiefly between the early sixteenth and mid-eighteenth centuries. My argument will have to contain, besides an account of the translators, *some* account – however foreshortened and simplified – of English poetry also.

A twentieth-century Hungarian poet, when asked to name the most beautiful Hungarian poem, replied, 'Shelley's "Ode to the West Wind" in the translation of Árpád Tóth.' I have sometimes dreamed of being asked 'What is the *greatest* English poem of the eighteenth century?' and of replying, 'Homer's *Iliad* in the translation of Alexander Pope.' And this comes close to what Pope's contemporaries thought: in the eighteenth-century Houbracken print of Pope's portrait, in a little scene inset on a stone structure halfway between an altar and a sarcophagus, it is Homer who leads Pope up to Apollo and the Muses to receive his poet's laurels.

Dr Johnson in his life of the poet refers to Pope's *Iliad* as 'that poetical wonder …, a performance which no age or nation can pretend to equal', and he looks at the prospect of poetry after its publication in the light of what Pope had achieved and made available to other poets: 'His version', writes Johnson, 'may be said to have tuned the English tongue, for since its appearance no writer, however deficient in other powers, has wanted melody'. In Johnson's nutshell here, in this '[tuning] of the English tongue', there is a short history of eighteenth-century poetry through Gray, Collins, Smart, Goldsmith, Johnson himself, even early Wordsworth, not to mention the beautiful hymns of Wesley.

Our received view of English poetry is characterised by the absence of any prolonged mention of translation and its effects. We do not immediately associate it with Apollo, though there are groups of specialists, like the Boston University Translation Seminar, who know that this must be wrong. It is usual, for example, to ignore the fact that young Mr Pope matured his comic vision through his dealings with the deviousness of Homer's gods and goddesses, and his sense of potential catastrophe (I am thinking of the climax of *Dunciad*, book 4) by his contemplation of the fall of Troy. A poet who, from his twentieth to his thirty-eighth year, has spent a sizeable portion of his life in the company of Homer, going on from the *Iliad* to complete the *Odyssey* with the help of assistants, can hardly have been unaffected by the experience. It might, in addition to the comic and the catastrophic, have also impressed upon him a sense of human grandeur in the presence of which that satire he is justly famous for must of necessity rise above the merely destructive. Pope without his Homer is – well, not Hamlet without the prince – but by ignoring the presence of Pope's major translation in the rest of his work and in the history of English poetry, we write defective history and partial criticism. And the same could be said of the accounts we have of other poets and their translations. Who, for example, is the first important American poet? Anne Bradstreet seems to have been engineered into that position. But why not George Sandys with his translation of Ovid's *Metamorphoses*, completed while he was treasurer of the Virginia Company between 1621 and 1626? Why do we demote our translations, while the Hungarians (say) are so grateful for theirs?

The simple answer, I suppose, is the sheer variety, the long-standing copiousness and continuity of English poetry – now English-and-American poetry. If one were a Russian, the history of one's poetry begins effectively in the eighteenth century. In the case of German – a literature which had dwindled into provinciality after the Middle Ages – we find Goethe, virtually single-handed, restoring its poetry to the centre of the European scene at the end of the eighteenth century. With no Elizabethan Renaissance behind him, no *grand siècle*, and no Augustan Age, he is technically in a situation far different from that of the English or French poets of his own era or the previous era. In the late 1780s, he confides to the notebook which became his *Italian Journey*: 'The main reason why, for several years, I have preferred to write prose is that our prosody is in a state of great uncertainty ... What has been lacking is any prosodic principle'. Dryden, a hundred years before, could hardly have expressed himself thus, as he reached back to free Chaucer, via translation, from the prosodic uncertainty *he* imagined Chaucer suffered. Though Dryden, of course, was not just correcting Chaucer: he was learning from him in astonishing ways. He thought of this poet three centuries back in his own tradition as a great forerunner and master, as the equal in his *Knight's Tale* of Homer and Virgil. Indeed, poets and certain key translators, as if sensing some vitamin deficiency in our literature, have intuitively gone back to Chaucer in an attempt to cure it. But this is to anticipate a theme to which I shall be returning in a moment.

We arrived at Chaucer down the vista of the long-standing copiousness of English literature – something the Russians and the Germans do not have in the same proportion. And it was that theme which had brought us to Goethe. Now, one of Goethe's most readable modern translators, Michael Hamburger, supplies a thought which has some bearing on this topic. He is underlining the literalness of his own translations and says with a disarming modesty: 'I am not offering "English poems in their own right" here, but pointers to the original texts, inductions to them for persons with little or no German. If one or two of my versions also stand up as poems in English, that is a bonus, a stroke of luck.' And he concludes: 'English poetry is so rich as to have little need or room for additions in the guise of translations.'

One feels obliged to respond to this conclusion by saying that English poetry happens to *be* so rich because of what it managed to incorporate into itself 'in the guise of translations', and that the creative translations of men like Oldham, Dryden, Pope, and, in our own century, Pound, helped English shed its provincialisms. Furthermore, these men, whose translation work is a meaningful part of the richness of English poetry, were seldom content to offer merely 'pointers to the original texts'; for the texts they were incorporating into English demanded an extension and enrichment of English itself if they were to be adequately and imaginatively embodied. Can it really be supposed, to borrow Hamburger's phrase, that 'persons with little or no German' – or Greek or Latin or Chinese – can be inducted into those poetries simply with the aid of 'pointers'? Dryden, on the other hand, out of a prolonged contemplation of Latin poetry, and through his versions of Ovid, Homer, Chaucer, Lucretius, Juvenal, and Virgil, permanently changed the scope of English poetry itself, and his originals, seen from the vantage of what he did with them, can never appear quite the same either. The phase of Dryden's greatest verse translations seems to have coincided with a spiritual crisis when he was actively seeking to confront and re-embody the spiritual values of classical poetry. Perhaps something of this nature – a serious and profound need brought to bear on a foreign text and by a great writer – is what accounts for the compelling power of some of our finest translators. Along with Dryden, his young contemporary John Oldham comes to mind, and Oldham's extraordinary re-creations of Horace, Boileau, and Juvenal. Yet Oldham is hardly read, and only very slowly has the full story of Dryden's genius as a translator come to be told. To others than Michael Hamburger, English poetry has appeared 'so rich as to have little need or room for additions in the guise of translations', and so the real news, in Pound's phrase, has been a long time in arriving.

Reflecting on this thought, I found myself wondering what my own generation was actually taught about such matters. The answer is: not much. At Cambridge the full glory of the English Renaissance was unquestionably felt to inhere in the Elizabethan–Jacobean drama. Erik Satie, asked why Beethoven was so famous, replied, 'Because he had such a good business manager' – meaning, of course, Beethoven himself. The business manager for Elizabethan–Jacobean drama was undoubtedly Shakespeare, and his great prestige seems to have reflected back and also forward over the whole era and fallen upon several lesser talents. 'Our' renaissance – that is, the renaissance of us students up at Cambridge in my day – took a broad look at Wyatt and Surrey, both translators, though this fact was never dwelt upon, and Surrey's partial translation of the *Aeneid* was evaluated less for its actual quality than for its having brought blank verse into English – blank verse with which others, principally the dramatists, were to do things of greater importance. One of the first essays I did at Cambridge was on Christopher Marlowe, which meant I read every bit of what he wrote, including such dramatic scraps as his *Massacre at Paris* and *Tragedy of Dido*. We were even persuaded that the scrambled and poorly written scenes in the middle of his *Doctor Faustus* were somehow gauged to show us the rather trite choices Faustus made when, having sold his soul to the devil, those choices could have been unlimited. No one told us to read Marlowe's splendid translation of Ovid's *Amores*. My copy contained these, and a curious fight went on in my own mind between the implanted idea that they 'were only translations' and the sense that I *liked* these poems – read rather hastily, because one's energies had to be invested elsewhere, in the dramas. It did not occur to me then that Marlowe's Ovid translations offered a quite alternative rhetoric to that of some of his most famous plays – something that might be said of other major Elizabethan translators in relation to the drama (I am thinking of Golding's *Metamorphoses*, the Sidney Psalter, and Fairfax's Tasso, all represented in the *Oxford Book*.) Just how translation could offer an alternative rhetoric, and thus another possibility for English poetry, did not become fully articulate for me for a number of years. This happened when, on 22 November 1956, Hugh Kenner delivered at the Royal Society of Literature, a remarkable paper with the title 'Words in the Dark' (*Essays by Divers Hands*, 1958, New Series, vol. 29). Kenner's dealings with Marlowe in that paper catalysed worries which had long jostled among my thoughts and which had to do with the sort of poetry I was at that time trying to write. The story is, once more, the relation between original poetry and what translated poetry has to teach the poet – in this instance myself, as I shall explain.

Kenner comments on two passages from Christopher Marlowe. Both of these passages were old friends to me, but I realised, as one sometimes does when brought up sharp by a perceptive critic, that I had never quite earned my right to those two bits of mental furniture which I could even quote. The first was half a dozen lines from Marlowe's translation of Ovid's *Amores*. The lover is addressing the coming day:

> Now in her tender arms I sweetlie bide,
> If ever, now well lies she by my side,
> The ayre is colde and sleep is sweetest now,
> And byrdes send forth shrill notes from every bow.
> Whither runst thou, that men and women love not?
> Hold in thy rosie horses that they move not!

Kenner is contending that 'there are potentialities in Chaucer that have never been developed since, because the Elizabethan drama had no use for them, and brought modern English to a working maturity without them'. He quotes Marlowe's Ovid to show how a poet, not serving a theatrical purpose and audience, could still tap those Chaucerian potentialities – namely a close fit between the word and its object and a certain plainness and clarity of sense and definition in the refusal to let every phrase run almost unbidden into metaphor. Kenner puts over against Marlowe the translator, Marlowe the dramatist – the famous passage in which Faustus gets his wish to see Helen of Troy and exclaims,

> Was this the face that launch'd a thousand ships,

> And burnt the topless towers of Ilium? –
> … O, thou art fairer than the evening air
> Clad in the beauty of a thousand stars;
> Brighter art thou than flaming Jupiter
> When he appear'd to hapless Semele;
> More lovely than the monarch of the sky
> In wanton Arethusa's azur'd arms;
> And none but thou shalt be my paramour!

Kenner's comment on this, with its 'bright halo of imprecision' around the incantatory words, establishes its fundamental difference from the more Chaucerian rendering of Ovid.

> These words … are a verbal substitute for the vision … What the audience *saw* was the costumed and painted boy; the words however don't encourage it to examine what can be seen, but to dream away from the visible. We are not told by what extent the face of the authentic Helen … would transcend what is shown: we are encouraged to ignore what is shown:
>
> > O, thou art fairer than the evening air
> > Clad in the beauty of a thousand stars –
>
> fairer than the evening air, not the evening sky; and that air not adorned with stars but clad in their beauty. These lines more than any others in the speech appeal to remembered delights of the senses, yet even their appeal to the senses is refined into ethereal abstraction by the operation of the words 'air' and 'beauty'. A 'face' is mentioned, but it is not shown … And while the words evoke hapless Semele and wanton Arethusa, Helen is not compared to either of them but to a brightness and a loveliness: the loveliness of the monarch of the sky and the brightness of flaming Jupiter.

Matthew Arnold, reflecting on the difficulties of a poet of the nineteeth century in achieving a unified style, complains about 'those damn'd Elizabethans' and the influence of 'their purple patches' on subsequent verse. Kenner is less belligerent than this as he goes on to trace the persistence of a rhetoric, an attitude to words and metaphors, evolved by the Elizabethan dramatists, continuing right through the romantics – he does not mention Wordsworth, who might have provided an interesting exception – on to Tennyson and ultimately even Eliot. 'These dramatists', Kenner says, 'virtually invented the procedures of nineteenth and twentieth century English poetry. Their tradition was slow in establishing itself – Dryden's *All for Love* may be noted as an episode of resistance – but by Coleridge's generation they were firmly established ... as seminal poets'.

What of the role of the business manager, Shakespeare himself, in Kenner's version of the history of English poetry? Shakespeare figures in this version as the author of the lines from *Antony and Cleopatra*:

> She looks like sleep
> As she would catch another Antony
> In her strong toil of grace.

Amid the magical suggestiveness of this, 'grace', says Kenner, 'is neither the theologian's grace nor the hostess's nor the dancer's but mingles the prestige of all three'. And he contrasts this calculated imprecision rich in connotations with the definition and de-notation of Ben Jonson's

> Underneath this stone doth lie
> As much beauty as could die.

A great translator, Ben Jonson invented a style that takes on something of the chiselled demarcation of his Latin originals. Suffice it to say of Shakespeare that *his* Latinity was not the Latinity of Jonson but often a glamorous over-plus, something magically produced in the words as another language transforms itself into our own:

> Nay, this my hand will rather
> The multitudinous seas incarnadine ...

Shakespeare's style left open many options – a fact Kenner does not dwell upon – including the reincarnation of the Chaucerian Duke Theseus from the *Knight's Tale* in *A Midsummer Night's Dream*, but these options did not prevent the development of English verse from Marlowe through Shelley, Tennyson, and Eliot along other lines – lines sometimes resistant (as in the case of Marlowe's dramatic verse) to what translation had to offer.

I can now say why Kenner's account struck me with such particular force in 1956 and how it then came to be borne out and even amplified by my dealings with translation and as editor of *The Oxford Book of Verse in English Translation*. In the first place, Kenner's lecture spoke to me principally as a poet. I had been writing poems that were influenced by Marianne Moore and were beginning to be influenced by William Carlos Williams, as I tried to blot out the golden voice of

Dylan Thomas and the 'halo of imprecision' around *his* words as he intoned:

> Altarwise by owl-light in the halfway house
> The gentleman lay graveward with his furies; ...

The result of my own American-prompted reaction as a poet to that was a general incomprehension from English publishers and an unplaceable manuscript that lay around for several years and was finally published in New York. You can perhaps imagine the warmth with which I responded to Kenner's concluding peroration where he brought on to the scene the names of both Marianne Moore and William Carlos Williams, suggesting that British readers might find them 'bare and astringent to the point of incompetence' because of British preconceptions about poetic resonance. 'They write', he explained, 'out of the logic of their real world, in which the Elizabethans in fact did not really exist'. If I was right in sensing the decadence of much of Thomas – a kind of fluent manipulator of the imprecise, a last inheritor of Tudorbethanry rather than a new direction – how heartening to be told from the podium of the Royal Society of Literature that British ears were still imprisoned by a tradition of stage rhetoric going back three and a half centuries, and that one had allies elsewhere.

Kenner's initial distinctions were drawn by placing side by side those two passages – Marlowe as dramatist and Marlowe as translator – and finding in the latter Chaucerian potentialities 'that have never been developed since'. 'Never' is perhaps to overstate the case, as a glance at Dryden and Pope will readily show. In going on now to speak more undividedly of the presence of translation in English poetry, I wish to touch on that persistence of the Chaucerian. Chaucer himself was no stranger to translation, although he was chiefly concerned with completely transforming what he took from others – most magisterially from Boccaccio – into his own thing. One of his most sustained passages of poetic translation is to be found in *The Legend of Good Women*, the episode from the first book of the *Aeneid* where Aeneas, along with Achates, meets his mother Venus in disguise:

> So long he walketh in this wildernesse,
> Til at the laste he mette an hunteresse.
> A bowe in hande and arwes hadde she,
> Hire clothes cutted were unto the kne.

But she was yit the fayreste creature
That evere was yformed by Nature;
And Eneas and Achates she grette
And thus she to hem spak, whan she hem mette,
'Saw ye,' quod she, 'as ye han walked wyde,
Any of my sustren walke yow besyde
With any wilde bor or other best,
That they han hunted to, in this forest …?'

The couplet tune is taken up again by Gavin Douglas in his complete translation of the *Aeneid*, finished 'apon the fest of Mary Magdalen', 22 July 1513. Gavin Douglas speaks of 'my mastir Chaucer', and one both sees and hears what he means when one reads this same passage in his version. It seemed only just to begin the *Oxford Book* with Douglas as the initiator of its Renaissance section – after all, Surrey knew his version and echoes it and still gets most of the credit because of his use of blank verse. Another piquant reason – culture is like this! – for beginning with Douglas is that his Virgil is not strictly speaking in English but Scots, a literature which through Henryson, Dunbar, and Lyndsay, from the later fifteenth century onward, deeply imbibed Chaucer's influence just when the English seemed not to know what to do with Chaucer. Thus the Scottish incorporation of Chaucer into another tongue becomes in essence an act of translation, across a divide as great almost as that between German and Dutch. Chaucer's couplet melody in Douglas's Scots now sounds like this:

Venus, eftir the gise and maneir thair,
An active bow apon hir schuldir bair
As scho had bene ane wild hunteres,
With wynd waving hir haris lowsit of tres,
Her skirt kiltit till hir bair kne,
And, first of other unto thame spak sche:
How, say me, yonkeris, saw ye walkand and heir,
By aventure ony of my sisters deir,
The cace of arrowis taucht by hir syde,
And cled into the spottit linx hyde …?

Ezra Pound, in his *ABC of Reading*, goes so far as to claim that 'Gavin Douglas … with his mind full of Latin quantitative metre, attains a robuster versification than you are likely to find in Chaucer'. Pound is, of course, a great and vocal admirer of Chaucer – he thinks Chaucer's culture 'wider than Dante's' – and yet he repeats, 'the

texture of Gavin's verse is stronger, the resilience greater than
Chaucer's'. Be that as it may, here we have a twofold translation – of
the lesson of Chaucer and the poetry of Virgil into Scottish verse.
Douglas's achievement was noted by Surrey when the latter did his
partial *Aeneid*, but Surrey made of Douglas a lesser thing, taking over
echoes into a more refined and yet ultimately less expressive English.
Douglas stands then on the threshold of the *Oxford Book* as something for the specifically *English* Renaissance to measure up to. His
particular challenge was not met. His *Aeneid* disappeared from view
– there was no edition between 1553 and 1710. When Dryden came
to translate Virgil's poem in the late seventeenth century, an edition
of Douglas was hard to come by. Dryden may, however, have laid his
hands on a copy, as William Frost in *Comparative Literature* 36 (1984)
has recently suggested, also quoting there from a periodical of 1693,
the *Athenian Mercury*: 'Gawen Douglas's Aeneads (if you can get it) the
best version that ever was, or we believe ever will be of that incomparable poem.' So once more, it does seem from this quotation that
the generally supposed neo-classical abhorrence of works of more
barbarous times has been exaggerated. And in saying that, while
thinking about translation, one is already tentatively sketching out an
alternative picture of seventeenth-century poetry itself.

If Douglas, via translation, carries to the brink of the Tudor era –
indeed, as far as the *Athenian Mercury* in 1693 – a fundamentally
Chaucerian possibility, a similar possibility crops up once more in the
Elizabethan era itself with the publication of Golding's translation of
Ovid's *Metamorphoses*. (This is the book that Shakespeare virtually
quotes from in *The Tempest*, in Prospero's invocation of the spirits of
act 5 – Ovid's passage is given in the *Oxford Book*.) I find it hard to go
along with Pound in claiming that Golding's *Metamorphoses* is 'the most
beautiful book in the language' – Dryden seems to me, by and large,
a finer translator of Ovid than Golding. But Golding is a fascinating
example of a poet in touch with Chaucer's simplicity, clarity, and
narrative verve, while suffering sporadic attacks of that logorrhoea
which afflicted the Elizabethans – as it does Chapman in his translation of Homer's *Iliad*. Yet there exists in the best passages of
Golding's ambitious translation something like an antidote to that
same logorrhoea, as when the giant Polyphemus woos the nymph
Galatea:

More whyght thou art then Primrose leaf my Lady Galatee,
More fresh than meade, more tall and streyght than lofty Aldertree,

More bright than glasse, more wanton than the tender kid
           forsooth,
Than Cockleshelles continually with water worne, more
            smoothe ...
More cleere than frozen yce, more sweete than Grape though
            ripe ywis,
More soft than butter newly made, or downe of Cygnet is ...

One might well, faced with passages like this or with the sheer spry-ness of Golding's best narratives, ask with Ezra Pound, 'Is Golding's Ovid a mirror of Chaucer?' and concur in the spirit of Pound's next question: 'is a fine poet ever translated until another his equal invents a new style in a later language?' Golding is hardly Ovid's equal, but in passages like this, he *is* the inventor of a new style – a new style rooted in an intelligent awareness of earlier English poetry. As Pound concludes, in his 'Notes on Elizabethan Classicists':

> ... Golding was endeavouring to convey the sense of the original to his readers. He names the thing of his original author, by the name most germane, familiar, homely to his hearers. And I hold that the real poet is sufficiently absorbed in his content to care more for the content than the rumble (Pound is fighting against Milton here); and also that Chaucer and Golding are more likely to find the *mot juste* than were for some centuries their successors, saving the author of *Hamlet*.

If what Pound says is true of Golding, then the discipline of transla-tion has brought to focus something that was rare enough in so-called 'original verse'.

Pound's tendency to measure later poets and translators against Chaucer – as he does in the case of Golding and Douglas – has an interesting bearing on our theme of alternatives to the rhetoric of Elizabethan drama – alternatives supplied during the Elizabethan age in (say) Marlowe's Ovid or the Sidney Psalter. As Pound writes of Chaucer in the *ABC of Reading*:

> Intending writers can read him with fair safety, in so far as no one can now possibly use an imitation of Chaucer's manners or the details of his speech. Whereas horrible examples of people wearing Elizabethan old clothes, project from whole decades of later English and American writing.

To Kenner's comment that 'Dryden's *All for Love* may be noted as an episode of resistance' to a given type of Elizabethan rhetoric, one might add that it was Dryden's own enthusiasm for Chaucer – 'Here is God's plenty', as he famously said – that enabled him in his later translations of that poet to touch ground and bedrock in a quite new way. He thought Chaucer's language 'followed Nature more closely' than Ovid's characteristic 'turn of words'. He thought Chaucer's *Knight's Tale* and Duke Theseus' vein of pity were superior in conception even to Homer because 'Homer can move rage better than he can move pity'. And he had a certain rather English dislike of heroic conceptions where pity is at a low premium, as when he spoke of 'those Athletick Brutes whom undeservedly we call heroes' and again of 'a mere Ajax, a Man-killing Ideot'. I do not believe there are enough of Dryden's translations of Chaucer in my anthology. The problem was chiefly one of space. You cannot demonstrate everything at once, and I had my eye on Dryden's Ovid, but perhaps an ideal anthology of Dryden could underline the fact that, practically simultaneously, he is doing two things – Dryden, an Anglican Christian and later a Catholic, is entering into a serious dialogue with paganism via his translation of Lucretius and Ovid, and is making re-available to a reading public that found the idiom and metre out of reach a large body of Chaucer's work: all of the massive *Knight's Tale*, *The Flower and the Leaf*, which was supposed to be by Chaucer, *The Character of a Good Parson*, *The Nun's Priest's Tale*, and *The Wife of Bath's Tale* (these last two, incomparable masterpieces of translation that would have to be printed complete in our imaginary ideal anthology). That both these tales are concerned with sex and sexual morality and that Venus should get special treatment (a more extended one than Chaucer's) in Dryden's version of *The Knight's Tale*, points to the way that Dryden in translating the pagans, in his dealings with Lucretius and Ovid, takes the power of Venus as seriously as that other 'neo-classical' author, Racine in *Phèdre*. The positive aspect of Venus appears in the *Oxford Book* in that lovely evocation from Lucretius rendered by Dryden before he came to do Chaucer:

> Delight of Humane kind and gods above;
> Parent of Rome; Propitious Queen of Love; ...
> All Nature is thy Gift; Earth, Air, and Sea:
> Of all that breaths, the various progeny,
> Stung with delight, is goaded on by thee.
> O'er barren Mountains, o'er the flowery Plain,
> The leavy Forest, and the liquid Main
> Extends thy uncontroul'd and boundless reign.

Through all the living Regions, dost thou move,
And scatter'st, where thou goest, the kindly seeds of Love ...

The 'Seeds of Love' may be 'kindly', but other words from this fragment of Dryden's Lucretius hint at the less amenable forces of Venus: 'stung', 'goaded', 'uncontroul'd', 'boundless'. 'Uncontroul'd' is what Myrrha's incestuous passion for her father is in Ovid's story from the *Metamorphoses*, which Dryden went on to translate in one of his supreme versions, where the fluctuations of the woman's mind and feelings in thrall to obsessive and forbidden love irresistibly remind one, in Dryden's rendering, of Racine's portrayal of the combined incandescence and shocked resistance in the mind of Phèdre. This is the Dryden Matthew Arnold and the Victorians preferred to forget, but the Dryden of whom Doctor Johnson said that he was 'not one of the *gentle bosoms* ... He hardly conceived [love] but in its turbulent effervescence with some other desires; where it was inflamed by rivalry, or obstructed by difficulties ...' Sir Walter Scott, in similar vein, speaks of Dryden's knowledge of 'the stronger feelings of the heart, in all its dark or violent workings ...' Johnson's phrase 'obstructed by difficulties' describes well the love of Palamon and Arcite for the same girl in Chaucer's *Knight's Tale*. Palamon, the worshipper of Venus, gets the girl: all's well that ends well, but in Dryden's temple of Venus (unlike Chaucer's) there are 'issuing sighs that smoked along the wall', and Dryden tops up Chaucer's list of those 'by love undone' by extending Chaucer's 'Th'enchantmentz of ... Circes' to 'Circean feasts / With bowls that turned enamoured youths to beasts'. Venus' worshipper, Palamon, having lost the tournament but won the girl because of a rather blatant divine intervention by Venus and Saturn, the goddess puts in an extended appearance in Dryden. She is there by implication in the great concluding speech of Duke Theseus, much reinforced by Dryden:

The Cause and Spring of motion from above
Hung down on earth the golden chain of Love.

And she comes on at the end in a passage of Dryden's devising (though it is devised in Chaucerian mode with its mixture of irony and sexual frankness):

Smil'd Venus, to behold her own true Knight
Obtain the Conquest, though he lost the Fight,
And bless'd with Nuptial Bliss the sweet laborious Night.
Eros, and Anteros (Cupid's brother), on either Side,

One fir'd the Bridegroom, and one warm'd the Bride;
And long attending Hymen from above,
Showr'd on the Bed the whole Idalian Grove.

I have spoken of Dryden's serious dialogue with paganism, and it seems to me that his engagement with Venus (powers, passions, ironies, and all), extending from his superb evocation of her in *Aeneid* book 8, from Lucretius to Ovid and Chaucer, is as deeply responsive as his re-creation of Lucretius' rather bracing atheism in *Against the Fear of Death*. This atheism, in Dryden's imaginative contemplation of it, while it abolishes any possible hope of an after-life, yet argues that since there is only one life, we should live it fully without bemoaning our lot. This optimistic atheism, as one might call it, finds an answering echo in the pagan philosophy of Duke Theseus, as previously imagined by Chaucer and now reincarnated in Dryden's words:

What makes all this, but Jupiter the king,
At whose command we perish, and we spring?
Then 'tis our best, since thus ordain'd to die,
To make a Vertue of Necessity ...
Enjoying while we live the present Hour,
And dying in our Excellence and Flow'r ...
When then remains, but after past Annoy,
To take the good Vicissitude of Joy?
To thank the gracious Gods for what they give,
Possess our Souls, and while we live, to live?

Here we have one of those moments of creative translation, when in the hands of a great writer, the text comes to speak his deepest feelings and convictions for him. It is comparable to that scene in Pound's version of Sophocles' *Woman of Trachis* when Herakles, suffering the effects of the shirt of Nessus and about to die, sees suddenly (for himself and for the translating poet) the logic and consequence of his life and cries out:

SPLENDOUR,
       IT ALL COHERES.

With all their differences, both passages – Dryden's Duke Theseus and Pound's Herakles – speak for the poets and yet speak for more than the poets, because these translators are, in their however freely adaptive way, finding and extending something which is demonstrably present in the original text. I feel myself that Dryden achieves this with far greater security than Pound: *Woman of Trachis*, with its uneasy hodge-podge of diction, does not really 'all cohere', as Dryden's *Knight's Tale*, and Duke Theseus' speech there do. What is interesting, though, is that Pound, Chaucer, and Dryden are trying to imagine how it could 'all cohere' for a pagan Greek. And that is what I mean by saying that the Catholic Dryden enters into a serious dialogue with paganism.

Dryden's Duke Theseus speech is translation, but it is also late seventeeth-century poetry at its full height, returning us to our initial theme that the story of English poetry cannot be truly told without seeing translation as an unavoidable part of that story. The editor of the recently published *New Oxford Book of Eighteenth Century Verse*, with a most courteous nod toward my own volume, resolves to avoid the translations of the age, preferring to stick to its 'original verse', though admitting 'imitations' whereby an old source is updated as in Johnson's use of Juvenal in *The Vanity of Human Wishes*. The trouble with this is that so much of the poetic vigour of the age went into great translations. Ignore them, and you get the whole picture out of proportion. And with this thought in mind, I come to my last major illustration of that theme – the work of another Chaucerian, Alexander Pope. I shall be touching on two aspects of Pope – his Chaucer translations and his *Iliad.*

Prompted by Dryden's example, the sixteen-year-old Alexander Pope turned to translating Chaucer. We hear much of the prodigy of a Rimbaud, with his marvellous visionary fireworks – for which he had, of course, to pay an early price, realising that his systematic derangement of the senses was costing too dear in human terms, so that he abandons art as precociously as he began to practise it. There is a lot more good old-fashioned common sense about our other sixteen-year-old prodigy – indeed, it is as if Pope went to two of Chaucer's creations that could tell him most directly what common sense was – *The Merchant's Tale*, with its clear-eyed view of what happens when the elderly marry the young, and *The Wife of Bath's Prologue*, where one of the unforgettable characters of literature tells us what marriage is like – or, at any rate, *her* conception of marriage.

Kenner, you will recall, spoke of certain Chaucerian potentialities 'that have never been developed since'. Yet one of the miraculous things is to hear Chaucer's couplet music still there in the translations of these two Augustans, Dryden and Pope. It helped tune *their* tongues, to borrow Doctor Johnson's phrase. As you well know, the imitation of the form and sound of a foreign text is often impossible and frequently unadvisable, yet in reaching back to English at an earlier stage in its development, Dryden and Pope were able to bring over something of Chaucer's music into their own contemporary idiom, and they were, after all, using the same basic form as Chaucer, the couplet. They 'made it new' (in Pound's slogan) in a way altogether more radical and convincing than those modern efforts to translate Chaucer – from Coghill's dreary versions downward, that we saw in the 1940s, 1950s, and 1960s, and that were written in a sort of no-man's-English. If we want to complain that the idiom of Dryden and Pope is much more four-square and balanced than that of Chaucer or that it lacks the freshness of Douglas or Golding, we should pause, with Coghill's example in mind, to consider the fact that it is a genuine idiom, consistent with its time, and not an attempt to cobble together medievalisms with coyly self-conscious modern turns of phrase.

In terms of tune and diction, what Dryden's modernisation had to offer Pope shows clearly enough in the way Dryden appropriates Chaucer's Chanticleer. Chanticleer enters Chaucer's text with a lyric clarity such as Golding was to inherit. Here is Chaucer's cockerel that

> In al the land of crowyng nas his peer ...
> His coomb was redder than the fyn coral,
> And betailled as it were a castel wal;
> His byle was blak, and as the jet it shoon;
> Lyk asure were his legges and his toon;
> His nayles whitter than the lylye flour,
> And lyk the burned gold was his colour.
> This gentil cok hadde in his governaunce
> Sevene hennes for to doon al his pleasaunce,
> Which were his sustres and his paramours,
> And wonder lyk to hym, as of colours ...

And here is Dryden – the countrified and the courtly less intimately at one perhaps, and yet why make excuses for what bids so undividedly for the ear's attention, discovering so infallibly its own substitutes where the vocabulary, word order, stress, and actual pace of English have altered over the years:

> High was his comb and coral red withal,
> In dents embattled like a Castle-Wall;
> His Bill was Raven-black, and shon like Jet,
> Blue were his Legs, and Orient were his Feet;
> White were his Nails, like Silver to behold,
> His Body glitt'ring like the burnish'd Gold.

This gentle Cock for solace of his Life,
Six Misses had beside his lawful Wife;
Scandal that spares no King, tho' ne'er so good,
Says, they were all of his own Flesh and Blood ...

As Marvin Mudrick put it many years ago in 'Chaucer as Librettist' (*Philological Quarterly* 38, 1): 'The moral seems to be that the Augustans were the last English poets who had sufficiently large command of technique and decorum, and sufficient trust in the versatility of their idiom, to be capable of turning Chaucer into a contemporary.' 'Into a contemporary' – that is the point. What twentieth-century poet has been able to reincarnate the Wife of Bath as the sixteen-year-old Pope did when she turns on her husband who is reading her, in bed, a book on the weaknesses of women?

When still he read, and laugh'd and read again,
And half the Night was thus consum'd in vain;
Provok'd to Vengeance, three large Leaves I tore,
And with one Buffet fell'd him on the Floor.
With that my Husband in a Fury rose,
And down he settled me with hearty Blows:
I groan'd, and lay extended on my Side;
Oh thou has slain me for my Wealth (I cry'd),
Yet I forgive thee – Take my last Embrace,
He wept, kind Soul! and stoop'd to kiss my Face;
I took him such a Box as turn'd him blue,
Then sigh'd and cry'd *Adieu my Dear, adieu!*

But after many a hearty Struggle past,
I condescended to be pleas'd at last ...

and she goes on to coax out of him mastery over both his person and his wealth:

– As for the Volume that revil'd the Dames,
'Twas torn to Fragments and condemn'd to Flames

If we were Hungarians (so to speak), a poem like this would be among our acknowledged masterpieces, and if we knew our *Iliad* (our greatest eighteenth-century poem, as I suggested), we might even catch an echo of Chaucer's comic vigour in the marital set-to's of Jupiter and Juno. True enough, in the first book of his *Iliad*, Pope – still the *young* Pope, he is now twenty-five – was perhaps too awed by his task to allow himself the full comic freedom of Dryden's dealings with the royal couple, or to risk calling their lame son, Vulcan, 'the rude Skinker' or barman. However, Pope's *Iliad* continually takes fire and increases in daring as it progresses. I wonder if those who have written on it have not perhaps underestimated just how comically devious the gods are shown to be. Jupiter (it has been said) stands too close to Milton's God the Father, yet his awful majesty is surely often qualified in a manner Milton would never have dreamed of for the supreme deity. There are many instances of this, including the tone of massive threat in which Jupiter reminds the restive Juno of how he had once had to hang her up in a golden chain from the ceiling of heaven. This (from book 15) follows on her deception of him in book 14, leading to the biggest family row in the whole poem. In an ideal anthology one would need both of these books, and if one could not have them both, then all of the marital comedy in 14.

In the *Oxford Book* I have tried to substantiate some of my claims for Pope's Homer. It seems to me that the array of epic similes there, the separate incidents – particularly the marvellous episode where the River Scamander attacks and fights with Achilles – and the whole sequence of the forging by Vulcan of Achilles' shield, go a long way to support Doctor Johnson's estimate with which I began: 'that poetical wonder ... a performance which no age or nation can pretend to equal.' But one thing *is* lacking in my *Oxford* choice (space precluded it) – namely, the high comedy of the interventions of the gods in the Trojan war and the sense of how this comedy – in Shakespearean fashion – is so mingled with and accentuates the tragic waste in the poem, reinforcing as it does, our awareness of how that is just the way things interact in the daily texture of life. In conclusion let me say a few words about books 14 and 15.

In his notes – a brilliant and unique addition to the translation – Pope has theological difficulties. He is worried that the Almighty (as he calls Jupiter) carries on the way he does in book 14. Pope's text, however, feels itself free to accept the power game and the marital scuffles of Jupiter and Juno and portrays them as not much more complex than the power game and the marital scuffles of the Wife of Bath. What really upset Pope is Jupiter's sexual passion for Juno (she's borrowed Venus' girdle to distract him while her brother Neptune helps the Greeks; Jupiter, of course, is favourable to the Trojans). The poem doesn't in the least reveal the embarrassment of its notes at this point, but splendidly pursues its course through Jupiter's almost operatic and self-blinding catalogue of Juno's charms to the consummation of his desire until

> At length with Love and Sleep's soft Pow'r opprest,
> The panting Thund'rer nods and sinks to rest.

Jupiter's famous nod, usually indicating his power, has become something else. We go from here to the horrors of battle and then we go back again to the marital quarrel once Jupiter wakes up to what is happening. You would imagine from certain critics that Pope's *Iliad* sounds all the same – the homogeniser of the heroic couplets blandly absorbing all those mighty hexameters and (to change the metaphor) making them come out like links of sausages. I suppose some such feeling as this was what prevented Ezra Pound from warming to Pope's *Iliad*, along with the evident influence of the detested Milton on Pope. It must be said, however, that the swiftness of Pope's couplets makes much lighter what he derived from Milton. He takes Milton's freight on board and yet manages to carry it at his own speed, which is often amazingly rapid. Books 14 and 15 are proof, if it were needed, of Pope's variety and of his ability to keep changing tone and focus in following his original. This ability – the context need not always be comic – is one that is shared by Homer, Virgil, Lucretius, and Ovid, as they move from close-up to long shot – an effect as of poetic montage, immersing themselves and then standing back and letting things re-group into perspective. It is a capacity the twentieth-century poet could learn from. Pope's rendering of one of Homer's great images in book 15 points the way. Here a child playing with sand and the wrecking of the Grecian wall by Apollo are accommodated side by side in (to keep up our cinematic image) three shots:

> Then with his Hand he shook the mighty wall;
> And lo! the Turrets nod, the Bulwarks fall.
> Easy, as when ashore an Infant stands,
> And draws imagin'd Houses in the sands;
> The sportive Wanton, pleased with some new Play,
> Sweeps the slight Works and fashion'd Domes away.
> Thus vanish'd as they touch, the Tow'rs and Walls;
> The Toil of thousands in a Moment Falls.

Had we but world enough and time, our story of the presence of translation would not end with the Great Augustans. It would need to be taken up again with Ezra Pound. That, in turn, would necessitate a leap across romanticism where the primacy of poetic translation begins to flag – with one important exception, Shelley. Shelley, who could write with all the ethereality of Marlowe's 'O, thou art fairer than the evening air', was marshalling, before his death, a suppler and intellectually more intricate style, much influenced by his own direct experience as a translator – of Euripides, Dante, Calderón, and Goethe. But all that – a little of it is told in the *Oxford Book* – would be an essay in itself.

The Poet as Translator

'With Poesie to open Poesie' – thus George Chapman on his aim as a translator of Homer. All good translators of verse seem to have worked in this spirit. Chapman having fallen foul of scholars who imagined only they could possess a definitive idea of what Homer was at, Dryden wrote in his defence, 'They neither knew good verse nor loved it.' It was out of this knowledge and this love that Rossetti declared, 'The life-blood of rhymed translation is this, – that a good poem shall not be turned into a bad one. The only true motive for putting poetry into a fresh language must be to endow a fresh nation, as far as possible, with one more possession of beauty.' To which Pasternak adds that a translation should 'stand on a level with the original and in itself be unrepeatable'. So the anthologist who goes to work in the light of such remarks will turn first to the great poets – say Wyatt, Jonson, Dryden, Pope, Pound – and establish his scale of values by seeing what they have made of translation.

Where to begin his choice? My own starts with Gavin Douglas's *Aeneid*, completed in 1513. If it seems tendentious to open *The Oxford Book of Verse in English Translation* with a Scot, I can only reply that it was Douglas's work which first established on this island the level at which great poetry can be translated. And why not Chaucer? If Chaucer was 'grant translateur', he translated mostly by incorporating and transforming other men's work in poems that are ultimately great originals. One could, of course, assemble fragments from here and there, including an early example of Petrarch in his *Song of Troylus*, but the results would be scrappy.[1] Perhaps only once do we find a stretch of translation as neatly excerptable as his free version in *The Legend of Good Women* of a passage from Virgil's first book, where Aeneas and Achates meet with Venus.

'My mastir Chauser', writes Gavin Douglas, who knew this passage, as can be seen by comparing it with his own translation of the same incident, where, once more, poesie opens poesie, in spite of Robert Frost's dictum, 'Poetry is what gets lost in translation'.

I admire the way George Steiner, in the introduction to *The Penguin Book of Modern Verse Translation*, finds a reply to that depressing, even

---

1   One might say the same of trying to extricate Ovid from Spenser's *Muiopotmos*.

self-satisfied, adage of Frost's. As Steiner says, 'Arguments against verse translation are arguments against all translation', since 'There can be no exhaustive transfer from language A to language B, no meshing of nets so precise that there is identity of conceptual content, unison of undertone, absolute symmetry of aural and visual association. This is true', Steiner concludes, 'of a simple prose statement and of poetry.'

Side by side with Frost's dictum, two other threats have persisted to admonish the translator of poetry. Both of them seem to be products of the academic milieu, distrustful still of the way the non-expert – usually meaning the poet – might set to work as translator. The first of these threats hints that the only true translation would be a kind of mirror image of the original, and therefore it is either best not to try, or best to leave it to the experts in the field of French, Russian or whatever. The second threat is the outwardly bullying, inwardly fearful child of the first – the preference for a rather staid but 'accurate' rendering into tame iambics of, say, Pushkin, so that nothing extraneous, as it were, should come between the reader and the original.

Dryden long ago took on this argument when he wrote: '… a good poet is no more like himself in a dull translation than his carcass would be to his living body.' And Dryden, being a poet and a person, not a mirror, admits with candour of his own translations – some of the greatest in the language: 'I have both added and omitted, and even sometimes very boldly made such expositions of my authors, as no Dutch commentator will forgive me.'

Dryden early in his career had entered into a debate on translation begun by the Royalist group of poets – Denham, Cowley, Fanshawe, Sherburne, and Stanley – who had been in French exile after the defeat of Charles I and thus had particular and daily reason to think in terms of translation. Sir John Denham, in congratulating Fanshawe on his version of Guarini's *Il Pastor Fido*, contrasted his achievement with the pedantry of those who stuck too closely to the original text:

> That servile path thou nobly dost decline,
> Of tracing word by word, and line by line …
> A new and nobler way thou dost pursue,
> To make Translations and Translators too:
> They but preserve the Ashes, thou the Flame,
> True to his sense, but truer to his fame.

Dryden had been at pains to draw out some distinctions from Denham's poem and also from the preface to his version of Virgil's second book, in which Denham had written, 'Poetry is of so subtile a spirit, that, in pouring out of one language into another, it will all evaporate; and, if a new spirit be not added in the transfusion, there will remain nothing but a caput mortuum.' What troubled Dryden was just how much should be added. Perhaps one could defend Cowley's free imitations of so 'wild and ungovernable' a poet as Pindar, but what of 'any regular intelligible authors' such as Virgil and Ovid? Dryden joined with Denham in refusing to trace 'word by word, and line by line' – metaphase, as he calls this. He distrusts imitation, or adaptation as we should say, and chooses 'paraphrase, or translation with latitude, where the author is kept in view by the translator, so as never to be lost, but his words are not so strictly followed as his sense; and that too is admitted to be amplified, but not altered'. Once one has put things like this, it is, as Dryden was to find, difficult in practice to limit the element of adaptation: 'I have both added and omitted', as he later confesses. Thus in his translation of Boccaccio's *Cymon and Iphigenia* appears the splendid interpolation about the Militia of Rhodes ('Mouths without hands, maintained at vast expense,/ In peace a charge, in war a weak defence'); Vulcan in *The Iliad* Book I becomes 'the rude Skinker' (a phrase purloined from a marginal gloss of Chapman's); memories of *Macbeth* are called on to describe the feast of the gods ('But Mirth is marr'd, and the good Chear is lost'); Vulcan pours and Crashaw's twenty-third psalm ('How my cup orelooks her brims') reinforces the result: 'The laughing Nectar overlook'd the Lid.' Here Dryden appears to have advanced beyond the modesty of Fanshawe's 'a Translation at the best is but a mock Rainbow in the clouds imitating a true one' towards Cowley's, 'I am not so enamoured of the Name Translator, as not to wish to be Something Better, though it want yet a Name'. Indeed, throughout the Augustan era, a philosophy of translation prevailed that permitted a wide freedom in abstracting from one's original and drew attention to its general nature rather than its local details, so that Stephen Barrett, whose *Ovid's Epistles* appeared in 1759, could write: '... if you take care to make sure of the true outlines, and strong likeness of your picture; the remainder is only drapery, and of no great consequence, whether exactly copied or not.'

   In the present anthology, I have excluded large-scale works of imitation like Johnson's *Vanity of Human Wishes* and Pope's *Imitations of Horace* – works that bear out Johnson's own definition of imitation,

'A method of translating looser than paraphrase, in which modern examples and illustrations are used for ancient, domestick for foreign.'[1] At the same time I have, from early on, included poems – Wyatt and Surrey are cases in point – where a foreign original is 'imitated' in terms of personal feeling and new possibilities have come into the language by way of the tension. However freely our older authors appropriated their originals, I can, at this point in history, see good reason for having at least a working definition of the word 'translation'. This is what Donald Davie calls for in a tightly argued paper for the Open University, 'Poetry in Translation'. He comes up with the formula: 'Translation is something which takes more liberties (i.e., takes on more responsibilities) than the "trot", but denies itself the liberties of the imitation and of other relations more tenuous still.' Davie is arguing against George Steiner's willingness to 'consider as "translation" any poem which makes a sustained allusion to a previous poem'. One sees the good sense in Davie's desire for clarity here and one admires the conduct of his argument. Among his examples of poetic translations appear two versions of part of Baudelaire's *Le Cygne* – one by Lowell and one by himself. The Lowell contains some very free and sometimes very odd inventions (from 'when Racine's tirades scourged our greasy Seine' to 'greening horses' teeth') and is surely a work of adaptation. Davie's own version is more literal, but where Baudelaire has the swan stretching its head towards the ironic sky 'Comme s'il adressait des reproches à Dieu', Davie writes 'as if to sue / (Its neck all twisted) God for damages'. Is not that phrase also adaptation in its purely fanciful relation to the original? And so one is back with the perhaps insoluble question of what degree of adaptation is necessary or desirable in a creative translation.

One thing is certain – translation of poetry is essentially a compromise between the original texts and the present interests and capacities of a given writer. Dryden says that the writer must be a poet. There is a difficulty here, in that some translators have shown no particular capacity as poets outside their translations, and others, like Gavin Douglas or Golding, are famous for a single extended work of translation – Douglas for his Virgil and Golding for his Ovid.

---

1   A shorter example of this comes in C.H. Sisson's imitation of Horace's *Carmen Saeculare* (No. 536) which forces one to ask oneself whether a closer translation of this poem could even begin to exist *as poetry* in our own time, and whether Sisson's is not perhaps the only way of remaining true to certain elements in Horace. Such 'straight' renderings as come to hand (from Bulwer Lytton to James Michie) suggest only the unbridgeable distance between us and the original.

Certainly our great poets have often been great translators, but perhaps the safest minimum prescription is that the translator of poetry must be a poet so long as he is engaged in that act and art.

In speaking of translation as a compromise between his original and the interests and capacities of a writer, I trust the word 'compromise' carries over no sense of timidity. Dryden's interests and capacities were those of a man in 'his great climacteric' who had written the masterpieces of his age. One of his modern admirers, the poet Charles Sisson, introducing his own translations, draws from Dryden's example what he calls 'an ineluctable law', namely 'that a verse translation has to be done in the only verse that the translator, at the time of writing, can make; and that if he could not make verse before he will not suddenly become so gifted because he is faced with a classical text'.

How elementary and yet salutory such a reminder is when one thinks of the enormous number of translations from classical texts, ranging from the marmoreal to the mushy, in which Greece and Rome were industriously buried by earnest but untalented people – people who 'could not make verse', people on whom the judgement of Sisson's 'ineluctable law' would be that no inner pressure of their own lives had revealed in them the gift of art.

It is the sense of inner pressure that makes vivid those versions of Marina Tsvetayeva done by another British contemporary, Elaine Feinstein – translations that embody for us the tortured years of pre- and post-revolutionary Russia, and the way they were suffered by a very un-English sensibility but a sensibility that has, at last, found for itself a style in English. Like Sisson, Mrs Feinstein knows there is no ideal mode of translation and that it is undertaken in the course of a life and amid contingencies. She is even frank enough to say: 'I am not sure ... how far a discussion of methods of translation attracts much useful reflection ... Poems are not translated *consistently*. Every line proposes a new set of possibilities.' What Mrs Feinstein aimed at, while facing this challenge, was, she says, 'to be sure the total move-ment had been sustained'. In similar vein, Henry Gifford has said that translation is resurrection, but not of the body. Introducing those versions from the nineteenth-century Russian, Fyodor Tyutchev, in which we both collaborated, he speaks of the flight or track a poem makes through the mind. 'Every real poem', he says, 'starts from a given ground and carries the reader to an unforeseen vantage point, whence he views differently the landscape over which he has passed. What the translator must do is to recognise these two terminal points, and to connect them by a coherent flight. This will not be exactly the flight of the original, but no essential reach of the journey will have been left out.' So, in the end, for any live translator, it is not a question of approaching a text with a defined method, but of eliciting definition from, and restoring to clarity that chaos which occurs, as, line by line, the sounds and patterns of the original crumble to pieces in the mind of the translator. Davie catches the challenge of that disconcerting moment brilliantly when, in his *The Poems of Dr Zhivago*, he writes of the professional poet as translator realising that 'in translating rhymed verse the rhyme is the first thing to go, and metre the second: whereas the amateur, wretched sceptic that he is, cannot be sure of having poetry at all unless he has these external features of it'. Predictably, Mrs Feinstein's versions when they first appeared were criticised for her neglect of Tsvetayeva's stanza schemes, yet by neglecting what cannot be convincingly reproduced in English the Feinstein versions went immediately to the heart of what can – that jagged, breathless, self-wearing tone of Tsvetayeva's poems.

Clearly there was common ground, a common sense of impending inner chaos perhaps, that drew Elaine Feinstein to Tsvetayeva. This personal aspect is a paramount one. Verse translation is not just a job to be got through. In the best translations there is an area of agreement between translator and translated, something they have spiritually in sympathy. The Earl of Roscommon in that very sensible poem, *An Essay on Translated Verse*, of 1684, puts it like this:

> Examine how your Humour is inclin'd,
> And which the Ruling Passion of your Mind;
> Then seek a Poet who *your* way do's bend,
> And Chuse an Author as you chuse a friend: …

Pound himself possessed this kind of ability. I am thinking of his versions of Li Po – Li Po seen as the outsider like himself – where he enters into the skin of his original through one of those combinations of the fortuitous and the creative that make art possible. In Pound's case the fortuitous aspect, the historic chance that deepened his very creativeness lay also in the fact of the First World War. Pound admired the implicitness of Chinese poetry – the silent eloquence underlying 'The Jewel Stairs' Grievance', for example – and those poems of parting and frontier service which make up *Cathay* clearly had their implicit link for him with the present campaigns in France. '*Cathay*', in Hugh Kenner's words, 'is largely a war-book, using Fenollosa's notes much as Pope used Horace or Johnson Juvenal, to supply a system of parallels and a structure of discourse … the *Cathay* poems paraphrase, as it were, an elegiac war poetry nobody wrote.' This confrontation, deepened by history between the personal and a text in a language distant in time and place, was of a kind that had happened to one of Pound's acknowledged forebears, Gavin Douglas in the Scottish–English conflict.

The success of translation depends, then, on a writer's confrontation with his given moment. It depends also on his capacity and readiness to undertake it and is thus, in some sense, a self-interested undertaking. In the doing of it, that writer is thrown up against a new scale of things, adding to his awareness of alternatives in literary expression, an awareness which carries over to his reader. This is what happened in the august cases from Wyatt to Ezra Pound. In their 'opening Poesie with Poesie', one hears English being drawn into a dialogue with other cultures, as when Pound, in Canto LII, translating the Chinese Book of Rites, gives us in magnificent processional rhythms something English and something irreducibly foreign and distant:

> Know then:
>   Toward summer when the sun is in Hyades
> Sovran is Lord of the Fire
>   to this month are birds
> with bitter smell and with the odour of burning
> To the hearth god, lungs of the victim
>   The green frog lifts up his voice
>   and the white latex is in flower
> In red car with jewels incarnadine
>   to welcome the summer

Thus, in all the great examples of how to do it, the matter is two way – the poet-translator is extending his own voice, is sometimes writing his finest work, and is performing a transmission of civilisation in the process of extending his own voice. Wyatt found his personal voice to some extent through Seneca, Petrarch, and the Psalms, Marlowe through Ovid – a voice that Donne seems to have learned from in the *Songs and Sonnets*. Where Wyatt was thought once to be most bluntly English, as in 'Madame withouten many words', it now turns out he was translating from the Italian of Dragonetto Bonifacio. And all the time English was gaining by these interchanges.

Think how Ben Jonson brings over the very cleanliness of Latin when he refleshes Catullus in 'Come, my Celia, let us prove / While we can, the sports of love,' where the famous *Nox est perpetua una dormienda* gets translated as:

> But if once we lose this light
> Tis with us perpetual night.

And here the loss of *dormienda* is made up for, by the succinct suggestiveness of the couplet and its brisk conclusive rhyming. Without these examples of intermarriage, English poetry would be the poorer – and so, in a sense, would Latin. Dryden talks about French having the nimbleness of a greyhound and English the bulk and body of a mastiff. And, very differently from Jonson, he sets precisely that bulk and body at the service of Latin when he translates Juvenal's *Sixth Satire*:

> In Saturn's Reign, at Nature's Early Birth,
> There was that Thing call'd Chastity on Earth …
> Those first unpolisht Matrons, Big and Bold,
> Gave Suck to Infants of Gygantick Mold;
> Rough as their Savage Lords who Rang'd the Wood,
> And Fat with Acorns Belcht their windy Food.

In all these examples the first thing one sees is the way that, having rejected the metres of their originals, these translators do not stop at a merely literal rendering of the unmetred words. Octavio Paz clinches our point about their opening of Poesie in an essay about translation where he says '… literal translation in Spanish we call, significantly, *servil*. I am not saying that literal translation is impossible, only that it is not translation. It is a device, generally composed of a string of words, to aid us in reading the text in its original language. It is somewhat closer to a dictionary than to translation, which is always a literary operation.' Our examples have invented a linguistic system as strongly organised as that of their originals, different as it must be in terms of music and metre, but comparable in terms of literary vitality – and, in Pasternak's word 'unrepeatable'. They have 'made it new' in the phrase Ezra Pound was so fond of. And to any discussion of translation Pound must sooner or later be admitted. He is significant in the way he has extended the resources of English in his handling of the Chinese, for instance, and he is significant also for his very active awareness of the creative problem – the transformation of the literal into the literary.

In an early essay, *I gather the limbs of Osiris*, Pound speaks about the way words transmit an electricity among themselves, generate and intergenerate certain qualities and combinations of energy by their very positions in a work. 'Three or four words', he says, 'in exact juxtaposition are capable of radiating this energy at a very high potentiality … [The] peculiar energy which fills [words] is the power of tradition, of centuries of race consciousness, of agreement, of association …'

What Pound's essay implies for a translator of poetry is that he must find a way of so placing his substituted words that the electric current flows and that there is no current wasted. If you fail *here*, at the level of the electric interchange of the words, you fail badly and this is the most common failure in translated poetry, even though you avoid howlers like 'le peuple ému répondit' Englished as 'the purple emu laid another egg'.

Pound was thinking particularly about the translation of Chinese poetry at that time. Now in H.A. Giles's *A History of Chinese Literature* of 1901, a book current, that is, during Pound's formative years, the reader was asked to believe that the great poet, Wang Wei, wrote the following:

> Dismounted, o'er wine
>   we had out last say;
> Then I whisper, 'Dear friend,
>   tell me whither away.'
> 'Alas,' he replied
>   'I am sick of life's ills
> And I long for repose
>   on the slumbering hills
> But oh seek not to pierce
>   where my footsteps may stray:
> The white cloud will soothe me
>   for ever and ay.'

Funnily enough, sinologists seem to have complained less about this kind of thing than about Pound's subsequent remarkable but free translations. Indeed, Arthur Waley praises Giles for uniting 'rhyme and literalness with wonderful dexterity'. His version has been thought presumably to be what is called 'accurate'. Half the trouble in this Wang Wei piece is the absurd tripping metre. In the last analysis the whole thing is a failure of ear, 'the ear', as Charles Olson says in his essay, *Projective Verse*, 'which is so close to the mind that it *is* the mind's, that it has the mind's speed'. For the mind's speed, surely, is what the translator is always seeking to catch *in his own language*, however much he may sacrifice the original metre and stanza form. And only according to the degree of his success in this attempt will his words carry the conviction of 'a man speaking to men'.[1]

In making my choice, I began with the great and worked my way down, but trust I have kept out of the *bas fonds* created by the no doubt inevitable but in some ways depressing translation boom of recent years. I did, however, spend more time than I enjoyed wading about down there. I have put in a few oddities and there are versions by different hands of the same text. If I had to give my vote to our greatest translator, it would go to Dryden. Had he lived to complete his *Iliad*, that would perhaps have made the future of English poetry a very different thing. If Pope looks down today on our literary doings he must think our relegation of his Homer very odd, and I have tried to atone for this. No anthology, however, would be big enough to hold all of his best feats of narrative skill (I should have liked all of Juno's deception of Jove in Book XIV, for example). The Bible, of course, forces the anthologist to similar arbitrarinesses of exclusion. And the same is true of all major translators. What, briefly, I have tried to do is reveal some of the outlines of an immense and, as far as past centuries are concerned, a largely forgotten literature.

1 In translating the poetry of the American Indians, in the late nineteenth century American anthologists were often writing better than the poets. It is curious that Pound, looking to Chinese and Japanese sources for a poetry of emotional compactness, should have been so unaware of the native product.

Classical Verse Translated

When, in the late 1970s, I was asked to edit *The Oxford Book of Verse in English Translation*, there was little in the shape of anthologies either to obstruct the view or extend it to past centuries. Looking back to *The Oxford Book of Greek Verse in Translation* of 1938, edited by T.F. Highman and C.M. Bowra, one found a desert spread before one, much of it of the making of the two editors themselves. From Pope's great *Iliad* there were four scraps, from his *Odyssey* there was nothing. Dryden's extraordinary *Iliad*, Book One, went unnoticed. Everywhere was 'horrid evidence', as Donald Carne-Ross has said, 'of what happens when people whose only claim is that they can read Greek, try to write English'. H.W. Garrod in his *Oxford Book of Latin Verse* (1912) had revealed a quicker eye and ear in the short section of 'Translations and Imitations' placed at the back of his anthology. But these, chiefly confined 'to the four principal Latin poets', consist of 'a few old favourites of my own', and Garrod confesses, 'I have made no systematic search in the literature of translation'.

In 1966 appeared George Steiner's *Penguin Book of Modern Verse Translation*. Steiner was perhaps the first to declare openly the inadequacy of Lattimore's long overestimated Homer, with its loose syntax and prosy vocabulary. His choice (despite a few dodos) was judicious, as far as the modern phase of translation goes, and his introduction lucidly defined what was at stake: 'The classic wanes to the status of the academic or falls silent unless it is re-appropriated by translation, unless the living poet examines and affirms its relevance to the current idiom (for want of a vital translation Lucretius is, at present inert).'

My own editorial work with OBVET (as I shall call it) had gone some considerable way when I made the discovery of a forgotten book, Mark Van Doren's *An Anthology of World Poetry* (1929). As one might expect from this Dryden scholar, his anthology (chiefly of translations) contained much that was suggestive and excellent, but its 1,270 pages were weighed down by a reliance on the Victorians and Edwardians and by Van Doren's own vaulting ambition. Poems from Japanese, Sanskrit, Arabic, Persian, Egyptian, Spanish, Scandinavian and Russian had been drawn from a dispiriting company of mediocre translators. However, there was enough seventeenth-century work to reinforce my own sense of the fineness of

Jonson, Cowley, Herrick and, above all, Dryden. Pope's Homer or anybody else's Homer were missing, as was Dryden's *Aeneid.* In short, an awareness of how much Van Doren had missed also proved encouraging in one's search for more.

In editing OBVET I rapidly became conscious of how little use had been made of our vast and neglected literature of poetic translation that had run along beside and, in the form of imitations and appropriations, often mingled unnoticed with 'original work' over the centuries. Of course, there was far too much to include all that one wanted. I even suggested two volumes, so that more justice could have been done to the twentieth-century revival after the doldrums of much of the nineteenth. The idea was turned down, but when the anthology was finally allowed to go out of print, I was able to make use of pieces that want of space had forced me to reject, along with some translations from OBVET itself that now would go underground (or so I imagined), in *Eros English'd* (1992), an anthology of classical erotic poetry in translation. Despite immense cuts in my Oxford anthology, I felt that I had been able to exhibit there much forgotten or undiscovered poetry in translation, with obvious high points in the work of Gavin Douglas, Jonson, Cowley, Dryden, Pope, Shelley, Tennyson and Pound. I also fought for a principle which has benefited the editors of *The Oxford Book of Classical Verse in Translation* now edited by Adrian Poole and Jeremy Maule – original spelling and not relentless modernisation. Indeed, OBVET ground to a halt for six months when I dug my heels in to gain this principle. 'I want modern spelling', my editor had said, 'because I do not underrate the future of this book as a Christmas gift.' He even sent me modernised versions, cobbled together in the office, of Spenser, a poet who deliberately wrote in an archaic English, to show me the way.

The Oxford Book of Classical Verse in Translation has the immediate advantage over OBVET of a narrower (though still wide) remit and two editors to sift the flow of translations. My eye fell first on the note on the wrapper and I imagine that both editors, when they read it, must have blushed with embarrassment. They cannot, of course, be held responsible for the work of an ignorant or amnesiac blurb writer. He, or she, gets underway by noting the existence of an 'astonishingly inventive tradition of translation to which some of the greatest English poets have contributed, including Chaucer and Jonson, Dryden and Pope, Tennyson and Ezra Pound'. 'How just,' I thought, 'the news is actually getting through.' But what riveted my attention was the phrase that follows: 'This anthology presents the wealth of this living tradition as it has never been seen before …' Never? I am sure the editors could scarcely have felt this way, since they both know my own work (to judge from their choice of quotations regarding translation in their introduction), including also my Clark Lectures, *Poetry and Metamorphosis* (given under the auspices of their own college, Trinity) with its concluding chapter, 'Metamorphosis as Translation'. The practice varies in Oxford Books, but Poole and Maule are scrupulous in acknowledging no debts to any of their friends, as if their book had sprung like Minerva fully armed from the head of Jove.

Anyone compiling an anthology of translations is faced by a choice. Either the arrangement is chronological under the names of the translators, or under the name of the poet being translated (thus Virgil, say, gets a montage sequence across the ages). The first method gives one a history of English translation in a fairly orderly fashion. The second opts for the drama of confrontation, as versions leap from translator to translator, century to century. Having used the first method in OBVET, I now found myself becoming a partial convert to the second through the sheer sense of historical collision. Aesthetically this method sometimes makes for a bumpy ride, compounded by the fact that, since the name of the translator does not precede but follows each extract, one does not always know whom one is reading without first turning the page – sometimes two pages. However, there are also unexpected pleasures to be experienced here.

The form of the anthology, as the introduction explains, is to divide the classical material into eight sections, four Greek and four Latin. 'The divisions', as we are told, 'are based mainly but not always on chronological principles. The first three sections of the Greek half also correspond to generic divisions between epic, lyric and drama…; the fourth section frankly embraces the heterogeneity of Greek verse after 400 BC …' The Latin part has at its heart the period which has had most effect on English literature, that of Virgil, Horace and Ovid. The introduction is written with vigour and wit, kindling at one point to a sort of raffish brio where we are told that 'this Oxford book will tell you, among other things, how to school calves, drown puppies, evade husbands, pick up boys …' This last item (though the list continues) would benefit from some value judgements. It leads one into an area of classical poetry where the idealised and the brutal, as do the Greek and Latin, fall into sharp contrast. I thought at once of the distinctions made by Guy Davenport in his essay 'Nabokov's Don Quixote' – he is talking about Lolita and her symbolic ancestry. 'She began', writes Davenport, 'as a seductive child in the first appearance

of romantic love in the West, boy or girl, Sappho's darlings or
Anakreon's striplings. Plato philosophised these hopeless loves into
something called the love of Ideal Beauty. The theme became sala-
cious and overbearing in the leaden hands of the Romans ...'

'The best classical verse in the best of English translations: this has
been our ideal', write the editors. And this ideal of Poole and Maule
has led them to versions that have been lost sight of in old books and
in manuscripts. You sense their industry at work, discovering,
comparing and contrasting. It is the contrast one is most aware of
when one considers (say) the Earl of Derby, Trapp, Ogilby and
Lauderdale and compares them with the likes of Dryden and Pope.
The first four are second-raters and offer nothing like 'the best classical verse in the best English translations'. They serve merely to
throw the best into even sharper relief, but you do not feel that the
editors are really conscious of this fact. There are times when they
seem to mistake small beer for 'the best of English translations': C.
Day Lewis reads as rhythmically commonplace, Fitzgerald's *Georgics*
feels underpowered, F.L. Lucas writes in no man's English, Thomas
Phaer's fourteeners (1573) turn Virgil into wordy slackness (though
I liked his adjective 'sowerskowling'), John Frederick Nims has a
moon that 'glamors the landscape' (Sappho) and his Horace ('your
riddled abdomen is raging', he says of poor old Lydia) is pretty dusty
here. I was amazed to find that old chestnut, Cory's 'They told
Heraclitus you were dead', a left-over from Highman and Bowra who
presumably culled it from Quiller-Couch's 1911 *Oxford Book of English
Verse*. Fifty years ago F.R. Leavis used to glance at this specimen of
Callimachus in his lectures, as an example of the inertly Victorian.
How right he was. Other odd choices occur and at least one of these
is part and parcel of these editors' montage way of working and
placing side by side snippets of a given work by different hands. The
case in point is Juvenal's Tenth Satire and its distressing passages on
old age. Instead of Dryden's version or Johnson's great imitation, *The
Vanity of Human Wishes*, we are turned over to Shadwell's burlesque
treatment of impotence:

Tho' all the Night he dallies, 'tis in vain.
It still does a poor Chiterlin remain.

Perhaps Robert Lowell's over-the-top sort of treatment works best
in a poem like the Tenth Satire. He does not appear in the above
montage, but is called on for Horace, of all unlikely poets. He leads
off with *Odes* 1.4, ending characteristically for Lowell, with a phrase

about 'girls in heat', rather an exaggeration of Horace's temperate 'will grow warm' (*virgines tepebunt*). Far more disastrous is Lowell's version of the ode on Cleopatra. She gets the full filmic treatment. According to Lowell, she aims 'to enthrone / her depravity naked in the Capitol', but ends up 'no queen now, but a private woman much humbled'. Between the sexy bit (not there in Horace) and the flat-footed conclusion, so many things are missed, it's difficult to know where to begin. This ode, which inspired Marvell's treatment of Charles I at his execution, hinges on one of those famous 'turns' of Horace, the poem veering away to celebrating her triumph – not (*pace* Lowell) her humbled status. She soberly contemplates the ruins of her palace and by her suicide scorns Caesar's triumph from her tomb. In all this, Horace sees the fineness and pride of one who 'nothing common did or mean / Upon that memorable scene' – as Marvell later said of King Charles, a figure whom he should not have been admiring while praising Cromwell, any more than Horace should have ended up admiring this anarchic female. Lowell gets it all wrong and even in small things. Our feelings are swayed by Horace as soon as he sees Caesar as the hunter of *molles columbas*, rendered by Lowell as 'the soft-textured dove', but these doves in Horace are merely 'soft' or 'tender' – their texture is neither here nor there.

I missed one or two things in this chiefly well-chosen section on Horace – Cowley's version of 'Ad Pyrrham' (his Anacreonticks are fully represented) and also the eighteenth century translator Philip Francis (?1708–73). His version of the Lydia poem (*Odes* 1.25) leaves John Frederick Nims standing, and the technical variety of his Horace is always surprising. Whatever happened to *Odes* 4.7 in Samuel Johnson's translations? The 1970 version here by Jim McCullock is by turns poetical ('the hour knells the riven day' – a lame echo of Thomas Gray) and floppy ('Graces and nymphs go dancing nude'). What a delight, though, to come upon Allan Ramsay's Pyrrha:

> What young Raw Muisted[1] Beau Bred at his Glass
> now wilt thou on a Rose's Bed Carress
> wha niest to thy white Breasts wilt thow intice
> with hair unsnooded and without thy Stays

– a version written c.1720, but not published until 1961.

When OBVET appeared in 1980, not many people were reading

1 Muisted; perfumed with musk

Pope the translator, and only recently has he crept back into the teaching syllabus. Poole and Maule display in all its glory his *Iliad*, 'that poetical wonder ... a performance which no age or translation can pretend to equal', as Samuel Johnson puts it. Our own age has managed to ignore it for the better part of a century, the Victorians having already begun to cool towards it, although they continued to print new editions. If Pope's Homer is the undisputed high point of the Greek portion of this anthology, Dryden's complete Virgil, together with substantial portions of Lucretius, Juvenal, Horace and Ovid, furnish the poetical wonder of the Latin – in fact, another performance 'no age or translation can pretend to equal'. Yet how many readers know the crowning glory of Dryden's Virgil, his *Georgics*? The Oxford editors do not disappoint us here, though the other translators of Ovid who accompany Dryden's major effort in that compilation by Dr Samuel Garth, *Ovid's Metamorphoses* of 1717, are thinly represented. Garth's edition is – *pace* Ezra Pound on Golding – perhaps the finest *Metamorphoses* we possess. But like the *Georgics* and Dryden's *Aeneid*, it is a neglected classic, one of the many victims to that romantic notion that translations cannot compete with 'original poems'.

After Virgil and his successors, Dryden is impatient with the course of Latin verse: 'It is littler wonder that rolling down through so many barbarous ages from the spring of Virgil, it bears along with it the filth and ordures of the Goths and Vandals.' What in fact lay ahead for Latin poetry and thus for its translators after Virgil, can be measured by the achievements of Ben Jonson, Cowley, Herrick, Vaughan, as the Oxford Book amply shows. There are good things here, too, from our own century.

Not 'as never before', but once again, the greatness of the English tradition of translating poetry into poetry stands vindicated. What remains to be done is for critics, aware of the centrality of translation to the whole history of English poetry, to revise our conception of that history. The presence of translation in it changes the balance of conventional assessments that still rate translation as a poor cousin of the real thing, poetry itself. But poetry itself is what the great translators were always looking for and finding.

The New Oxford Book of
Sixteenth-Century Verse

When C.S. Lewis divided sixteenth-century poetry into 'the drab' and 'the golden' – purely descriptive terms, he insisted – he was in fact making a value judgement that betrayed something of his Victorian prejudices. This kind of prejudice was already evident in the volume Emrys Jones' splendid anthology at last replaces, namely Sir Edmund Chambers' *Oxford Book of Sixteenth-Century Verse*, first published in 1932 and reprinted several times since. It has taken many years for us to see how radically nineteenth-century taste distorted our view of the sixteenth century. I recall the pleasure and salutory shock experienced at first reading a reproving article on Lewis' *English Literature in the Sixteenth Century* by that great American critic Yvor Winters (now in the process of being forgotten, along with F.R. Leavis, Lionel Trilling and other leading critics of his generation).

Winters was writing in *The Hudson Review* in 1955. His opinion was that Lewis' scholarship was formidable, but that he did not know which the best poems were: 'he likes the pretty so profoundly that he overlooks the serious.' A truly practical critic, Winters supplied a list of 'a minimal number of poets and poems' representing his own taste. Most of these appear in Emrys Jones' anthology, plus many more. But Winters' centre of interest turned on the short poems of the period and Jones clearly sees that to represent it by these alone, for all their technical and spiritual fineness, falsifies the picture. It was an era of the extended poem and also, importantly, of translations – and of translations that are not always acknowledged as such:

> Let's then meet
> Often with amorous lips, and greet
> Each other till our wanton kisses
> In number pass the days Ulysses
> Consumed in travel, and the stars
> That look upon our peaceful wars
> With envious lustre. If this store
> Will not suffice, we'll number o'er
> The same again, until we find
> No number left to call to mind.

This masterly imitation of Catullus' 'Vivamus, mea Lesbia', attributed to Sir Walter Ralegh, is entitled simply 'To his love when he had obtained her'. Ralegh (if Ralegh it was) took over Catullus as audaciously as he set out for the Orinoco, and with a good deal more success. Other translators add their own mite to their authors; some (Wyatt's Petrarch, for example) deconstruct the original to accommodate new and bitter meanings; Gavin Douglas's *Aeneid* – the greatest long poem of the early sixteenth century and one I should have dearly liked to find represented by Jones – has a new ending invented by its Scottish author. Scottish! That's why Douglas does not appear in these pages. Yet, given that he influenced Surrey's Virgil which does, and that Douglas's translation was still prized as late as the 1690s as 'the best version that ever was of that incomparable poem', perhaps readers should have been forced to brave its Scots idiom. And what of Dunbar? Henryson, alas (d.1506), is a bit early, though other early and latecomers (among the latter Ben Jonson) have been discreetly smuggled in.

Of course, it is only too easy to give advice to anthologists or to put them right. It is, at this date, easy also to be unfair to Chambers who, though he excluded Marlowe's Ovid from his anthology along with Chapman's Homer, did print a sizeable chunk of Golding's version of the *Metamorphoses* (the lovely story of Baucis and Philemon) together with some twenty stanzas of Fairfax's Tasso and another twenty of Harington's Ariosto, both massive undertakings we have too long agreed to forget. Chambers, though, never focuses the fact that translation is central to this period, something that Jones brings out with bold inclusions (almost four hundred lines of Golding, sixty-three stanzas of Harington and forty-eight of Fairfax). I, for one, could have taken more extracts from Golding – Ezra Pound was surely right in 'Notes on Elizabethan Classicists' to show his many facets with half a dozen contrasting snippets. But there is plenty to be going on with here, and now that OUP do not intend to reprint *The Oxford Book of Verse in English Translation* – a triumph of accountancy over literacy – we shall need to have recourse to anthologies like Jones' to keep alive our awareness of the importance of translation in the whole history of our poetry.

Jones prints many favourite pieces and many that will come as a surprise to non-specialist readers – 'Scottish Field', for example, an extended anonymous poem celebrating the English victory at the Battle of Flodden in 1513. What is striking about this is its being written in alliterative metre, 'the last surviving poem', says Jones, 'to

use alliteration as a metrical system in the old way' – the old way being
that of the author of *Sir Gawain and the Green Knight* and Langland.
(Interestingly enough, it was in the sixteenth century that Langland
was printed for the first time.) 'Scottish Field' is only one example of
the overlap of medieval and Renaissance modes in this anthology,
modes of thought as much as metrical ones. We travel from the
familiar inspired doggerel of Skelton on the death of Jane Scrope's
pet sparrow (shades of Catullus once more) –

> Some time he would gasp
> When he saw a wasp;
> A fly or a gnat
> He would fly at that;
> And prettily he would pant
> When he saw an ant.
> Lord, now he would pry
> After a butterfly …

on to the majestic gloom of Fulke Greville's

> Sion lies waste, and thy Jerusalem
> Lord, is fall'n to utter desolation …

Verse satire (a genre neglected by Chambers) is copiously and justly
represented and the idea (Chambers once more) that Elizabethan
poetry is 'characteristically a light-hearted poetry that plays upon the
coloured surface of things' receives many challenges. Donne, on
these grounds, was excluded by Chambers as being 'Elizabethan' only
by chronology! He is restored by Jones to his place in the 1590s along
with other impressive poets of that decade of anxiety.

It is a general trade mark of the Oxford anthologies that they are
in modernised spelling. Those who like a smooth read will rejoice at
this and others will regret the loss of that floating feel of a language
that has not yet been finalised into dictionary shape and for which
'correct English' is a distant concept. People who wrote of ciperstrees,
mushrumps and porpentines had a very different sense of language
from our own. And what do we gain by exchanging Skelton's
'huswyfe' for the phonetic 'hussif'? Rhyme sometimes throws up a
barrier against Oxford's practice. 'Wordes' has to stay because it is
two syllables. Spenser has sensibly been left alone, since he wrote in
a consciously archaic diction – though in one current Oxford
anthology his spelling too has been modernised. This is rather like
modernising Chatterton.

But for the general reader (if this is not a polite fiction) these are matters that will not provoke his or her animosity. For general and specialist readers – and also for poets – there are things in these seven hundred and more pages of verse that will quicken the pulses as they bring home a sense of the immense resources and variety of our poetic inheritance.

Some Aspects of Horace in the Twentieth Century

It would be impossible today for any writer to identify his poetic concerns so completely with those of Horace as did Alexander Pope. Pope's *Imitations of Horace* counted on a familiar acquaintance with that poet among its readership – after all, he was, from school days, in the possession of most literate males and evidently also of some educated women. For Mrs Aphra Behn, Lady Mary Wortley Montagu and Anna Seward, the Swan of Lichfield, all wrote imitations of one of Horace's most famous odes, 'Ad Pyrrham'. The ground had been prepared for an English Horace ever since Ben Jonson put him into couplets and an Horatian tone entered his own original poetry. Previously both Surrey and Sidney had tried their hand at Englishing him, but it was not until the creative effort initiated by Jonson and continued by Fanshawe, Cowley, Oldham and Dryden that Horace became, so to speak, a fully fledged English poet. Dryden's version of *Odes* 3.29 ('Descended of an ancient Line / That long the Tuscan Scepter sway'd ...') is perhaps the greatest single translation of a Horace poem to date – the date of its publication and, one might add, the present time. Thus, when Jacob Tonson in 1715 brought out his edition of Horace, translated by numerous hands, he could assemble from chiefly contemporary writers a team of remarkable quality. The balance, but also the audacity of Horace, had entered into the bloodstream of many of these, so that the term Horation can be applied to much original English poetry of the seventeenth and eighteenth century in a way that would not fit our contemporary verse. Most readers of poetry do not know Horace even in translation; the several Penguin versions of the odes, epodes and satires do little to convey the verbal corrugation of the original; in my own lifetime, universities have ceased to require Latin for student entrance. So the generalisation with which I began seems set to be confirmed, since poets of future generations are the products of educational requirements. Individuals, of course, will diagnose and seek to remedy their own cultural vitamin deficiencies. For example, in 1979 and in America, where the high schools had long since abandoned any pretence of a humanistic education, the young poet Robert Pinsky, in making his debut with the ambitious book-length poem *An Explanation of America* (Princeton, 1979), incorporated into this work a version of Horace's *Epistles* 1.16 where, says Pinksy, Horace

> Implies his answer about aspiration
> Within the prison of empire or republic.

He then goes on in a meditation on Horace's poem to discover common ground with this Roman freedman's son whose youthful enthusiasm had found him, 'Along with other enthusiastic students/ (Cicero's son among them)', on the wrong side at Philippi:

> Horace came back to Rome a pardoned rebel
> In his late twenties, without cash or prospects,
> Having stretched out his wings too far beyond
> The frail nest of his freedman father's hopes,
> As he has written.

Pinsky's poem is in some ways an Horatian reply to the subjectivity implicit in those psycho-dramas of the self, the poetries of Lowell, Berryman, Sexton and Plath. Given the moment of its appearance, perhaps there is even something honourable in its running the risk of seeming at times verbally somewhat undernourished. It is Horatian in the democratic moderation of its imaginings of a possible future for Pinsky's country and his children, and also in the unapocalyptic tone in which it patiently 'explains' the present, avoiding the Manichean black and white of ready simplifications (Vietnam was one of the uneasy issues whose visionary yeast had activated much bad poetry). Pinsky's 'two lame cheers for democracy that I /Borrow and try to pass to you' and his suspicion of 'that tyrant / And sycophantic lout, the majority' are given force and context by his real-isation that

> Denial of limit has been the pride, or failing,
> Well-known to be shared by all this country's regions,
> Races and classes; which all seem to challenge
> The idea of sufficiency itself ...

His 'idea of sufficiency itself' finds tempered scope in the expression of the Horation epistle that precedes this statement. In a poem addressed to his children (who, as he realises, may never read it), it is right and proper that questions of family and of paternal regard should be primary:

Horace's father, who had been a slave,
Engaged in some small business near Venusia;
And like a Jewish or Armenian merchant
Who does well in America, he sent
His son to Rome's best schools, and then to Athens
(It's hard to keep from thinking, 'as to Harvard')
To study, with the sons of gentlemen
And politicians, the higher arts most useful
To citizens of a Republic ...

Pinsky opts for the 'middle style'. His unshowy, even relaxed way of writing, derives from the epistolary Horace and not from the denser, more compacted style of the odes. It was this latter style that appealed to a number of literary modernists born earlier in the century than Pinsky, namely Pound, Bunting and Auden (though Auden also has an Horatian epistle in 'The Sea and the Mirror', Alonso's 'Dear Son, when the warm multitudes cry ...'). Pinsky's style harks back, with whatever differences, to the Horatianism of an American belonging to an older generation than all these, Robert Frost, and aims, like Frost, at an effect of almost casual conversation. Frost himself had been anticipated in this vein by Emerson and also in the use of a convention whereby the man who lives close to the soil – shades of Horace's Sabine farm – can chasten the rootless townee with his own more elementary satisfactions. There is even an Horatian touch, when in Emerson's 'Hamatreya', Death puts in an appearance among these rural solidities:

'Tis good, when you have crossed the sea and back,
To find the sitfast acres where you left them.'
Ah! the hot owner sees not Death, who adds
Him to his land, a lump of mould the more.

Emerson, however, cannot sustain this unity of tone and before long we have left the world of Horatian nature and are listening to the spirit of Earth purveying a rather different kind of wisdom. It was Frost himself who, as Reuben Brower[1] has remarked, Americanised the Horatian *sermo*, Pope's couplets suggesting the technical means, as in a poem like 'The Lesson for Today' where Frost considers the historic gap between quantitative verse such as that used by Horace and the reversion in medieval Latin poetry to stress and end rhyme:

1   Reuben Brower, *The Poetry of Robert Frost* (Oxford, 1963), Chapter III.

> Yet singing but Dione in the wood
> And ver aspergit terram floribus
> They slowly led old Latin verse to rhyme
> And to forget the ancient lengths of time,
> And so began the modern world for us.

'The ancient lengths of time', of course, refers to the quantitative measures of Roman verse – the medieval 'ver aspergit terram floribus' with the addition of 'And' at the beginning of the phrase, makes a perfect modern accentual iambic pentameter. Two speakers are imagined as exchanging views in this poem, a common device in Horace's (and Pope's) satires. 'The dramatic mode of the debate', says Brower, 'is also Horatian', as Frost addresses an aristocratic poet of a previous epoch:

> Let's celebrate the event, my distant friend,
> In publicly disputing which is worse,
> The present age or your age.

However, 'And so began the modern age for us' ushers in elsewhere a somewhat bleaker prospect (Horace, of course, could be bleak, but not with the lonely and romantic nihilism of the post-Nietzschean generations). New Hampshire, whatever earthy wisdom it had to teach, was hardly the Sabine farm for Frost. Sheer endurance, the sense of being alone up there, are the marks of both Frost and his protagonists. The Horatian modes are social and often convivial, but in a poem like 'Directive' Frost has to face out the overmastering awareness of geological ages – those disappearing quantities, the cancellation of 'ancient lengths of time', are more than simply a metrical matter:

> There is a house that is no more a house
> Upon a farm that is no more a farm
> And in a town that is no more a town.
> The road there …
> May seem as if it should have been a quarry …
> Besides the wear of iron wagon wheels
> The ledges show lines ruled southeast northwest,
> The chisel work of an enormous Glacier
> That braced his feet against the Arctic Pole.

This is a vaster and more troubling universe than that of Horace and in 'Directive' the sustaining fiction of dialogue has fallen away. The voice in the poem addresses 'you', meaning us, but we have no more chance of replying than the aristocratic poet from years back. Although the protagonist in the poem, exploring this deserted spot, takes up a broken drinking goblet which he likens to the Grail, we know this Grail does not contain Christ's blood, and we know also that the 'you' at the poem's conclusion, while it gestures towards a community of listeners, falls on the lonely desertion of Panther Mountain:

Here are your waters and your watering place,
Drink and be whole again beyond confusion.

Yet the confusion was endemic to Frost and to his time and not to be got rid of by an invented ceremony among the ruins. He finds himself, before taking refuge behind the persona of the bluff, no-nonsense New Englander (his formative years until the age of twelve were spent in San Francisco), a houseless spirit threatened by the aftermath of a thinker whose perception of Horace is part of our story, that is Nietzsche himself.

Nietzsche, like the early Frost, was a divided man, a product of the Protestant north who yearned towards the Mediterranean. Having begun by endorsing the music of Richard Wagner and its re-embodiment of Teutonic mythology, he succeeded in persuading himself that the music which really appealed to him was that of Bizet with its evocation of the unsubjective south (of a Spain, in fact, on which Bizet had never set foot). Here was the opportunity to 'be whole again beyond confusion': 'How such a work [*Carmen*] brings one to perfection. One becomes a "masterpiece" oneself', as he wrote to the composer Peter Gast. The south, he tells us, in *Beyond Good and Evil*, is 'a great school of recovery for the most spiritual and the most sensuous ills' and teaches us to be 'somewhat on guard against German music'.[1] As far as literature goes, in his rejection of Wagnerian subjectivity (he sees Wagner as poet as well as musician), his attraction towards the south and 'the Mediterranean clearness of sky' leads, according to the testimony of his later years, to Roman in preference to Greek culture: 'We do not *learn* from the Greeks: their mode is too foreign, it is also too unstable to operate imperatively or "classically". Who would ever have learned to write from a Greek!' It is as a writer that Nietzsche is speaking, and when he says of the

1 Friedrich Nietzsche, *Beyond Good and Evil*, trans. Helen Zimmern (T.N. Foulis, Edinburgh and London, 1907), pp. 216–17.

Greeks, 'they *cannot* be to us what the Romans are', the Roman he
particularly thinks of is Horace. The section 'My indebtedness to the
Ancients' in *The Twilight of the Idols*[1] contains a passage on the effect
of Horace's style very different from anything expressed or incorporated by a poet like Frost into his own mode of writing. The insights
in Nietzsche's account of Horace, uncannily accurate in defining the
way the original Latin works, point forward to what it was that drew
Pound, Bunting and other moderns to the Horatian ode rather than
the *sermo*. D.M. Hooley in his book *The Classics in Paraphrase*[2] speaks
of the odes giving 'some crucial stimulus to the modern poet's technical artifice', and goes on 'Horatian metrical virtuosity, its mosaic
cohesiveness, its love of contrast and surprising turns – all find their
analogues in *Briggflatts* and Bunting's two books of *Odes*'. The word
'mosaic' in this come from Nietzsche's passage:

> Up to the present I have not obtained from any poet the same
> artistic delight as was given me from the first by an Horatian ode.
> In certain languages that which is obtained here cannot even be
> hoped for. The mosaic of words in which every word, by sound,
> by position and by meaning, diffuses its force right, left, and over
> the whole, that *minimum* in the compass and number of signs, that
> *maximum* thus realised in their energy, – all that is Roman, and if
> you will believe me, it is *noble par excellence*. All other poetry becomes
> somewhat too popular in comparison with it – mere sentimental
> loquacity.

Before going on to see how this conception of a 'mosaic of words'
affords 'some crucial stimulus to the modern poet's technical artifice',
in Hooley's phrase, first an example from Horace himself of what
Nietzsche has in mind. Dr Frank Stack includes in his *Pope and Horace*[3]
an account which can scarcely be bettered of the first eight lines of
Odes 4.1, a poem made familiar to us by both Ben Jonson and Pope
and which exists in an elegant contemporary version by James Michie.
Dr Stack begins by quoting from the poem:

1   Friedreich Nietzsche, *The Case of Wagner, Nietzsche Contra Wagner, The Twilight of the
    Idols, The Antichrist*, trans. Thomas Common (T. Fisher Unwin, London, 1899),
    pp. 233–4. I have amended one or two awkwardnesses and touches of late
    Victorian rapture.
2   D. M. Hooley, *The Classics in Paraphrase* (Susquehanna, 1988), p. 109.
3   Frank Stack, *Pope and Horace* (Cambridge, 1985), pp. 103–4.

> Intermissa Venus diu
> Rursus bella moves? parce precor, precor!
>   Non sum qualis eram, bonae
> Sub regno Cynarae: Desine, dulcium
>   Mater saeva Cupidinum,
> Circa lustra decem flectere mollibus
>   Jam durum imperiis: abi
> Quo blandae juvenum te revocant preces.   (1–8)

(Christopher Smart's trot runs: After a long cessation, O Venus, again are you stirring up tumults? Spare me, I beseech you, I beseech you. I am not the man I was under the dominion of good-natur'd Cynara. Forbear, thou cruel mother of soft desires, to bend one bordering upon fifty, now too harden'd for your soft commands: go whither the soothing prayers of youth invoke thee.[1])

Our scholar and critic comments:

This is what Nietzsche calls the mosaic of words. Adjectives are placed well before the nouns they modify, suspended to arouse interest in what it is they refer to and only 'completed' when their nouns are discovered: '*Intermissa* ... *bella*' ('suspended ... warfare'), '*bonae* ... *Cynarae*' ('good ... Cynara'), '*dulcium* ... *Cupidinum*' ('sweet ... desires'), '*mollibus* ... *imperiis*' ('soft ... commands'), '*blandae* ... *preces*' ('wheedling ... prayers'). Contrasting words are yoked together: '*dulcium* ... *saeva*' ('sweet ... fierce'), '*mollibus* ... *durum*' ('soft ... hardened'). The words '*imperiis*' ('commands') and '*durum*' ('hardened') are juxtaposed without syntactical connection in order to emphasise the paradox. But within this complex pattern how powerful is alliterative '*parce precor, precor*' ('Show mercy, I beg and beseech you'); and how simple and haunting is '*Non sum qualis, eram bonae / Sub regno Cynarae*' ('I am not the man I was under the rule of good Cynara'). Finally, how distinctive is the rhythm: the metre is the Second Asclepiadean, a graceful metre used, significantly, in many of Horace's earlier love poems:

$$- - - \smile \smile - \smile \overset{\smile}{-}$$
$$- - - \smile \smile - \parallel - \smile \smile - \smile \overset{\smile}{-}$$

The heavy syllables at the beginning of every line tend to give strength and calm, the light syllables movement and grace.

---

1   C. Smart, *The Works of Horace Translated Literally into English Prose* (London, 1752), Vol. 1.

Ezra Pound, beginning with the curious proposition that Horace was 'the first Royal Academy', moves reluctantly away from his ambivalence about him, and at the end of his poetic career, writes three masterly versions of the odes to which I shall return later. A sense of 'the mosaic of words' and an awareness of the role of metre, comparable with that in Stack's analysis, already appear in an article Pound published in *The Criterion* for 1929–30, where we read: 'Apart from Catullus, he was the most skillful metrist among the Latins ... [He gives pleasure] to the connoisseur by his verbal arrangements ... This literary pleasure is not due to the passion of Horace, but to the order of words and their cadence in a line measured by the duration of syllables.[1] Basil Bunting, never having doubted the mastery of Horace, admonishes another Poundian, Louis Zukofsky, in a letter of 1948, 'Horace works wonders with a word order which was crabbed even to his contempories, as one may see by reading Lucretius and Ovid on either side of him. It is not right to banish such effects ...' Like Frost, both Pound and Bunting were exercised by the fact that verse had 'forgotten the ancient lengths of time'. Discussing Horace's genius in 'changing the whole mood of a poem in a single line', Bunting says,

> Quantity is no doubt one element in it – there are semibreves as well as crotchets etc., in music. To write pure quantitative poems in English, as Sidney, Spenser, Campion sometimes did is very difficult because the stress in English is so strong that people, at least in the south of England, don't notice anything else. Besides, the stress sometimes modifies the quantity. English phrases with stress on a short syllable are not common. But a poet ought to be always aware of the quantities and it is a very good exercise to imitate quantitative patterns.[2]

That people 'at least in the south of England' can hear nothing *but* accent and gloss over the differentiation of vowel lengths, points to the fact that perhaps only a northerner could have achieved the differentiations in the opening lines of Bunting's masterpiece *Briggflatts*:

> Brag, sweet tenor bull,
> descant on Rawthey's madrigal ...

1 Ezra Pound, 'Horace', *The Criterion* 9 (1929–30), pp. 217–18.
2 Basil Bunting, 'An Interview with Basil Bunting', *Scripsi* (Summer / Autumn 1982), p. 30.

'I'd see what could be done in the way of adapting Greek quantita-
tive patterns into English', he had already advised a young poet
George Marion O'Donnell in 1934. In his own work, in translating
Horace's *Odes* 1.13 he bases his accentual English cadences on the
Second Asclepiadean metre, that is used also in 'Intermissa Venus diu
/ Rursus bella moves'. Pound even half persuaded himself, 'I think
the desire for vers libre is due to the sense of quantity reasserting itself
after years of starvation'. His own response to this was the metre of
Homage to Sextus Propertius. 'As to quantity', mulling over the same
question in 1913, he had written: 'it is foolish to suppose that we are
incapable of distinguishing a long vowel from a short one.' He wanted
to know when he first read Marianne Moore's syllabic verse 'whether
you are working in Greek quantitative measures …' Eliot, as D.S.
Carne-Ross has recently reminded us, said of Pound's poem 'The
Return' that it was 'an important study in verse which is really quantitative. Carne-Ross in this same *Arion* article audaciously argues that
in this poem where Pound sets out to resurrect the presences of classical poetry –

> See, they return; ah, see the tentative
> Movement, and the slow feet,
> The trouble in the pace and the uncertain
> Wavering!

– there is an attempt to reconstitute the effect of that very Sapphic
stanza Horace adapted from the Greek:

> The tentatively moving feet we are called on to see are those of
> the ancient gods, returning to us after their long absence. On the
> poem's secondary level we are invited to *hear* the feet of the ancient
> poems that celebrated their presence, the Greek poems composed
> in the quantitative measures now returning to assume new forms
> in English verse.[1]

The mosaic of words, Horace's ability to '[change] the whole mood
of a poem in a single line' (Bunting's phrase), the role of quantity in
achieving this, all these elements in the ongoing drama of a Horace
poem, derive their complete force from the fact that Horace is writing
in an inflected language, whose positioning of adjective in relation to
noun, for example, cannot easily be reproduced in our uninflected

1   D.S. Carne-Ross, 'Jocasta's Divine Head', *Arion* Third Series Vol. 1 No. 1 (1990),
    pp. 135–6.

English. But what of the all-over form of an Horatian ode, in terms, that is, of its track from start to finish? Can its movement be transposed into English poetry and how can that movement be defined? An attempt to answer these questions brings into our account another American poet, but one of a rather different constituency from that of Pound and his friends, J.V. Cunningham.

Cunningham, having published *The Helmsman* in 1942, went on to write a commentary on the poems this book contains, *The Quest of the Opal* (1950).[1] The title poem 'The Helmsman' is, very consciously, an Horatian ode and Cunningham's reflections on the form contain some of the most enlightening insights about it I have come across. Like Frost and Pound, Cunningham has pondered the loss of 'the ancient lengths of time' and the poem is an attempt 'to achieve in English the effect of the Alcaic strophe' by combining disyllabic and trisyllabic feet, rhyme being 'admitted here and there as a figure of diction'. My own feeling is that the substance of the experiences alluded to in 'The Helmsman' is more successfully handled in the accentual metres of two other poems, 'August Hail' and 'Montana Pastoral'. The trouble with Cunningham's Alcaics is that (unlike, say, Tennyson's imitation of this stanza in his tribute to Milton, 'O mighty-mouthed inventor of harmonies') the lines lack metrical bite, and the occasional appearance of rhyme has the effect, in so controlled a poem, of seeming almost desultory. However, Cunningham's reflections on 'the track' of the Horatian ode contain a most arresting passage. He located, he says, the unity of the ode in 'the unformulable feeling that, as the poem unfolded, its length and the arrangement of parts were proper and inevitable: "that just now is said what just now ought to be said."' And then comes – he speaks of himself in the third person – the most brilliant insight and simile of the entire commentary: 'He found that the progression from detail to detail was by a kind of imagic shift or transformation image which, like a train through a tunnel, brings one to a new prospect on the other side of the divide.'

One has only to look, say, at *Odes* 1.37, the so-called Cleopatra ode (the poem Marvell imitated in that portion of his own 'Horatian Ode' which deals with the execution of Charles I), to see the justice of Cunningham's image. 'Nunc est bibendum', we are told, and what we

---

1   J.V. Cunningham, *The Helmsman and the Quest of the Opal* (The Colt Press, San Francisco 1942 and Alan Swallow, Denver 1950, bound together and issued, unpaginated, presumably by Alan Swallow).

are drinking to is the defeat of Cleopatra's navy at Actium and of her 'contaminated gang' in Smart's prose version. Caesar has brought her back to reality, her mind swimming in Mareotic wine. His pursuit of her is compared to the hawk pursuing the tender doves or the nimble hunter the hare in the plains of snowy Thessaly. A certain sympathy is here reserved for the 'molles columbas' and the 'leporem', but we are not allowed to forget that this is 'a destructive monster of a woman who' (and here the synatax takes an unforeseen turn, prompted perhaps by that note of sympathy and by the way Caesar has forced her mind back to reality). This is the kind of thing Bunting alludes to when he speaks of Horace 'changing the whole mood of a poem in a single line'. We are, in Cunningham's image, coming out of the tunnel to our new prospect: 'who' introduces 'seeking to die a more generous death / displayed no womanish fear ...' And the concluding portion of the poem, twelve lines of it, show us a woman with as steady an eye as Marvell's Charles, gazing at her ruined palace and, with courage and fortitude, taking hold of the asps that will kill her, rather than letting herself be dragged off by the Liburnian sailors ('rough Liburnian tars', says Smart). The triumph is entirely hers – she whose defeat the poem had begun by calling on us to celebrate.

A contemporary poet who seems to have taken careful note of Cunningham's image of the tunnel is Donald Davie, in a poem that follows the turns of the Horatian ode in dealing with, of all improbable themes, the miners' strike under Arthur Scargill (Davie and Scargill are both Yorkshiremen). Unlike Cunningham, he does not try to imitate Horatian metre, but Horatian syntax. He writes in free verse of a neo-American variety, verse guided (as in Horace) to its unpredictable goal by the firmness of its syntactic connectives:

Wombwell on Strike

Horace of course is not
a temporiser, but
his sudden and smooth transitions
    (as, into a railway tunnel,
      then out, to a different landscape)

It must be admitted elide,
and necessarily, what
happens up there on the hill
    or hill-ridge that the tunnel
      of syntax so featly slides under.

I have been reminded of this
when, gratefully leaving my native
haunts, the push-and-pull diesel
            clatters into a tunnel
            under a wooded escarpment:

Wentworth Woodhouse, mounded
or else in high shaws drifted
over the miners' tram-ways.
            Horace's streaming style
            exhorts me never to pause;

'Press on,' he says, and indeed his
suavities never entirely
exclude the note of alarm:
            'Leave the unlikely meaning
            to eddy, or you are in trouble.'

Wombwell – 'womb well': it is
foolish and barbarous word-play,
though happily I was
            born of this tormented
            womb, the taut West Riding.

Yours was solid advice,
Horace, and centuries have
endorsed it; but over this tunnel
            large policemen grapple
            the large men my sons have become.[1]

When, over thirty years ago, I first discovered Cunningham's image of the tunnel and the 'new prospect on the other side of the divide', a piece which immediately came to mind was Marianne Moore's 'Poetry'. Did this follow the formal path of an Horatian ode? I soon realised that it didn't quite, but the abruptness of the transitions, whether intentionally or not on the part of the poet, recalled Horace, and the heavily Latinate diction together with the indented syllabic lines of the stanza form, eschewing traditional accentual verse, reinforced the association. The Moorish style suggests rather than exemplifies classical practices – hence Ezra Pound's puzzlement as to 'whether you are working in Greek quantitative measures'. She was

1   Donald Davie, *Collected Poems* (Manchester,1990), pp. 447–8..

not, and presumably one of the few ways of doing so in English would be to follow Swinburne's approach in his 'Sapphics', allowing stress and quantity to coincide and keeping to the same syllable count as Sappho's hendecasyllabics:

All the night sleep came not upon my eyelids,
Shed not dew, nor shook nor unclosed a feather,
Yet with lips shut close and with eyes of iron
    Stood and beheld me.

This is precisely what Bunting did in his version of Catullus' imitation of Sappho's most famous ode, No. 20. Bunting, who must be one of the very few major twentieth-century poets (Pound was another) to be an enthusiastic admirer of Swinburne as metrist, uses the same method in his translations of Horace's *Odes* 1.13 and 3.12. The first of these, as noted above, is in the Second Asclepiadean, and Bunting's accentual cadence is hewn close to the rhythm of Horace's Latin:

Please stop gushing about his pink
    neck smooth arms and so forth, Dulcie; it makes me sick …

Odes 3.12 is in the *ionic a minore* (˘ ˘ – –/˘ ˘ – –) which Bunting once more effectively mimes, letting the metre show from time to time, rather than governing every turn of the poem:

Yes, it's slow, docked of amours,
    docked of the doubtless efficacious
bottled makeshift …

His version of *Odes* 2.14 is far darker in tone, as befits its subject, and an excellent example of the way Bunting follows out the winding inevitability of Horace's syntax. This was written in Bunting's seventy-second year:

You can't grip years, Postume,
that ripple away nor hold back
wrinkles and, soon now, age,
nor can you tame death

not if you paid three hundred
bulls every day that goes by
to Pluto, who has no tears,
who has dyked up

giants where we'll go abroad,
we who feed on the soil,
to cross, kings some, some
penniless plowman.

For nothing we keep out of war
or from screaming spindrift
or wrap ourselves against autumn,
for nothing, seeing

we must stare at the dark, slow
drift and watch the damned
toil, while all they build
tumbles back on them.

We must let earth go and home,
wives too, and your trim trees,
yours for a moment, save one
sprig of black cypress.

Better men will empty
bottles we locked away,
wine puddle our table,
fit wine for a pope.

In a recorded interview made for the New York Center for Visual History in 1984, Bunting both reads and comments on this poem. We have heard much of Pound's stress on 'the ideogrammatic method', a technique whereby he juxtaposes many verbal fragments in his *Cantos* on the basis of his understanding of Chinese characters. Bunting is sceptical about Pound's reliability in this area and, asked to comment on the nature of the ideogrammatic method, he replies

> It ultimately has nothing whatever to do with the Chinese character. Though Pound saw an instance of it there, you could find it just as well in Horace … It is as if you set two things side by side … But it's not the case of one ideogram against another. It's the case of a whole page of ideograms one against another so to speak … In Horace you find this continually . … . He leaves you to fill in the connections.[1]

---

1   Basil Bunting, Recorded Interview (The New York Center for Visual History, 1984.

The example he then reads is 'You Can't Grip Years, Postume'. Aren't we back once more ('set side by side, a whole page of ideograms one against another') with Nietzsche's idea of 'the mosaic of words'? – the difference between Bunting's and Pound's (also between Horace's and Pound's) construction of the mosaic being, that Bunting believes in syntax and that Pound, at any rate in the *Cantos*, believed in the paratactic confrontation of a poem's elements, with the rôle of syntax greatly diminished.

Bunting, of course, spent a very small portion of his life actually translating Horace, but the Horatian presence in his own work is very audibly there. The Horatian cast of thought and the attention to the inter-meshings of sound pattern, have caused one critic, David Gordon, in *Paideuma*, to call Bunting 'A Northumbrian Sabine'.[1] As to sound and rhythm, Gordon writes of the Horatian cross-fertilisation in *Briggflatts*:

> In Bunting's own *vers libre* we find a rough and irregular metric pattern, unusual sequences of trochees, spondees and dactyls, as well as of long or heavily stressed syllables, eg., 'tíght / néck córds? Áxe rústs. Spíne / pícked báre.' And we hear arresting echoes of bits of the logaoedic measures of Horace, which Bunting formed according to the rhythmic needs of his poem, eg., 'Loáded wĭth mái̇l ŏf lĭnked lié̇s' (an aristophanic from the Second Sapphic); 'kĭ́ng lĭ́ft tŏ fĭ́ght' (from the Alcaic); 'spíne / pícked báre bŷ rávĕns' (from the Alcaic); 'inért braĭn nĕvĕr wíse' (from the Fourth Asclepiadean). 'Thére wĭll bĕ hŏthĭng ŏn Stáĭnmóre tŏ híde' (from the Second Pythiambic); 'stópped tĭll lŏng flíght' (from the Alcaic); 'endĕd ĭn bále ŏn thĕ féllsĭde' (from the Alcmanic).

The moral austerity and stoicism of the Northumbrian Sabine draw this comment from Gordon: 'certainly Bunting would have found this stern morality, self-reliance, self-mastery, this equanimity in facing life or death in Villon and in the Persian poets, but he undoubtedly found them first in Horace.'

In the twentieth century the influence of Horace and of classical poets generally has led to a far more widespread modification of English metrical form than it did in the seventeenth and eighteenth centuries, those great ages of classical influence and translation. The linguistic intrusion of another poetry is most radically felt in some of

1 David Gordon, 'A Northumbrian Sabine', *Paideuma* Vol. 9 No. 1 (1980), pp. 83, 85.

Pound's versions in his *Confucian Anthology* where he gives us something English and something irreducibly foreign and distant. A compromise, but also a meeting of cultures, comes in the reconciliation of accent and quantity. Hardy, our third Swinburnian, tried this – his scansion of 'Sapphics' is to be seen in his own copy of Swinburne's poems – and conceivably the influence filtered to W.H. Auden, though there was a further element needed for the full intrusion of foreignness in the 'Horatian' Auden. This came about through his adoption of the Moorish style in the syllabics of 'In Memory of Sigmund Freud'. Eventually he will combine Moore's syllabic lineation with an increasing regard for that imagined reader he speaks of who can recognise choriambs and bacchics. Line and sentence length are also to become important, line emphasising the cruxes of meaning and sentence lengthily deploying a complex syntax, while rhythm, playing across the two, dances through ingenious equivalents of Latin spondees, dactyls and anapaests. For my own money this use of the long sentence, miming aspects of Latin syntax, achieves its most striking display of artistry in 'In Transit', a poem which memorably re-creates the homeless feeling of a stop-over in a strange airport in a landscape we shall never get to know:

> Let out where two fears intersect, a point selected
>   Jointly by general staffs and engineers,
> In a wet land, facing rough oceans, never invaded
>   By Caesars or a cartesian doubt, I stand,
> Pale, half asleep, inhaling its new fresh air that smells
>   So strongly of soil and grass, of toil and gender,
> But not for long: a professional friend is at hand
>   Who smiling leads us indoors; we follow in file …

And the sentence of this first stanza winds to completion four lines on into stanza two with an Horatian audacity. Appositely to the effect here, Richard Johnson in *Man's Place, an Essay on Auden* comments:

> The pattern of internal rhymes helps to create both the music and the spatial pattern of the poem. It almost serves as a system of inflections, drawing words together across the patterns of line and phrasing [and] our attention to connections and resemblances, which, because the pattern is neither schematic nor familiar, as in end-rhymed forms, come to the reader as sudden discoveries.[1]

---

1   Richard Johnson, *Man's Place, an Essay on Auden* (Cornell, 1973), p. 92.

'In Praise of Limestone', 'Ischia' and 'Ode to Gaea' also contain elements of Horatian procedures and evidence of a growing taste for Horatian attitudes – a distrust of romantic extravagance, the selection of a modest Mediterranean hideaway (a house on Ischia, later to be exchanged for more northerly premises at Kirchstetten in Austria), and a preference for 'moderation' (sometimes getting to sound a little too satisfied with itself as in 'Read *The New Yorker*, trust in God; / And take short views.'). 'The Horatians' decides that 'Flaccus and [his] kin' are to be found not in Grand Opera or Opera Buffa, but are more likely to turn up as the amateur detective in a whodunit who solves the murder 'thanks to your knowledge of local topography' (by this point the poem is getting a little 'gabby', an adjective Frank Kermode once used to describe Auden's 'The Aliens'). Auden's Horatians are also to be found among 'Natural bachelors / and political idiots',

> Zoological and Botanical Gardens,
> museum-basements displaying feudal armour
>   or old coins: there too we find
>   you among the custodians.

> Some of you have written poems, usually
> short ones, or kept diaries, seldom published
>   till after your deaths, but most
>   make no memorable impact

> except on your friends and dogs …

Is not all this making Flaccus and his kin slightly twee and the 'Horatian' just a formula for resolutely minor achievements? One takes the point that the tastes of Horatians 'run to/ small dinner parties, small rooms, / and the tone of voice that suits them'. Though whether Auden himself ever quite attains that tone of voice consistently is another matter, for the compulsive talker tends just to chunter on. Horace is never a tour guide to the Sabine villa; Auden even takes us into his lavatory.

The aim of this paper has been to touch on certain saliences. These would be incomplete without mentioning two more, the versions of C.H. Sisson and also Ezra Pound's late tribute to a poet about whom he had once been ambivalent. Before rendering a number of Horace's odes, Sisson had been concerned with seeing how much pressure might be brought to bear on the unadorned declarative sentence. His verse was then being honed towards precision in his versions of Catullus. The declarative sentence which can sometimes be telling for

Catullus is less helpful in Englishing Horace, though Horace also, for all his polish, often chooses the unresonantly prosaic phrase to counter our over-emotive expectations. Sisson's choice of a still plain but now slightly more elaborate style dwells on this side of Horace, a stylistic trait that combines with a certain relish for Horace's no-nonsense attitudes ('a poet invaluable in our time not least because of his lack of sympathy with our most current prejudices!).

The most surprising item among Sisson's odes is his attempt at the *Carmen Saeculare* which 'comes near to being a new start from the old original', in short an imitation rather than a direct translation, often with old instances which are updated and re-applied as in Johnson's use of Juvenal in *The Vanity of Human Wishes.* An imitation of Horace's most Virgilian poem, celebrating the emporer as the lineal descendant of Anchises and Venus, the head of Church and State, permits some interesting parallels. One of the pleasures of classical imitation being the pleasure of recognition, there is a parallel here that gains both wit and point if the reader sees it. In 'The Secular Ode' Aeneas sails from Troy to Rome and finds it better than what he left behind him. Sisson's British parallel to this is a legend David Jones makes much of in *The Anathemata* – the legend of the Trojan Brutus who, according to tradition, came to settle in England. What Sisson's poem brings home is that it could only have been written by an Englishman, and by an Englishman for whom Christianity and the monarchy continue to matter. Sisson can still write out of a profound sense of national unity – of England not just as the sum of economic developments, oil finds and balanced budgets, but 'England as a poetic idea', as Donald Davie put it. This phrase implies the idea of inherited unity that, as a nation of monarchists, we invest in the symbol of the crown. Sisson, once Under Secretary at the Ministry of Labour, spells out much of this in his prose work, *The Spirit of British Administration* of 1959. His version of Horace's 'Secular Ode' unselfconsciously celebrates the idea of unity as he looks at London in the perspective of Rome, but without any plangent evocations of vanished imperial splendours, though the fact of empire enters this poem as part of England's story and part of the poem's story. England 'as poetic idea' must here also balance itself against the ironies of history and the sense of both human frailty and human fragility:

> The ways that have led here are multifarious,
> Even Brutus from Troy, our ancestors believed,
> But whatever they left they found better here.

We have been through it all, victory on land and sea,
These things were necessary for your assurance.
The King of France. Once there was even India.

Can you remember the expression 'Honour'?
There was, at one time, even Modesty.
Nothing is so dead it does not come back.

There is God. There are no Muses without him.
He it is who raises the drug-laden limbs
Which were too heavy until he stood at Saint Martin's …

He bends now over Trafalgar Square.
If there should be a whisper he would hear it.
Are not these drifting figures the chorus?

Besides his odes, I must mention in passing Sisson's translation of
the *Ars Poetica*, written in long lines which seem to owe something to
the hexameters of Arthur Hugh Clough in *Amours de Voyage*.

When in 1964 Pound's anthology *Confucius to Cummings*, compiled
with the aid of Marcella Spann appeared, it contained three translations of Horace by Pound, *Odes* 1.31, 1.11 and 3.30, done respectively
in 1963, 1964 and 1964. Here we have what Hopkins meant when he
wrote of poetry's power to 'bid' us:

By the flat cup and the splash of the new vintage
What, specifically, does the diviner ask of Apollo? Not
Thick Sardinian corn-yield nor pleasant
Ox-herds under the summer sun in Calabria, nor
Ivory nor gold out of India, nor
Land where Liris crumbles her bank in silence
Though the water seems not to move …

Great translators have sometimes found support in their spiritual
crises by expressing them through another mouth. Dryden did this
via Lucretius and Ovid, Cowley via Anacreon. In the twentieth
century perhaps the most moving example is Ezra Pound. Amid the
wreckage of his late years, his *Cantos* a botch (or so he thought), we
see him turning to Horace and away from trying to save the universe.
In his version of *Odes* 1.11,

Winter is winter
Gnawing the Tyrrhene cliffs with the sea's tooth.

Take note of flavors, and clarity's in the wine's manifest.
Cut loose long hope for a time.

In 1.31, contenting himself with 'olives ... endives and mallow roots' ('Delight had I healthily in what lay handy provided') he asks

> Grant me now, Latoe:
>   Full wit in my cleanly age,
> Nor lyre lack me to tune the page.

The third version rephrases a famous Horatian boast: 'This monument will outlast metal and I made it' and qualifies with 'Bits of me, many bits, will dodge all funeral' – using Horace's own qualification to point to Pound's scattered triumphs and the nuggets in the sprawling *Cantos*. How few people know these three masterpieces of translation – a pity, for they alter our sense of Pound and reveal his capacity for humility.

These three poems tell us less about Horace's original text and its dense implications than Pope's more extended work, but like the Pope, they are activated by a personal electricity. At the same time, there is a putting aside of the merely personal. D.M. Hooley says well when he sums up this phase of Pound's activity. 'The three translations', he writes,

> form as effective a 'crown' to Pound's career ... as any he could devise. And it is significant, not just curious, that so fitting a closure comes through translation. It is not just that Pound thought best through the matrices of other languages, literatures, traditions. Rather, through resigning himself to their influences, he transfigured their impulses into startling new creation ... in both the Propertius and the Horace there is some resignation of self, of dogmatism ... Horace dictates a kind of reorientation of the poet to his verse and the verse to the world. Horace, the master of technique, pressures Pound just as he does Bunting ...[1]

Pound's Horace does not exactly dispose of the generalisation that stands at the head of this essay, but it leaves a salutory dent in it; so that perhaps the claim should be modified, with also Bunting's and Sisson's versions in mind, to say that, given our angle of approach – inevitably a more fragmented business than Pope's – we must rest content with 'bits ... many bits that will dodge all funeral'.

1 D.M. Hooley, *The Classics in Paraphrase*, p. 121.

Martial in English

Within my own lifetime, Latin has disappeared in Britain as a requirement for entry into university. The publication of a new edition in the renowned Loeb Classical Library of the Epigrams of Martial – Latin verse and English prose *face à face* – affords the pleasant reflection that someone somewhere is still studying the language, and also offers an occasion for thinking about the way Martial's presence shows itself in English poetry and about the poet in person.

A reliable English version is always good to possess and here we have one that gives us access to many a dark and difficult corner of the original Latin. To anyone, like myself, who has only fitfully kept up his Latin, I cannot exaggerate the usefulness of an unpretentiously accurate approach to the meaning such as this. It helps the reader to the mental possession of the original and it also makes one conscious anew of how splendidly some of our English poets responded to Martial.

Marcus Valerius Martialis was born round about AD 40 at Bibilis in Spain, a sort of first-century Pittsburgh, famous for its iron mines and the manufacture of steel, and a centre of Roman culture. Like most cities in the ancient world, Bibilis lay within easy access of the countryside and when, in later life, Martial returned there, a local patroness whom he refers to as Marcella provided him with a rural property that sounds rather like Horace's Sabine retreat.

Patronage was a lifelong necessity and concern for Martial who, having left Bibilis for Rome in 64, soon abandoned the idea of a career in law for a career as a writer of epigrams. Compliments in verse, addressed to prospective patrons, may have formed the staple of his early poetry which has vanished. Later poems make much play with the stinginess of those who provide or fail to provide handouts.

The time of Martial's arrival in Rome was not an auspicious one if, as is likely, he sought for help from the house of Seneca, another Spaniard and tutor to the emperor, Nero. For no sooner had Martial set foot in the capital, than Seneca was forced by his former pupil to commit suicide after having been involved in an unsuccessful plot against Nero. Another writer, Lucan, Rome's last great epic poet, author of *Pharsalia* and Seneca's nephew, perished in the aftermath of the same foiled conspiracy.

So Martial was on his own, and we must not, in our protective age, dwell too insistently on his propensity to flatter those in power. Among these was another monster, the Emperor Domitian, who granted Martial the *ius trium liberorum*, the Right of Three Children, that is to say the important privileges of a citizen who had three children – Martial had none. The poet's shameless petition for this appears in his second book of epigrams. Ben Jonson in 'To the Ghost of Martial' wittily flatters James I while disapproving of the other poet's flattery:

> Martial, thou gav'st far nobler epigrams
> To thy Domition, than I can my James:
> But in my royal subject I pass thee,
> Thou flatterd'st thine, mine cannot flattered be.

In his first book, *On the Spectacles*, Martial had already sung the praises of the public shows presented by the Emperor Titus along with the Colosseum he had built. Later, the poet reflected on the gloomy form of that structure and, by implication, the gloomy goings-on inside it. He also went back on his praise for Domition to whom, after his assassination, the senate had refused public burial. But it was becoming too late for Martial to ingratiate himself with rulers like the milder Nerva and the military Trajan, and in the year 100 he returned to Spain, to spend his declining years at Bibilis. The rural retreat he had long sung in verse, he now had in his native place. But he was not content, though protesting his happiness to his friend Juvenal who remained in the capital he missed.

I first heard about Martial while reading Subsidiary Latin at school. This was from an older boy who was doing Scholarship Latin (which meant he might, if lucky, obtain a scholarship that would send him to university). I gathered that Martial was one of the filthiest writers who had ever lived and mentioned sexual practices which were a mystery to us. This had troubled his nineteenth-century readers, too. However, Henry G. Bohn in his 1865 edition of Martial in English, writes by way of moral counter-offensive, 'It must be premissed that his constant and severe castigation of the two grand vices which prevailed in his time … has given him the reputation of an obscene poet.' The two grand vices? Martial sometimes writes of sodomy and of fellatio, but he is not much exercised by these in moral terms and, *pace* Bohn, often deals with them in a somewhat carefree manner. He is repetitious here and can be boring. Bohn, in his edition, used a 1782 Italian translation of those poems he considered obscene and dangerous for the unqualified person to read. This practice also persisted in the Loeb Library up to W.C.A. Ker in 1925, though in reprints plain English was silently substituted. D.R. Shackleton Bailey in this latest and thorough edition, has rephrased the translations from Italian and used as many four letter words as he thinks fit. The trouble with that blunt instrument 'fuck' is that it remains so musically invariable – an 's' is about all you can add to it in the present tense, whereas in Latin (even without counting fancy things like subjunctives) *futuere* possesses six variations in the present indicative.

Some of the obscene poems are downright funny, others – despite their metrical expertise – of a schoolboy crudity. One of the very best, the comically un-P.C. XI, 104 – instructions to a wife on going to bed – exists in an excellent modern verse translation by Peter Porter (*After Martial*, 1972). Even this boisterous affair was kept in Italian until our own days: 'Moglie mia va fuori, o pratica i nostri costumi.'[1] Graglia's eighteenth-century prose achieves a rather fine onset with something of the thrust of real verse. I do not know about Graglia's general accuracy as a translator, but in Bohn's extracts his versions are as readable as any I have come across, consistent in idiom and rhythmically convincing.

Martial writing in person about his risqué poems (XI,16) is more charmingly funny than *they* sometimes are. In the seventeenth century, Herrick showed the right lightness of touch in his English renderings:

To read my Book the Virgin shy
May blush (while Brutus standeth by),
But when he's gone, read through what's writ,
And never stain a cheek for it.

Of that other body of poems – those that complain of patrons and of the stingy meals they provide – Peter Porter has given us some amusing versions, whose snap and crackle rise above those indispensible plain prose renderings such as in Bohn or Loeb. Of Mancinus in I, 43,

this was the order of dishes
you pampered us with:
    NO late-gathered grapes
    NO apples sweet as honeycomb
    NO ponderous pears lashed to the branch
    NO pomegranates the colour of blowing roses …

1 Wife, get out of it, or give us what we're used to.

The American J.V. Cunningham is Porter's equal in some of the briefer epigrams and in his own imitations of Martial's manner – his gigolo, adept 'with either sex at either end', is a very Martial-like invention.

Some of those anti-patron poems (as with their opposites, the poems on friendship) are in a vein that brings the full force of Martial's imagination into play. There is at least one of them that anticipates the imaginative inventiveness of a Swift or Pope, even perhaps a Lewis Carroll, XI, 18. The gist of this comes over in a prose version, but verse takes it up a notch. There is no translation to match Ben Jonson's, Sir John Denham's or Abraham Cowley's of other poems, but Bohn has tracked down an anonymous publication of 1856:

> Lupus, a farm near town you gave to me;
> A larger plot I in my window see;
> Such scrap of earth a *farm* 'twere hard to prove
> When one small rue-plant makes Diana's grove.
> This, which a locust's wing might overlay!
> Whose crops would feed an ant one single day!
> This, which a folded rose-leaf might have crown'd,
> Where not a herb can any more be found
> Than eastern scents or fragrant spices rare
> To please the palate or perfume the hair:
> Where e'en a cucumber must crooked lie;
> A snake to coil its tail would vainly try.
> Such garden scarce one caterpillar feeds.
> The willow bed no second insect breeds ...
> The devasted land a mouse lays low ...

And so it goes on, with a deliberate delight in the absurdity of scale which quite exceeds any desire to satirise or complain. The imagination has made its own place of this minute estate, one that you might dream of visiting, like Alice's looking-glass world, or like Pope's when he imagines the giant girl in his friend Swift's book searching desperately for her charge, the lost Gulliver. It is not so much her desperation that matters as the poetry made possible by the distortion of scale. Here the local topography of Brobdignag, to Glumdalclitch as minute as Martial's farm, is of jungle-like extent to Gulliver:

> Dost thou bewilder'd wander all alone
> In the green thicket of a mossy stone ...

Dost thou, embosom'd in the lovely rose
Or sunk within the peach's down, repose?

There is an imaginative generosity in Martial's poem on a patron's meanness, and this generosity of mind shows nowhere more richly than in III, 58 which celebrates his friendship with Faustinus whose Baian villa reconciles beauty and use, grain 'tightly crammed in every corner and many a wine jar … fragrant with ancient vintages'. Faustinus is a good landlord and master surrounded by reconnaissant neighbours. In the Shackleton Bailey version,

> Nor does the country caller come empty handed. He brings pale honey with its comb and a cone of milk from the woods of Sassina: one proffers drowsy doormice, another the bleating offspring of a hairy dam … Strapping daughters of the honest tenant farmers present their mothers' gifts in wicker baskets.

How all this struggles to get itself into verse, moving towards octosyllabics and two iambic pentameters in Shackleton Bailey's prose! Bohn, who aims to print a translation in verse whenever he can find one, comes up with what he labels 'Old Ms. 16th Cent':

> No farmer there doth empty handed goe
> To visit you. – One honny in a combe,
> Another curds and creame from his owne home
> By th' next wood's side; some sleepy doormice give,
> A kidd, or capons forced chaste to live;
> And with their baskets the plumpe girles are sent
> Their mothers' gifts and service to present.

Was Bohn's author actually writing after the turn of the century, and had he perhaps read the poem that truly translates – carries over – Martial into English and into the English scene, Ben Jonson's praise of the Sidney household, 'To Penshurst'?-

> … all come in, the farmer and the clown:
> And no one empty handed, to salute
> Thy lord and lady, though they have no suit.
> Some bring a capon, some a rural cake,
> Some nuts, some apples; some that think they make
> The better cheeses, bring 'em; or else send
> By their ripe daughters, whom they would commend
> This way to husbands …

Penshurst, like Faustinus' farm is the great good place that never was on sea or land, something to stretch the imagination in Jonson's course for civilising English aristocrats. In other poems he is quite frank about what he expects from Sir This or Sir That. Here, the ideal is not too ideal, and when the king and his son turn up at Penshurst unexpectedly, the lord and lady of the house aren't wholly ready for them – 'What (great I will not say, but) sudden cheer', comments Jonson. It was Martial who enabled Jonson's almost laid-back sense of opulence, encouraged his zest for the specific (listing foods in 'Inviting a Friend to Supper', as Martial likes to do), inspired him via those complaints about being invited to an aristocrat's house, but not getting the same food as the master, or even sitting at the same table – to a series of generous opposites that can be expected at Penshurst,

> Where comes no guest, but is allowed to eat,
> Without his fear, and of the lord's own meat …
> Here no man tells my cups; nor standing by,
> A waiter, doth my gluttony envy …

Martial is re-located in an English setting, after more than a thousand years. Pope, in a vein close to Jonson, can equal Martial's complaints in the grotesque dinner episode of the visit to Timon's Villa in 'Epistle to Lord Burlington'. He, too, is a son not only of Ben but of Martial.

Jonson, by way of imitation, commandeers Martial for his own quarrel with the architect and designer of masques, Inigo Jones, refashioning the Roman poet's insulting epigram on Ligurra (XII, 61) and achieving a comparably concise put-down. It is in an instance like this that one sees how right Bohn was to look for a verse equivalent to his plain prose versions. Of course, this was easier to do in his case, since, unlike the Loeb, he does not print the valuable additions of the Latin text, and so has more room. He finds some good examples from Oldham, Sedley, Byron, even Thomas Moore. Some of the best of all are by Cowley who stands next to Jonson in sheer finesse of handling and to him I shall return later on.

Bohn helps one see how Martial entered English poetry down the centuries, but he comes to grief, alas, by reprinting acres of the abominable Elphinston, a poetaster whose complete version of the epigrams once seemed important. Bohn even admits that these versions are 'very indifferent, to say no worse of them'. Clearly there were not enough good translations to further his laudable intentions.

The century and more that has elapsed since his edition would not afford him much help, as anyone will realise who has leafed through the dreary obscenities and the flaccid diction evident in *Epigrams of Martial Englished by Divers Hands*, edited by J.P. Sullivan and Peter Whigham. I have quoted Marvin Mudrick on modern translators of Chaucer and do so once more: 'The moral seems to be that the Augustans were the last English poets who had a sufficiently large command of technique and decorum, and sufficient trust in the versitility of their idiom, to be capable of turning [and here I must replace Mudrick's Chaucer with] Martial into a contemporary.' We can take Ben Jonson as the founding father of the Augustan tradition and Byron as its dissolute heir. Even an Augustan as minor as Elijah Fenton can produce a lively imitation of Martial's manner:

> Milo's from home; and, Milo being gone,
> His lands bore nothing, but his wife a son:
> Why she so fruitful, and so bare the field?
> The land lay fallow, but the wife was till'd.

Porter and Cunningham – there are few others – achieve their happiest results by finding a modern equivalent for Augustan wit.

Martial wrote a number of poems on the deaths of children – a barber's boy, a boy stabbed through the throat by an icicle falling from overhead, a six-year-old slave girl called Erotion. Porter has an excellent version of IV, 18, the icicle episode. His attempt at the greatest of the three – perhaps Martial's greatest short poem – the one on death of Erotion (V,34) – fails, as all versions I have seen of this poem fail. Porter pops in details from other poems, as if this one were not good enough in itself, and his dragging free verse does not help much either. We seem to have lost the art of genuine pathos, controlled as Martial's is, by the handling of metre, of sound and sense. Here is the Loeb's prose:

> To you, father Fronto and mother Flaccilla, I commend this girl, my pet and darling. Little Erotion must not be frightened by the dark shades and the montrous mouths of Tatarus' hound. She was due to complete the chills of a sixth midwinter, no more, if she had not lived that many days too few. Let her now play and frolic with her old patrons and lispingly chatter my name. Not hard be the turf that covers her soft bones, be not heavy upon her, earth; she was not heavy upon you.

The syntax of the third sentence here, clear in the Latin, gets contorted in the English, and I am not sure that 'my pet and darling' is much of an improvement on Bohn's less gushing 'my joy and delight'. The archaism of 'Not hard be' and 'be not heavy' isn't really prepared for by the more or less modern register of the rest. Archaism dogs Shackleton Bailey elsewhere ('look you', 'would fain', 'wont to', 'is a-wooing', 'not found therein', 'do you not think', the use of the obsolete subjunctive as in 'pray that it not please too much'.) However, this version gives a sketch of Martial's intentions and doesn't commit the sort of errors of taste K. Flower Smith is guilty of:

> She's such a little lassie – only six –
> To toddle down the pathways to the Styx
> All by herself!

It's precisely that note Martial avoids. The poem is heart-felt, but does not wear its heart on its sleeve. I used to imagine, perhaps sentimentally also, that Erotion (a love child, hence her name) was a love child of Martial's own. Shackleton Bailey is surely nearer the mark in his comment on the touching introduction of the poet's own parents, that Erotion might have been a memory from Martial's young days in Bibilis. But he sensibly adds that the poem might well be 'a figment' (perhaps 'fiction' would have been a kinder word).

It took a great poet to do anything in English with Erotion. And this was not in a direct translation, but by incorporating a memory of the poem, and some of its vocabulary, into a lament that was wrenchingly personal – that for the death of Ben Jonson's own daughter, Mary:

> Here lies to each her parents' ruth,
> Mary, the daughter of their youth …
> This grave partakes the fleshly birth.
> Which cover lightly, gentle earth.

Jonson very consciously metamorphoses the original into a Christian poem – there is no Cerberus here – and the child's name is part of this process:

> Mary, the daughter of their youth …
> Whose soul heaven's queen (whose name she bears)
> In comfort of her mother's tears
> Hath placed amongst her virgin train …

This loveliest of all Jacobean laments does not exhaust Jonson's debt to Martial. He concludes the poem on the death of his son which, like that on Mary is both lament and traditional Christian *consolatio*, with:

Rest in soft peace, and asked, say here doth lie
Ben Jonson his best piece of poetry.
For whose sake, henceforth, all his vows be such
As what he loves may never like too much.

The final couplet is a borrowing from Martial VI, 29, a lament on the death of a loved child servant: *quidquid ames, cupias non placuisse nimis* (whatever you love, pray that it doesn't please too much). Jonson's epitaph on Salomon Pavy, the boy actor of old men, reads:

And did act (what now we moan)
    Old men so duly,
As, sooth, the Parcae thought him one,
    He played so truly.

We track him once more in Martial's snow. In X, 53, Martial laments the death of the thirty-year-old Scorpus, 'the glory of the circus': 'Envious Lachesis [the Fate among the Parcae who assigns to a man his term] ... counting my victories, believed me an old man.' The beauty of this kind of allusion is something we largely forgo in our Latinless present.

Matrial's true Penshurst world was the villa of and the precious hours spent with his friend, Julius Martialis (IV, 64). The meaning of friendship and the human waste which is its obverse, are the last of Martial's themes I now have space to touch on. His friend's place has all the frank largesse of the Sidneys' acres, but there is nothing about a happy peasantry in Martial here (they are kept out of sight) or the functional nature of a properly run estate. You cannot hear the traffic on the Flaminian and Salarian Way, or the noise of the boatmen's cries on the nearby Tiber. All is courtesy and liberality, and the landscape an emblem of those qualities of ease and friendship the poet most admires. Shackleton Bailey complains that 'Martial's idea of living seems to have amounted to little more than loafing'. But the man who wrote more than 1500 poems could not have been loafing all the time – perhaps needed to loaf at times, with a nervous system keyed to major effort. What he seems to have regretted most was time not spent in the company of friends like his namesake – time consumed in playing the Roman games of opportunism and dining out. He dreams in (V, 20) of 'carefree days' when both he and Martialis would 'have leisure for true living' – true loafing, as Shackleton Bailey might say – 'riding, chatting, books, the Field, the colonnade ...' Then they would know nothing of 'the halls and mansions of the great'.

Instead, however, 'We feel our good days slip away and leave us'. Putting off until tomorrow what life and the riches of friendship offer was a theme Horace had already rehearsed in his Epodes, poems Martial obviously admired:

Our yesterday's tomorrow now is gone.

The translator of that line of Horace was the poet destined to feel most keenly the force of Martial's own regrets – Abraham Cowley:

Life for delays and doubts no time does give,
None ever yet made haste enough to live.   (II, 90)

Excelled only by Jonson, Cowley can reach the true Martialian note, especially on this theme, as in his version of V, 59:

Tomorrow you will live, you always cry,
In what far country does this tomorrow lie,
That 'tis so mighty long ere it arrive?
Beyond the Indies does this morrow live?
'Tis so far fetch'd this morrow, that I fear
'Twill be both very old and very dear.
Tomorrow I will live, the fool does say:
Today itself's too late; the wise liv'd yesterday.

Cowley makes one of the great English poems out of the piece I have already quoted from in fragments of Shackleton Bailey's helpful prose, V, 20. There is a certain amount of Augustan tidying up of the original, but this is a true rediscovery of a past poem's insight, just as Martial was rediscovering and reworking some of the most ungain-sayable reflections from Horace's Epodes – in Pope's phrase, 'What oft was thought, but ne'er so well expressed'. Cowley greatly expands Martial's fourteen lines, so I must be content to end with merely a sample:

If, dearest friend, it my good fate might be
T'enjoy at once a quiet life and thee,
If we for happiness could leisure find,
And wand'ring time into a method bind,
We should not, sure, the great men's favour need,
Nor on long hopes, the court's thin diet, feed,
We should not patience find to daily hear
The calumnies and flatteries spoken there,
We should not then lords' tables humbly use,

Or talk in ladies' chambers love and news;
But books and wise discourse, gardens and fields,
And all the joys that unmixt Nature yields.
Thick summer shades, where winter still does lie,
Bright winter fires that summer's part supply.

Why Dryden's Translations Matter

'Dryden', as Doctor Johnson famously says in his life of the poet, 'may be properly considered as the father of English criticism.' It would be gratifyingly symmetrical, but a slight exaggeration, if one could go on to claim him as 'the father of English translation' – translation of poetry, that is. Dryden is rather the most brilliant heir to that legacy of creative effort, initiated by Ben Jonson, and continued throughout the seventeenth century by such poets as Fanshawe, Cowley and John Oldham, to make new the classics – Horace, Virgil, Juvenal, Lucretius – as part of the live current of English poetry.

'Make it new', in the twentieth-century modernism, has often meant a violent break with the past, of the sort inaugurated by cubism and surrealism. What the seventeenth-century poets sought to achieve was a break with merely literal translations from the classics and with that timid habit of reducing texts to moralistic tags, a mode beloved of seventeenth-century school masters. English poets set out to recover as translators the kind of energies which re-appeared in France, out of a vivid awareness of Martial and Horace, in the poetry of Boileau, admired by Dryden and by his own heir, Alexander Pope. Dryden appeared on the scene just as the English part of the undertaking was gathering momentum, and the artistic impetus his own presence guaranteed 'made it new', not only for himself, but for a succeeding generation of poet-translators. As a practitioner, his prose formulations about translation always carry the conviction of authority, as when in the Preface to *Sylvae* (1685) he tells us, '... a good Poet is no more like himself, in a dull translation, than his Carcass would be to his living Body. There are many', he continues, 'who understand Greek or Latin, and yet are ignorant of their Mother Tongue. The proprieties and delicacies of the English are known to few: 'tis impossible even for a good Wit, to understand and practice them without the help of a Liberal education, long Reading, and digesting those few good Authors we have amongst us ...'

I want to look at the perspective I've just been sketching under three heads – in relation to Dryden's immediate forebears and contemporaries; in relation to Dryden's personal case and the fact that the last fifteen years of his life were chiefly dedicated to poetic translation; then, finally and very briefly, in relation to the younger

poets over whom he was so influential and whose work he super-
vised, in a rather Ezra Poundian way, with enabling criticism. For, as
Congreve tells us 'He was extreme ready, and gentle in his correction
of the errors of any writer who thought fit to consult him'. So if
Dryden was the father of English criticism, he also looked on the act
of translating as both a creative and a critical act: 'Thus ... a Man
shou'd be a nice Critick in his Mother Tongue, before he attempts to
Translate a foreign Language.' And to cap this: 'to be a thorow
Translatour, he must be a thorow Poet.'

First, then, his poetic forebears and contempories, and the way in
which their voices are heard in the struggle against the merely literal
translation of poetry, which at the time was called 'verbal interpretation'. I'm afraid the ghost of this literalism is still with us, despite all
attempts to lay it. Speak to many a classicist and mention Dryden's
Horace or Pope's Homer, and you realise very quickly by their glazed
expression that what they have in mind is something closer to Richard
Lattimore's *Iliad*, packing in all the words Homer used, regardless of
the fact that the resulting idiom is one 'that never *was* on sea or land',
in what Donald Carne-Ross referred to definitively almost thirty years
ago as 'a mistaken ambition of exactness'.

Samuel Johnson evidently thought this sort of thing could never
happen again, when in his 'Life of Dryden', he speaks of translation
of verse 'struggling for that liberty it now enjoys'. 'Why', he goes on,
'it should find any difficulty in breaking the shackles of verbal translation [word for word translation, that is] which must for ever debar
it from elegance, it would be difficult to conjecture, were not the
power of prejudice every day observed.'

Now poets had long known this. We find Aurelian Townshend,
who flourished between 1601 and 1643, writing in 'To the Right
Honourable, the Lord Cary ...',

> Verball Translators stick to the bare Text,
> Sometimes so close, the Reader is perplext,
> Finding the words, to finde the wit that sprung
> From the first writer in his native tongue.

The debate was carried on by the seventeenth-century group of
royalist poets, including Denham, Cowley and Fanshawe. Sir John
Denham – author of the 1656 Virgilian translation, *The Destruction of
Troy*, cautions in the preface to that work, that, since there are 'Graces
and Happinesses peculiar to every Language, which gives life and
energy to the words ...' these cannot be taken over and forced against

the grain of differently constructed language as 'Verbal Translation' tries to do.

It was precisely in the spirit of this preface that, when Dryden emerged as a major translator in the volume *Sylvae* of 1685, where splendid versions of Lucretius, Horace and Theocritus appear, he wrote in his own preface,

> Where I have taken away some of their expressions, and cut them shorter, it may possibly be on this consideration, that what was beautiful in the Greek *or* Latin, *wou'd not appear so shining in the English*: And where I have enlarg'd them, I desire the false Criticks wou'd not always think that those thoughts are wholly mine, but that either they are secretly in the Poet, or may be fairly deduc'd from him: or at least, if both these considerations should fail, that my own is of a piece with his, and that if he were living, and an Englishman, they are such, as he wou'd probably have written.

Poet-translators – think of Pound versus the sinologists and the Latin professors – seem to experience the need to recover this kind of confidence in almost every generation.

Sir John Denham once more. He is congratulating Sir Richard Fanshawe on the latter's version of Guarini's *Il Pastor Fido* (*The Faithful Shepherd*) of 1658:

> That servile path thou nobly dost decline,
> Of tracing word by word, and line by line …
> A new and nobler way thou dost pursue,
> To make Translations and Translators too:
> They but preserve the Ashes, thou the Flame,
> True to his sense, but truer to his fame.

Denham, always an acute writer on this topic, clearly means, when he sees Fanshawe's aim as 'To make Translations and Translators too', that the bold and capable translator like Fanshawe was opening a future possibility to other translators, which is exactly what Dryden was to achieve for a younger generation of poet translators, his own superb *Aeneid* preparing the way for Pope's even greater *Iliad*. Here Dryden's *Aeneid* set the standard, sealing the fate of one Doctor Brady's subsequent version in blank verse which, says Doctor Johnson, 'when dragged into the world, did not live long enough to cry'.

Denham in another poem offers congratulations to that absurdly underrated poet and translator who was 'the darling of my boyhood', says Dryden – namely Abraham Cowley, whose versions of Horace and Virgil precede and alert Dryden's own. Here is Denham on Cowley:

> Horace's wit and Virgil's state
> He did not steal, but emulate!
> And when he would like them appear,
> Their garb, but not their cloaths, did wear.

Here we have an alternative to T.S. Eliot's dictum to the effect that great artists steal and minor only borrow – not theft but emulation: Cowley, Denham is surely implying, in the act of translating, is penetrating to the very spirit of classical authors; his translations by interpreting them however freely, bring them to life, because Cowley does not come away from the encounter wearing their bits and pieces, but can emulate an entire civilisation by his unerring sense of its style or styles. Singling out this passage in a very different context, Donald Davie commends the razor edge of Denham's diction, and writes, 'It had not occurred to the reader that the distinction between "garb" and "clothes" was so fine yet so definite'.

But to return to Abraham Cowley, Dryden's admired predecessor, who, says Dryden, 'must always be thought a great poet'. Milton, Pope, Johnson all concurred in this judgement. Our own century has thought otherwise, perhaps because some of Cowley's most brilliant work is in the form of translation, an art which only recently has begun to receive its grudging due. Even at the age of thirteen, Cowley, a Mozartian wonder had found his way to that side of Horace which was to appeal so strongly to poets who had experienced the civil war and its aftermath or who, like Cowley later on, were disappointed courtiers wishing to withdraw to a world of personal probity and quiet self possession, away from the duplicity and obsequiousness of court circles. Doctor Johnson, in his life of Dryden, registers the corruption that such a milieu involved for the poet, when he comments on one of Dryden's royal dedications that it is 'in a strain of flattery which disgraces genius, and which it was wonderful that any man that knew the meaning of his own words, could use without self-detestation'.

The thirteen-year-old Cowley – prematurely and ironically in view of the effect of the civil war on his life and fortunes – was already responding to that vein of Horace which appealed to other subsequently disabused royalists, rewarded late if at all for their adherence to the Stuart cause, or, like Dryden, in his post as poet laureate and historiographer royal, with salary unpaid and often up to two years in arrears. The boy Cowley responded to Horace with lines that imitate

and wear the garb of the Roman poet in his search for ease of mind
and an inner contentment at having lived fully and true to oneself:

> I would not fear nor wish my fate,
>   But boldly say each night,
> Tomorrow let my sun his beams display
> Or in clouds hide them; I have lived today.

This conclusion, says Cowley, 'is taken out of Horace'. These characters, he adds, were early engraved within him: 'They were like letters
cut into the bark of a young tree, which with the tree still grow propor-
tionately.' Cowley's beautiful image says much about the effects of
early learning, and of learning the right thing, on the mind and
memory of the individual. It says much about teaching by way of the
classical languages and daily translation practice which was the mode
throughout English grammar schools and specifically at Westminster
School where Ben Jonson, Cowley and Dryden were all pupils at
different periods.

Cowley was to continue, not only to translate Horace, but to
imitate him in later life, saying, 'I am not so enamoured of the Name
Translator, as not to wish to be Something Better though it want a
name.' One result of this approach was his masterpiece, an imitation
of Horace's tale of the town and country mouse whose lightness of
tone carries with ease the moral theme of being true to oneself. The
country mouse offers his town guest something from the unconta-
minated bounty of nature, but the Londoner opts for more
sophisticated products and the luxury of court.

Cowley, along with his contemporaries and in tune with Horace,
keeps reverting to the idea of rural self-sufficiency. Here Virgil enters
the picture with Cowley's translation of *Georgics*, Book 2:

> O happy (if his happiness he knows)
> The country swain, on whom kind heav'n bestows
> At home all riches that wise Nature needs;
> Whom the just earth with easy plenty feeds.

Cowley also renders a similar dream of sufficiency from Horace's
Epode 2:

> Happy the man, whom bounteous gods allow
> With his own hands paternal grounds to plough!
> Like the first golden mortals happy he,
> From business and the cares of money free!

These Virgilian sentiments are undercut at the conclusion of Horace's poem – and also of Dryden's own version of it – where we see that they are just the daydreams of a usurer who soon hastens back to pecuniary transactions. Cowley omits this final bit of the original, because the same dream he had found in Virgil's *Georgics* evidently appealed to him so deeply. Dryden, too, speaks of 'the greatest poem of the greatest poet', in referring not to Virgil's *Aeneid* but to the *Georgics* themselves, surely his outstanding triumph of translation from the Virgilian canon. Both Cowley and Dryden are warmly attracted to that figure of the morally upright agriculturalist as against the thankless court milieu they had known. The image of the Virgilian small farmer would have had its obvious resonance, too, for Latin-reading country gentlemen in civil war and post-civil war England. Despite Virgil's directions about when to plough or how to handle your bees, there was also a kind of mythic overplus about this figure, something transferable from the Roman to the English scene. He isn't, for all the apparent basis of realism in the poem, an entirely realistic character. As Alistair Elliot tells us in his edition of Dryden's *Georgics* plus Latin text (1981): 'He is a richer, vaguer figure, more like the universal farming ancestor, the greater, grander and grander grandfather who lived when Adam delved (if not Eve).' Translation soon ensured his existence in an English moral context.

The desire for moral self-sufficiency clearly played a main role in the career of Dryden, to whom I now turn at the time of his crisis of the mid-1670s onwards, as he grows more and more conscious of wasted powers and of the artistic futility of his attempt to live by serving up to the London theatre the plays that would be box-office successes.

Two names of friends appear in the context of Dryden's energetic transference of interest from the theatre to translation, Jacob Tonson the publisher and Wentworth Dillon, Earl of Roscommon, to whose *An Essay on Translated Verse* of 1684 Dryden wrote a preface, also in verse, where he sees English poetry, and by implication, translation of poetry into English, as making our own literature equal to the classics, so that the poets – 'the few belov'd by Jove' – will

> On equal terms with ancient Wit engage,
> Nor mighty Homer fear, nor sacred Virgil's page;
> Our English palace opens wide in state,
> And without stooping they may pass the gate.

With his customary incisiveness, Donald Carne-Ross has argued against the translator setting up English 'on equal terms with ancient Wit', and he insists that a translator ought to leave signs of the irreducibly foreign element in texts from other languages, as Ezra Pound does in translating the Confucian Odes. I find this idea persuasive, though I don't think I would accuse Dryden as Carne-Ross does, of 'a certain provincial arrogance', of '[setting] over the door of the house of translation a sign announcing, "English only spoken. No foreign tricks allowed here."' This charge of provincialism seems, perhaps, slightly unfair when, as we know, translations in the seventeenth century were frequently read side by side with the Latin originals, so that the reader could compare and contrast. As for 'foreign tricks', Dryden and his contemporaries were Latinists from a tender age, so 'English only spoken' would have seemed a provincial attitude to them also. This over-riding desire to get things into English, chiefly from Latin, but also from Greek, is, I believe, an historic attempt to morally reinforce English from classical sources – sources whose profound literary insights could be educative and sustaining – at a time when English culture was suffering from the terrible schisms of the civil war. If you could engage 'on equal terms with ancient Wit', then maybe all was not lost, and England and English could draw on and re-align fractured potential.

One of the things that shows an exceptional linguistic awareness in Dryden is the way he dramatises the explosive meeting of Saxon monosyllables with the superior melopoeia (as he saw it) of polysyllabic Latin. His Saxon monosyllables actually emphasise the barbarism which stalks the classical text. The foreign element – the Latin – is brought out in Dryden's Ovid and Virgil in a head-on collision with a decidedly atavistic English. Eric Griffiths, in a 1993 British Academy lecture gives an excellent example of this, where Aeneas sees the ghost of Hector, and Greco-Latin is confronted by Anglo-Saxon:

> Such as he was, when by *Pelides* slain,
> *Thessalian* Coursers drag'd him o'er the Plain.
> Swoln were his feet, as when the Thongs were thrust
> Through the bor'd holes, his Body black with dust.

But let us return to the Earl of Roscommon and that *Essay on Translated Verse.*

Dryden's sympathy for Roscommon's *Essay* must have been deepened by the latter's sense that translation is not just another piece of literary business, and for the finest translation to take place there must be an affinity between translator and original author. Playing with the Pythagorean idea of the transmigration of souls, Dryden came to feel that, just as Milton had inherited the soul of Spenser, and Spenser imagined 'that the Soul of Chaucer was transfus'd into his Body', he, John Dryden, also had 'a Soul congenial to [Chaucer's]'. In translating that poet, as he was to do in his final book, *Fables*, Dryden half-jestingly implies that the transmigration of souls (metempsychosis) is at work specifically in the act of translation, so that you had better choose a text where you are the soul-mate or perhaps the transfus'd soul of the previous author. This ability to identify oneself with one's original is a theme that evidently attracted him to Roscommon's poem and, especially, one imagines, to these lines of baroque sprezzatura:

> Then seek a *Poet* who your *way* do's bend
> And chuse an *Author* as you chuse a Friend.
> United by this *Sympathetick Bond*
> You grow *Familiar, Intimate* and Fond;
> Your thoughts, your *Words,* your *Stiles,* your *Souls* agree,
> No longer his Interpreter, but He.

We also get a glimpse from Roscommon of the seventeenth-century way of translating, using every hint you can from previous translators and commentators – Dryden, when he came to translate Virgil, used up to nine previous editions and their commentaries. Thus Roscommon writes:

> Take pains the *genuine* Meaning to explore,
> There *Sweat,* there Strain, tug the laborious *Oar:*
> Search *ev'ry Comment,* that your Care can find,
> Some here, some there, may hit the Poets Mind.

So what Roscommon is offering is not translation theory, but a practical guide on how to do it, to which Dryden, as a practitioner, could respond. It is surprising how little James Anderson Winn found to tell us about the Roscommon connection and circle in his biography of Dryden, *John Dryden and His World* of 1987.

Scholars have discovered more for us of another relationship that shored up Dryden in his years of difficulty, that with Jacob Tonson, an emerging publisher who was to become the Faber and Faber of his day and the leading publisher of translated literature. Tonson was the effective force making possible in financial terms this renaissance of the classics in English, combining in his list an impressive range of both prose and verse in translation, together with editions of the chief English poets, including Milton, Cowley, Shakespeare and Spenser, not to mention Tonson's Miscellanies in which much contemporary work, including Dryden's, appeared. Without Tonson, Dryden would not so easily have rescued himself either financially or morally from his dilemma.

At the height of this crisis Dryden was drawn more and more into translation, not merely as a way of making a living, but also as a means of self-exploration. Concerning his plays he would come to say, 'I knew that they were bad enough to please, even when I wrote them.' And in his *Ode* on the death of the youthful poet, Mrs Anne Killigrew, we hear the unmistakable note of self-disgust that had undermined all hope of an Horatian quiet mind:

> O Gracious God! How far have we
> Profan'd thy Heav'nly Gift of Poesie!
> Made prostitute and profligate the Muse,
> Debas'd to each obscene and impious use,
> Whose Harmony was first ordain'd *above*,
> For tongues of *Angels* and for *Hymns* of *Love!*
> Oh wretched We! Why were we hurried down
> This lubrique and adultr'ate age,
> (Nay, added fat pollutions of our own)
> T'increase the steaming Ordures of the stage?

Dryden, at this time, seems to be passing in review the terms of his moral crisis. Made poet laureate at the age of thirty-seven, here he was beyond the middle years of his life, the author of some powerful poems, but guilty of the unevenness of which Johnson complains – 'faults of affectation ... faults of negligence ... beyond recital. Such is the unevenness of his compositions, that ten lines are seldom found together without something of which the reader is ashamed'. He was coming gradually to see the unparalleled achievement of Milton's *Paradise Lost* as a living reproach to him. 'This Man', he is reported as saying, 'Cuts us All Out, and the Ancients too', the irony being that Dryden was to go on to ask Milton's permission to turn *Paradise Lost* into yet one more work for the stage, *The State of Innocence*. The death of a young compeer of Dryden's the poet and translator John Oldham, also deeply affected the former's sense of lost things and lost opportunities:

> Farewell too little and too lately known
> Whom I began to think and call my own

For sure our Souls were near ally'd; and thine
Cast in the same Poetick mould as mine.
One common Note on either Lyre did strike,
And Knaves and Fools we both abhorr'd alike:
To the same Goal did both our Studies drive,
The last set out the soonest did arrive ...

In short, the youthful genius of John Oldham had led him, ahead of
Dryden, to see how verse translation could be a major undertaking
for the poet. Oldham had already, by the time of his early death at the
age of thirty in 1683, translated into lively English substantial quantities of Horace, Juvenal, Lucretius, Ovid and (among the moderns)
Boileau.

Oldham's central influence had been Abraham Cowley, from
whose favourite types of translation he had learned much – the two
types defined by Dryden as 'paraphrase or translation with latitude,
where the author is kept in view by the translator, so as never to be
lost, but his words are not so strictly followed as his sense and that
too is admitted to be amplified, but not altered.' The second type was
imitation, where the translator (if he has not lost that name) assumes
the liberty not only to vary from the words and sense, but to forsake
them both as he sees occasion; and 'taking only some general hints
from the original, to run division on the ground-work, as he pleases'.
Dryden's words bring to mind those of Cowley we have already heard,
'I am not so enamoured of the Name Translator, as not to want to
be Something Better ...' Following Cowley's hint, Oldham produces
one of the masterpieces of that Horatian-Virgilian tradition that
Dryden was to extend and that I have touched upon, the 'Beatus Ille'
(Blessed the Man), the Adamic agriculturalists of Cowley's and
Dryden's versions of *Georgics*, Book 2 and of Cowley's Epode 2 from
Horace. Oldham's masterpiece is also from Horace – Ode XXXI,
Book 1, an ode Ezra Pound was to translate beautifully in his latter
years, and where the blessings this time belong to the poet, defined
like those of the country mouse in terms of the basic bounties of
nature, 'olives, succories and emollient mallows'. The things the poet
doesn't want are given as the names of commodities to be had from
around the Mediterranean and the East. These are all changed by
Oldham as he '[runs] division on the ground-work, as he pleases' and
Englishes the whole onset:

What does the Poet's modest wish require?
What Boon does he of gracious Heav'n desire?

> Not the large Crops of Esham's goodly soil
>   Which tire the Mower's, and the reaper's toil:
> Not the soft flocks, on hilly Cotswold fed,
> Nor Lemster Fields with living fleeces clad ...

No wonder, in the light of work like this, Dryden found an exceptional poet to mourn, a poet whose quality was to be saluted by Pope
and whose imitation of Juvenal's Satire 3 supplied the ground-work
for Samuel Johnson's own imitation of Juvenal in his poem *London*.
Paul Hammond's exceptional book *John Oldham and the Renewal of
Classical Culture* speaks of 'the urgent thinking that takes place as
Oldham composes his translations, that establishes their independ-
ence from their models', and he underlines for us these translations'
'abiding values and their function as a critical preparation for the work
of Dryden, Pope and Johnson'. Towards the end of Oldham's imitation of Horace's Ode XXXI, Book 1, after a rich evocation of the
copious variety supplied by the natural world, we come to wish for
'sound Health, impair'd by no Disease' – a line which must have
carried deep personal meaning for the consumptive Oldham.
Hammond comments: 'What happens in Dryden's versions of
Horace, and ... in Oldham's is that the poet evokes the sensuous
delights of life with a greater zest and discrimination because he is
reappraising their value in a world menaced by Fortune and death.'
   Dryden's elegy for Oldham, 'Farewell too little and too lately
known', tolls the bell of an inner significance for Dryden himself, as
he passes through the critical years that see the culmination of his
disgust with crown and theatre, as he perhaps reflects on other deaths
of major poets – Cowley, Rochester, Milton. There is a dramatic rightness and a montage swiftness for the reader of the Kinsley edition of
Dryden in that, turning the page of Dryden's elegy for his friend, one
comes immediately upon the title *Sylvae* (1685), that wonderfully
compact collection of poems in which Dryden emerges in his mid-
fifties as the finest poetic translator of his age.
   Sylvae opens with passages translated from Lucretius and these
replicate once more that sense of the copiousness of life in the lovely
evocation of Venus, 'Delight of humane kind, and gods above, /
Parent of Rome, Propitious queen of love', and then follows 'Against
the Fear of Death', that amazing and exultant celebration of death,
not as the way aloft, as one might have expected from a Christian and
Catholic, but as the end of all things:

We, who are dead and gone, shall bear no part
In all the pleasures, nor shall feel the smart ...
And last, suppose Great Natures voice shou'd call ...
To thee, or me, or any of us all ...
Thou hast enjoyed, if thou hast known to live,
And pleasure not leak'd thro' thee like a Seive,
Why dost thou not give thanks, as at a plenteous feast
Cram'd to the throat with life, and rise and take the rest?

The way Dryden edits his chosen fragments of translation involves
us in a world of mighty opposites: love and death, the love that is
delightful, the love that is ferocious, the love that combines both
pleasure and a kind of desperation, as in (from Lucretius still)

Our hands pull nothing from the parts they strain,
But wander o're the lovely limbs in vain:
Nor when the Youthful pair more clossely joyn,
When hands in hands they lock, and thighs in thighs they twine;
Just in the raging foam of full desire,
When both press on, both murmur, both expire,
They gripe, they squeeze, their humid tongues they dart,
As each wou'd force their way to t'others heart:
In vain; they only cruze about the coast,
For bodies cannot pierce nor be in bodies lost.

One sees here what Johnson meant when he said that Dryden was
not one of the gentle bosoms and that love appealed to him 'in its
turbulent effervescence'. But Lucretius also has his Horation side and
Dryden warms to this, too, translating a passage that contains
Horace's image of the boat moving safely close to the shore, along
with thoughts of the quiet mind sufficient unto itself,

To Vertues heights, with wisdom well supply'd,
And all the magazines of learning fortifi'd ...
A Soul serene, a body void of pain.
So little this corporeal frame requires;
So bounded are our natural desires.

The equanimity of this is of a piece with the equanimity of Dryden's
greatest Horatian translation, Ode XXIX, Book 3, where with Horace
he urges his aristocratic friend to lay aside 'the busie pageantry / That
wise men scorn, and fools adore'. We are back with that side of
Horace the boy Cowley seized on, but for Dryden Horace's lesson

comes home to him with all the force of adult life and years of political and personal vicissitude:

> Happy the man, happy he alone,
> He, who can call to day his own:
> He, who secure within, can say
> To morrow do thy worst for I have liv'd today ...
> Fortune that with malicious joy
>   Does Man her slave oppress
> Proud of her Office to destroy
>   Is seldome pleas'd to bless ...
> I can enjoy her while she's kind;
> But when she dances in the wind,
> And shakes her wings, and will not stay,
>   I puff the Prostitute away ...

And we end the poem in that safe Horatian boat, 'Contemning all the
blustring roar',

> Within some little winding Creek;
>   And see the storm a shore.

From the violence of parts of his Lucretius to the balance of his
Horace may seem a far stride. But 'Without contraries is no progression' and Blake's aphorism expresses for us the apparent anomaly of
Dryden and his mighty opposites: here is a Royalist who satirises
kings, a Catholic who despises priests, a lover of the quiet life and the
quiet mind who delights in the vivid description of fire, flood, battle,
sex, and who uses translation to extend his range with these very
subjects. Poets are often the least conventionally accountable of creatures, like small children, 'Their aim as much the wonder as the cause',
as one of them writes. Dryden can even wonder at the sleazily phal-
locentric Charles II, thinly disguised as King David in *Absalom and
Achitophel*.

> When Nature prompted, and no law deny'd
> Promiscuous use of Concubine and Bride;
> Then, Israel's Monarch, after Heaven's own heart,
> His vigorous warmth did, variously impart
> To Wives and Slaves: And, wide as his command
> Scatter'd his Maker's image through the land.

When Dryden comes to translate Juvenal's sixth Satire (published in
1693) there is something of the same 'gust', as he calls it, in his treat-

ment of the Empress Messalina. Challenged, he might reply to the
question of why he chose to wonder at her, as he did to that of why
he translated the love passages in Lucretius: 'I own it pleas'd me.'
Messalina, like Horace's Cleopatra, is a creature to be marvelled at, a
strange monster. Yet if anybody ever believed Juvenal was an
improving writer, chiefly intent on exposing and curing the ills of
Rome, Dryden's version soon gets rid of that pious myth, with his
astonished and astonishing portrait of this woman who slips out of
the royal bed and takes on the customers of a brothel:

> At length when friendly darkness is expir'd,
> And every Strumpet from her Cell retir'd,
> She lags behind, and lingering at the Gate,
> With a repining sigh submits to Fate:
> All Filth without and all a Fire within,
> Tir'd with the Toyl, unsated with the Sin.
> Old Caesar's Bed the modest Matron seeks;
> The steam of lamps still hanging on her Cheeks
> In ropy Smut; thus foul, and thus bedight,
> She brings him back the Product of the Night.

Like King David, Messalina is as much a cosmic force as a human
being, and it is this obsession with cosmic forces, swirling around the
precariously human, that makes Dryden the perfect translator of
Virgil's *Georgics*, with its linxes, wolves, stags and horses, turned frantic
by the seasonal force of spring. The same is true of his versions from
Ovid's *Metamorphoses*, and its series of instinctually driven characters,
its violent not-too-be resisted transformations, its dwelling on
murder, incest, lust. The philosophical side of Ovid, 'the Pythagorean
philosophy', also mirrors Lucretius' sense of 'this everchanging
Frames decay / New things to come and old to pass away', translated
by Dryden previously.

Dryden had to put to one side the Ovid versions he had been
working on for the young publisher, Jacob Tonson, to undertake the
more lucrative complete Virgil, and some of these were to turn up in
his final and greatest volume – largely one of translations – *Fables
Ancient and Modern*, published just two months before his death in
1700. I have time only to mention the superb rendering of Ovid's first
book plus assorted metamorphoses that came out in Dryden's
Examen Poeticum (*A Swarm of Poems*) of 1693. The harvest of Dryden's
Ovidian efforts was not to appear in one publication until 1717 when
Doctor Samuel Garth re-activated the Dryden–Tonson project of a

complete *Metamorphoses*, and called on the young Alexander Pope and more minor poets to contribute to what I believe to be the most splendid *Metamorphoses* we have, outclassing that book Pound considered the loveliest in the language, Arthur Golding's version of 1565–7. One third of the poems in what one might call Garth's Ovid are by Dryden himself.

It would be foolish at this point to embark on a blow by blow account of Dryden's *Aeneid*, facilitated by the pull away from Ovid, and the ways in which it suited him and the ways it didn't. I have already mentioned in passing the masterly *Georgics* with which he began his complete translation of Virgil. There is a sense of the universal human involvement in natural and animal processes here which parallels a theme which had drawn Dryden to that work he had to defer, Ovid's *Metamorphoses*, and it is Dryden's rôle in that venture that must lead me towards my conclusion.

Like the *Georgics* the *Metamorphoses* deal with universal laws and processes in (and here I must quote from my book, *Poetry and Metamorphosis*) an 'imaginative vision of a world where all things are inter-related, where flesh and blood are near kin to soil and river, where man and animal share common instincts'. After he had experienced Ovid, Metamorphosis for Dryden (as it was for Darwin) becomes the universal law that is of most interest to him. By one of those cunning extensions of his author, Dryden sees the law of metamorphosis as including not only history where 'former things / Are set aside like abdicated Kings', but also the specific act of translation itself. To look at it the other way round, what is the metamorphosis of the universe, continually recycling itself, but one unending act of translation too?

> All things are alter'd, nothing is destroy'd,
> The shifted Scene for some new Show employ'd …
> Those very Elements, which we partake
> Alive, when dead some other Bodies make:
> Translated grow, have Sense, or can Discourse;
> But death on deathless substance has no Force.

The wit and imaginative dash with which Dryden inserts the word, 'Translated', into Ovid there, is the act of a man who used the 'very Elements' of Lucretius, Horace, Virgil, Ovid, Chaucer, and metamorphosed these old poems into new poems, just as the universe re-uses and re-shapes its basic constituents.

I cannot, alas, deal in detail with Dryden's narrative brilliance in retelling Ovid's stories, or in re-telling stories from Boccaccio and Chaucer which are also to be found in *Fables*. The book is a marvellous collection of short stories in verse, full of suggestion for future narrative poets. I have time only to illustrate a little further the notion of metamorphosis as applied by Dryden in the context of translation.

Chaucer's *Knight's Tale* might seem an unusual sample to publish beside Ovid. Once again Dryden uses it to illustrate the operations of two of those mighty opposites behind nature's laws – Mars and Venus, with Venus winning the day. Metamorphosis, however, enters into the way Dryden looks at Chaucer's types as being human constants despite all the changes history imposes on humanity. This is a theme he celebrates in his preface to *Fables* when he sees once more how 'All things are alter'd, nothing is destroy'd'. 'For mankind', runs Dryden's preface, 'ever is the same, and nothing lost out of nature, though everything is alter'd.' The idea of metamorphosis enters into Dryden's most famous exclamation here as he looks at Chaucer's characters:

> Here is God's plenty. We have our Fore-fathers and Great Grand-dames all before us, as they were in Chaucer's Days; Their general Characters are still remaining in Mankind, and even in England, though they are call'd by other names than those of *Moncks*, and *Fryars* and *Chanons*, and *lady Abbesses* and *Nuns* ...

If Dryden had never translated Ovid ('All things are alter'd, nothing is destroy'd') he would not perhaps have seen Chaucer's types in the way he did, and arrived at the insight that they are part of a universal metamorphosis which is basically indestructible. The freshness of insights like these are all part of his ability to 'make it new' in translation.

Dryden delighted in mirroring his authors one in another – Horace in Virgil, Virgil in Horace, Spenser in Ovid, Lucretius in Chaucer. Instances of an author reflecting or modifying the voice of another author (think of T.S. Eliot and Baudelaire) are a fact of literary history – of literary metamorphosis, one might say, and this is a principal feature of the metamorphosis that takes place when one poet acts as the translator of another. I have a further example for you and this must be my last.

If I now place Chaucer next to Dryden's translation, you can actually hear an acoustic process of metamorphosis taking place. Even Chaucer's title *The Knyghtes Tale* has to change into *The Knight's Tale*.

What maketh this but Juppiter the Kyng,
The which is prince and cause of alle thyng ...
Thanne is it wysdom, as it thynketh me,
To maken vertu of necessitee ...
And certeinly a man hath moost honour
To dyen in his excellence and flour ...

So Dryden bringing Chaucer into his seventeeth-century reader's acoustic range, metamorphoses a very corrupt text into the lucidity of :

What makes all this, but Jupiter the king
At whose command we perish, and we spring?
Then 'tis our best, since thus ordain'd to die,
To make a Vertue of Necessity . .. .
Enjoying while we live the present hour
And dying in our Excellence and Flow'r.

These words are those of Duke Theseus, that somewhat Prospero-like figure who speaks for the poet within the poem on (in Nietzche's phrase) 'Dying at the right time'. They mirror for us and they meta-morphose for us Dryden's own rendering of Lucretius which I have already quoted from *Sylvae* of fifteen years earlier,

Thou hast enjoy'd, if thou hast known to live,
And pleasure not leaked through thee like a Seive,
Why dost thou not give thanks as at a plenteous feast
Cram'd to the throat with life and rise and take thy rest?

Dryden's metamorphosis of Chaucer's lines has for its neighbour in *Fables* his versions from Ovid's *Metamorphoses*. After his death these were to take their place in the already mentioned translation of a complete *Metamorphoses* brought together by Doctor Samuel Garth, the Queen's physician in 1717. This drew on the work of several poets for whom Dryden had set a standard, some of whom are little known today though they rose to the occasion as translators then – Croxall, Eusden, Harvey, Maynwaring, Rowe, Stonestreet, Tate, Vernon and Doctor Garth himself. Congreve is also there and so is Addison. The most famous younger presence is Alexander Pope, who at the age of sixteen was inspired by Dryden to his own metamorphosis of Chaucer, his sparkling versions of *The Merchants' Tale* and *The Wife of Bath her Prologue*. Ahead of him lay the *Iliad* and the *Odyssey*, challenged into being by Dryden's Virgil. Some of the younger poets in Garth's

Ovid were writing in Dryden's own life-time and for all we know Dryden himself may have revised their versions, since he was the editorial presence behind this book that he was never to see completed and in print.

The success of Garth's Ovid says much about the imaginative climate in the eighteenth century. That this book (still available in popular editions in Victorian times), with its powerful erotic charge, should have appeared in the middle of what used to be called 'our age of prose and reason', dispels somewhat that misconception of Matthew Arnold's on which many of us were brought up, and power-fully illustrates how the idea of metamorphosis laid hold on the Augustan imagination.

By 1700 Dryden, then, had created that part of the idiom and tradi-tion from which the individual talent could take wing and he had done it largely through translation. Alexander Pope, we all agree, was the most significant individual talent of the coming era. Paying tribute to Dryden's final volume, *Fables Ancient and Modern*, that cornucopia of some of his finest translations, Pope could say, writing to the old dramatist, William Wycherley,

> ... Those Scribblers who attack'd [Dryden] in his latter time, were only like Gnats on a Summer's evening, which are never very trou-blesome but in the finest and most glorious Season; (for his fire, like the Sun's shin'd clearest towards it setting.)

Pope's tribute was to a work mainly of translation, emphasising what we still choose to forget, namely the centrality of poetic trans-lation to the whole history of English poetry. That history has to be re-written because the presence of translation in it changes the balance of conventional assessments that still rate poetic translation as a poor cousin of original verse. For too long Dryden was looked on merely as satirist and controversialist (which he magnificently was), but the fire of which Pope speaks that 'shin'd most clearly towards [Dryden's] setting' was that of a great poet, the measure of whose greatness can only be taken if we see him as a great translator, too.

Shelley and Translation

Some poets often achieve in their translations work which equals or even surpasses their original verse. Dryden was one of these and so, in his very different way, was Shelley. It is strange that, except for the customary note on the influence of the Homeric *Hymn to Mercury* on *The Witch of Atlas*, Shelley has received so little attention as a translator. Or perhaps not so strange when one considers the neglect of our classic works of translated poetry. Dryden's versions from Ovid's Metamorphoses go commonly unread in departments of English; the fact that he translated the first book of the *Iliad* can even cause surprise, and that he did so magnificently elicits scepticism; Pope's Homer is not now cheaply available to the general reader, whereas in the nineteenth century popular editions were still appearing in print.

Nineteenth-century readers seem also to have made more of Shelley's translations than our contemporaries. Arnold, indeed, preferred them to the other poems; 'Except', he says, 'for a few short things and single stanzas, his original poetry is less satisfactory than his translations, for in these the subject-matter was found for him.' Thus Arnold, though one might add that the subject matter was often very close to that of the original poetry. Lockhart also believed that having a model of style before him and the ideas supplied, kept Shelley's besetting vices at bay: 'When he translated, whether from the Homeric hymns, from Euripides, from Calderón, or from Goethe, he had every requisite for the attainment of excellence. The vague and idle allegories in which he delighted ... were banished for the moment from his fancy ...' The truth of the matter was not quite so simple and Dr Webb's valuable study *The Violet in the Crucible: Shelley and Translation*, illustrates in detail the inextricable and salutory relationship between the translations and the rest of Shelley's work.

Shelley's theory of translation seems initially as defeatist as Robert Frost's notion that the poetry is precisely what gets lost. A Platonist, he sees poetry as '[stripping] the veil of familiarity from the world' to lay bare 'the spirit of its forms', whereas the translation of poetry works in the opposite direction: he is tempted by the Greek plays and certain dramas of Calderón, he says, 'to throw over their perfect and glowing forms the grey veil of my own words'. However, once Shelley goes to work as a translator, theory never comes between him and his own practicality – the *Hymn to Mercury* goes into ottava rima, not because that was the shape of the original, but because, as a stanza, it serves to capture the original's wit and humour. A marvellous instinct subdues even his errors to the element he works in – namely, to the general atmosphere of a given poet. A random example occurs in the *Faust* fragment in what he makes of *unvollkommne* (not yet full), which he mistranslates as 'unwelcome', accommodating the error in a context which is psychologically finely exact:

> But see how melancholy rises now,
> Dimly uplifting her belated beam,
> The blank unwelcome round of the red moon ...

So, although Shelley says of translation, 'it were as wise to cast a violet into a crucible', he adds: 'The plant must spring again from its seed', which is precisely what happens here. Dr Webb is alert to the creative value of such re-workings and conscious that 'The inscape of the original admits of only one existence'. 'The point is made', he writes, 'by Borges's fable of a man translating *Don Quixote*, sentence by sentence and word by word.' The point is Dr Webb's and not, as he supposes, Borges's. For Pierre Menard, in that celebrated fable, is engaged in a much more fantastical undertaking than translation – actually to *compose* 'a few pages which would coincide – word for word and line for line – with those of Miguel de Cervantes'.

Dr Webb traces Shelley's work through five languages with enviable expertness and he does something more in making us aware of the background and cohesiveness of Shelley's interest in other literatures. The sense of sheer absorption that must have preluded the translations comes over well in Hogg's description of Shelley reading the Grenville edition of Homer: 'He devoured in silence, with greedy eyes, the good and legible characters, often by firelight, seated on a rug, on a cushion, or on a footstool, straining his sight, and striking a flame from the coals with a shovel, or whichsoever of the fire-irons he could first seize upon, remaining in front of the fire until the cheek next to it had assumed the appearance of a roasted apple.' Despite his devotion to the *Iliad* and the *Odyssey*, it was the Hymns he in fact translated as a kind of therapeutic exercise. For Shelley's confidence as a poet was severely damaged by the propensity of reviewers to snarl at the new before rushing back to their hammocks. The pastoral Greek world he entered in the Hymns Dr Webb links with the influence of Peacock, Hunt and Hogg on Shelley, and their preference for a pre-Nietzschean view of Greek culture. Shelley's urbanity (Donald Davie's phrase, echoed by Dr Webb) received much healthful exercise in finding the tone in which to render his completist masterpiece of translation, *The Hymn to Mercury* of 1820, and, if Shelley were escaping his detractors in working at this, he was also learning new resources as a poet. The same is true of his version of Euripides' satyr play, *The Cyclops*, probably done in the year previous to the Hymns, and again a minor work and not one of the tragedies. It is surprising to find a poet, capable of the excited and lax Shakespeareanising of parts of *The Cenci*, producing the admirable blank verse of this short drama as, later on, the evocative but lithe verse of *Faust* and the dryly ratiocinative speeches of Cyprian in Calderón's *Magico Prodigioso*.

Goethe and Calderón clearly answered to darker pressures then the Hymns and Dr Webb relates them, among a wealth of bibliographical connections, to the relationship with Byron and the mutual concern of both poets for the demonic and for the theme of the devil as Doppelgänger. Besides this he provides much of interest on the English fortunes of Goethe – viewed, initially, as yet one more representative of 'the corrupting influence of German literature on the public taste and national morality of Englishmen', the scenes Shelley chose to translate being omitted as blasphemous in such versions of *Faust* as were available. Dr Webb sees Mephistophiles in the Goethe fragment as taking on a tone of voice close to the Satan of Byron's *Vision of Judgement* – a more gentlemanly figure, perhaps, than Goethe's devil, but admirably adapted by Shelley. Webb feels the angels' chorus to be one of Shelley's great successes. It is certainly energetic, but how convincing is the forced rhyme 'even' of line three and the wrenched word order in line six of the opening?

> The Sun makes music as of old
>   Amid the rival spheres of Heaven,
> On its predestined circle rolled
>   With thunder speed: the Angels even
> Draw strength from gazing on its glance,
>   Though none its meaning fathom may:–
> The world's unwithered countenance
>   Is bright as at Creation's day.

A similar wrenching for the sake of rhyme – 'Though no one comprehend thee may' – occurs in the final stanza. Shelley appended an arresting 'literal version' in a footnote to this chorus, fearing that his translation might be a *caput mortuum*. Although we lose 'The world's unwithered countenance', the footnoted lines move splendidly. Would that all literal translations read like this:

The sun sounds, according to ancient custom,
  In the song of emulation of his brother-spheres.
And its fore-written circle
  Fulfils with a step of thunder.
Its countenance gives the Angels strength
  Though no one can fathom it.
The incredible high works
  Are excellent as at the first day.

Has not Shelley created here poetry more original and commanding than his rhymed version – inventing free verse, as it were, without noticing it?

The scenes translated from Calderón's *Magic Prodigioso* belong, like *Faust*, to 1822, the last year of Shelley's life. It was not only the character of the devil which attracted Shelley to Calderón, but also Calderón's other-wordly feeling for the deceptiveness of reality: *la vida es sueño*. Before translating him, Shelley already 'Calderónized', as Mary calls it, in his letters and even in conversation, consciously imitating the other's baroque imagery and his way of developing this in series. A reader familiar with the changing metaphors for the runaway horse at the opening of *La Vida Es Sueño* – hippogriff, wind, dark lightning, dull-plumed bird, scaleless fish – will remember Shelley's manner of deploying imagery in 'To a Skylark'. The ripples spread much further, into 'Ode to the West Wind' (as Salvador de Madariaga showed long ago), through the spider and silk-worm passage in 'Letter to Maria Gisborne', the stanza form of the 'Hymn to Mercury', 'The Witch of Atlas' and, most bleakly 'The Triumph of Life'. Dr Webb describes Shelley's world as abstracted and mathematical where Calderón's is intangible and schematic. The abstracting he compares, following Wilson's *Shelley's Later Poetry*, with the art of Cézanne. But was there ever art so unlike Cézanne's in its final effect on the reader of palpitating intensity? Turner is, at times, a more likely choice, as in the Calderónesque *episodio* of the cloud in 'Ode to the West Wind':

                    Thou dirge
  Of the dying year, to which this closing night
  Will be the dome of a vast sepulchre,
  Vaulted with all thy congregated might

  Of vapours from whose solid atmosphere ...

This is wonderfully adjusted to the *terza rima* (Dante merging with Calderón), so that one feels the architectural build-up right across the rhymes and stanza, and then – most dramatically – comes the enjambement over the stanza-break: 'Of vapours.' Shelley's Calderónizing here is tempered by his own rapid perceptual vision: that move from the clinched rhyme *night* and *might* which cements, so to speak, the firm architecture of the dome, suddenly confronts one with 'congregated might/Of vapours'. Then immediately the vapours become 'solid atmosphere': so true to one's sensation of the ambiguity of cloud, as in Turner's paintings.

John Holloway, in a fine essay on Shelley, has remarked of the poetry, 'It is difficult because there is, with trying regularity, a tension and an eagerness about it that leads the reader hardly to expect the control which he very often finds.' Dr Webb's examination of the minutae of word choices Shelley confronted in translating, increase one's insight into the way the art brought into fine reciprocation instinct and control. The two interact powerfully in 'The Triumph of Life' where Shelley's debt to Calderón and Dante is greatest, yet where he has transformed them into something new. Here Rousseau, metamorphosed to an old root, his mysterious Dantescan vision dissipated in his despair that life is simply a dream, says that if he had not spiritually lost his way

> Corruption would not now thus much inherit
> Of what was once Rousseau – nor this disguise
> Stain that which ought to have disdained it ...

The verbal echoes here are something any poet might instinctively turn up – they seem close to the word play in the final couplet of Dryden's *Aeneid*, for instance, depicting the death of Turnus:

> The streaming blood distained his arms around;
> And the disdainful soul came rushing through the wound.

Shelley compels word play into his familiar and Platonising obsession with stains ('Stains the white radiance of eternity'). His control in the lines on Rousseau, the curious almost anagrammatic effect of 'disguise stain' and 'disdained', brings out Rousseau's mingled horror and disgust, as the very sounds – 'disguise stain' and 'disdained' – seem to seep into each other. The 'disdaining' *ought* to have kept him free of the stain but, failing to disdain, he took on this disguise which is now staining him. In context it is accurately forceful and the situation stains the words right through.

If the presence of Calderón broods over the final phase of Shelley's work, Dante's influence runs parallel. Dante, in turn, undergoes the softening influence of Petrarch. This is a Petrarch somewhat distorted by Shelley's characteristic and self-intoxicating habit of rhapsody and Dr Webb perhaps underestimates the habit and the influence in his extended account of a poem like 'Epipsychidion'. Although Shelley did not begin his four-year residence in Italy until the April of 1818, he had embarked on the language probably as early as 1813 and even then, so Hogg tells us, Petrarch was his chief devotion, Shelley having taken 'the soft infection' from 'a most engaging lady'. By 1814 he had moved on to Alfien, Guarini, Tasso and Ariosto. A year later he translates with real verve Dante's sonnet to Cavalcanti, catching – despite the too insistent alliteration of line four – something of the original's tone of high courteousness and restrained fantasy:

> Guido, I would that Lapo, thou, and I
> Led by some strong enchantment, might ascend
> A magic ship, whose charmed sails should fly
> With winds at will where'er our thoughts might wend,
> So that no change, nor any evil chance
> Should mar our joyous voyage; but it might be
> That even satiety should still enhance
> Between our hearts their strict community …

Magic and *charmed* there, and *wandering* later in the poem, are Shelley's additions but so, less predictably, is *strict*. The fantasy of the magic boat awaits its moment to be expanded from the fourteen lines of the sonnet to the daunting two hundred line *invitation au voyage* to Emilia Viviani that closes 'Epipsychidion'. About the same time, Shelley went on to translate Calvacanti's sonnet of reproach to Dante, 'I' vegno il giorno a te infinite volte', which, as Dr Webb shows, also anticipates the form and manner of another of Shelley's poems, his admonitory 'To Wordsworth'. An act of translation that strikingly prepares the way for Shelley's own development is his rendering, probably in 1820, of the first Canzone of Dante's *Convito*, 'Ye who intelligent the Third Heaven move', 'perhaps the most perfect instance', writes Webb, 'of how Shelley's translations interlock with his original work.' This translation, though it contains gaps and was never brought into final shape, is metrically ingenious and its concluding stanza done with exceptional grace:

> My song, I fear that thou wilt find but few
> Who fitly shall conceive thy reasoning,

Of such hard matter dost thou entertain;
Whence, if by misadventure, chance should bring
Thee to base company (as chance may do),
Quite unaware of what thou dost contain,
I prithee, comfort thy sweet self again,
My last delight! tell them that they are dull,
And bid them own that thou art beautiful.

Dr Webb sees this poem as providing Shelley with 'a scenario of the heart', namely a mode in which to write about an idealised relationship between man and woman like that explored by Dante and the poets of *il dolce stil novo*. Dante himself seems to have been uneasy in his prose interpretation of this Canzone, anxiously allegorising out of existence the *bella donna* in question. Shelley follows the same tack in explaining that descendant of Dante's poem, 'Epipsychidion', to John Gisborne: 'The Epipsychidion is a mystery – As to real flesh and blood, you know that I do not deal in those articles, – you might as well go to a ginshop for a leg of mutton, as expect any thing human or earthly from me. I desired Ollier [his publisher] not to circulate this piece except to the Σύνετοι [cognoscenti], and even they it seems are inclined to approximate me to the circle of a servant girl and her sweetheart.' Of course, there is a certain stoical humour in this, but Shelley after all had only himself to blame if even the Σύνετοι mistook him. Art cannot so easily divorce itself from history – as Mary Shelley must have painfully felt – when it bears an epigraph such as that with which Shelley prefaces 'Epipsychidion': 'Verses Addressed to the Noble and Unfortunate Lady. Emilia V____, Now Imprisoned in the Convent of _____', this being followed by a high-flown phrase about 'the loving soul' labelled 'HER OWN WORDS'. Shelley seems to want things all ways round and so at this point in his book does Dr Webb. He speaks of Shelley's 'slightly lush quality' in one passage of the poem and also of his 'natural propensity for idealised infatuation', but neither of these judgements is brought to bear squarely on the piece as a whole. For it is this – merely hinted – vulgarising that blurs Shelley's Dantescan intentions, as they veer into something like a Romantic caricature of Petrarch, and drag the poem far below the level of achieved excellence that Dr Webb assumes it to possess in its entirety. Shelley chose to read Dante in Milan Cathedral 'where', as he told Peacock, 'the light of day is dim and yellow under the storied window'. Dr Webb comments on his 'eagerness to achieve the authentic medieval feeling' and 'the appropriate location', though what is particularly authentic about this eyesight punishing act, in a building that was not begun until sixty years after Dante's death, goes unsaid. It savours a little of that self-consciousness and strain involved when Shelley tries, in this long poem, to renovate Dante's convention of the *gentil donna*:

> Woe is me!
> The wingèd words on which my soul would pierce
> Into the height of Love's rare Universe.
> Are chains of lead around its flight of fire –
> I pant, I sink, I tremble, I expire!

There seems to be no necessary relation between this kind of thing and 'the fluency and grace' (Dr Webb's words) which appear elsewhere in 'Epipsychidion':

> True Love in this differs from gold and clay,
> That to divide is not to take away.
> Love is like understanding, that grows bright
> Gazing on many truths ...

The entire passage, which begins with this, certainly earns Dr Webb's later tribute when he says that 'like so much that is best in English poetry, [it] results from a fruitful grafting of the imported bloom on to the native stock'. He is rewarding on Shelley's own importation of the *terza rima*, on his use of it in the translation of the Matilda scene from *Purgatorio* as against Cary's blank verse, and on its absorption into 'Ode to the West Wind' and 'The Triumph of Life'. He prints a version of 'Matilda Gathering Flowers' freed from Medwin's editorial improvements. Shelley's flexibility here was a remarkable achievement in his reintroduction of a form long in disuse (Gray translating from *Inferno* had, like Cary, hammered it in Miltonics) and the tone has a kind of chaste intentness far from any mere excitability:

> My slow steps had already borne me o'er
> Such space within the antique wood, that I
> Perceived not where I entered any more;

> When lo, a stream whose little waves went by,
> Bending towards the left the grass that grew
> Upon its bank, impeded suddenly

> My going on – ...

The virtue of Dr Webb's study lies in its ability to evaluate the

intrinsic merit of such passages in their own right and also to relate
the translations to currents in Shelley's life and to the development
of his original poetry. He is sensitive both to the major examples and
to the slighter ones – the twenty-one line translation, for instance, of
a fragment from Virgil's Fourth Georgic with an underwater setting
– where the creative imagination recognises a geography, familiar and
yet other, and incorporates it through the artist's subtle union of
imperiousness and deference into the mind's own place:

> And the cloven waters like a chasm of mountains
> Stood, and received him in its mighty portal ...

Poetry and Metamorphosis

1 An English Ovid

The theme I wish to open with is Ovid in translation. This will give me the opportunity to speak of that neglected classic, Sir Samuel Garth's composite edition of Ovid's *Metamorphoses* in English of 1717. Garth's edition represents the completion of a *Metamorphoses* begun in the 1690s during the business collaboration of the publisher Jacob Tonson and John Dryden. These two had recruited a team of (often young) translators for Ovid and other projects. This *Metamorphoses* was left unfinished at Dryden's death, after he himself had tackled many of the greatest parts of the poem. When I reach Ovid in metamorphosis you will, I hope, see how this grows out of and is intertwined with Ovid in translation.

Dryden seems to me the Poundian figure of his age, invigorating the talents of others – the young men he and Tonson had gathered round them – by his example and by his personal urging. Ovid seems to me a chief ancestor of literary modernism, and if the case of Joyce's *Ulysses* appears to deny that assertion, one can reply that Joyce's *Ulysses* is *The Odyssey* metamorphosed, and that Joyce, a directive influence on both Eliot and Pound, himself set forth on seas unknown emboldened by an epigraph concerning the artificer, Dedalus, from *The Metamorphoses,* Book VIII. We read on the title page of *Portrait of the Artist* 'Et ignotas animum dimittit in artes': 'And he abandoned his mind to obscure arts.' These obscure arts led Joyce to a point, some two decades later in *Finnegans Wake,* where opposites 'by the coincidence of their contraries reamalgamerge', and to the famous conclusion of Part I in which a couple of washerwomen on the banks of the Liffey undergo Ovidian metamorphosis into a stone and an elm. But this is to anticipate.

I take it that the wisdom of *The Metamorphoses* inheres in its imaginative vision of a world where all things are interrelated, where flesh and blood are near kin to soil and river, where man and animal share common instincts, where vegetarianism is poetically the only defensible philosophy of life. This last point – quaint, as one might think it in the abstract – draws eloquence from Ovid and a comparable spread and sweep of the imaginative wing from Dryden in Book XV:

While Kine to Pails distended Udders bring,
And Bees their Honey redolent of Spring;

> While Earth not only can your Needs supply,
> But lavish of her Store, provides for Luxury,
> A guiltless Feast administers with Ease,
> And without Blood is prodigal to please [...]
> If Men with fleshy Morsels must be fed,
> And chaw with bloody Teeth the breathing Bread
> What else is this, but to devour our Guests
> And barb'rously renew Cyclopean Feasts!

In this vision of the animals as 'our Guests', the speaker is Pythagoras, and there is a dramatic rightness in the way Ovid can allow him to rehearse the vegetarian argument, and later on the argument of metempsychosis (that hard word which in Joyce's *Ulysses* Molly Bloom asks Leopold Bloom the meaning of). For Ovid – and I imagine we have no evidence to show that he was either vegetarian or believed literally in metempsychosis – is using both arguments as a kind of imaginative wit, a 'dallying with surmise', to lead him to the climax at which his own voice and that of Pythagoras tally in a vision of cosmic unity, where, to quote Joyce, the 'coincidence' of 'contraries reamalgamerge', where time is

> Still moving, ever new: For former Things
> Are set aside, like abdicated Kings:
> And every Moment alters what is done,
> And innovates some Act, 'till then unknown.

And Dryden moves to one of the great climaxes of his version of the poem with:

> All Things are alter'd, nothing is destroy'd,
> The shifted Scene for some new Show employ'd [...]
> Those very Elements, which we partake
> Alive, when dead some other Bodies make:
> Translated grow, have Sense, or can Discourse;
> But Death on deathless Substance has no Force.

The audacity, the *sprezzatura,* with which Dryden throws in the word 'Translated' here – he who *translated* Chaucer into modern English and who said he expected someone to do the same for him one day – wittily incorporates the notion of literary translation into the conception of an ongoing world empowered by the metamorphosis of its own elements – mud and stones into flesh and blood, flesh into trees, human into divine. Dryden himself, it is not too much to say, metamorphosed – translated – elements from his own life into the imaginative splendour of his English Ovid. Thus the political Dryden – and it is a besetting sin of commentators to thrust the political references to the forefront of an imagination which digests political 'innovation' and 'act' to its own purposes – the political Dryden brings to the realisation of Ovid in English (Ovid translated) the power of his own hard-won wisdom, a wisdom then reaching, with Ovid, beyond politics towards (one is tempted to say) the origin of species:

> The Face of Places, and their Form, decay;
> And that is solid Earth, that once was Sea:
> Seas in their Turn retreating from the Shore,
> Make solid Land, where Ocean was before;
> And far from Strands are Shells of Fishes found
> And rusty Anchors fix'd on Mountain-Ground.

Origin of species? If that is to exaggerate, perhaps one can redeem the exaggeration by adding that Darwin, beginning his career with works like *Structure and Disappearance of Coral Reefs*, was to go on to write, in *On the Origin of Species*, a book which dwells insistently and imaginatively on the universal fact of metamorphosis.

In Ovid's universe, with its 'manifold variety', as one of his editors has it, the metamorphoses come as reward, punishment, means of escape. Among the most beautiful are two celebrations of married love – the change of the old couple Baucis and Philemon into trees (Book VIII), so they shan't experience separate deaths, and that of Ceyx and Alcyone into sea-birds (Book XI). Alcyone, the daughter of Aeolus, god of the winds, has tried to dissuade her husband, Ceyx, from his sea-journey, and when her premonitions of his drowning are fulfilled she, too, expresses the desire of Baucis and Philemon – that of dying together:

> Happier for me, that all our Hours assign'd
> Together we had liv'd; ev'n not in Death disjoin'd!

She finds the drowned body of Ceyx, attempts to drown herself and is metamorphosed:

> A Bird new-made, about the Banks she plies,
> Not far from Shore, and short Excursions tries;
> Nor seeks in Air her humble Flight to raise,
> Content to skim the Surface of the Seas [...]
> Now lighting where the bloodless Body lies,
> She with a Fun'ral Note renews her Cries:

> At all her Stretch, her little Wings she spread,
> And with her feather'd Arms embrac'd the Dead.

The translator again is Dryden, moving easily through imaginative regions that Van Doren long ago said he was incapable in – a measure of Dryden readily concurred with by Eliot in his stress on the poet's lack of 'insight'. That judgement still seems to be with us, a left-over from the era when Dryden was convicted on insufficient evidence, of contributing to a dissociation of sensibility that was never more than a handy literary myth. Dryden – and the stories of Deucalion and Pyrrha and of Baucis and Philemon are the other supreme examples – as the poet of the tenderness and pathos of married love! But, you will say, it took Ovid to make him that. No doubt it did. Yet it would be no exaggeration to say of Dryden that, in writing about marriage, he *translated* Ovid on to a higher plane. And Dryden proved capable, as no translator before or since, in providing the imaginative effort to find the exact tones for this delicate yet profound piece of wish-fulfilment in the Ceyx/Alcyone story:

> Then flick'ring to his pallid Lips, she strove
> To print a Kiss, the last Essay of Love.
> Whether the vital Touch reviv'd the Dead,
> Or that the moving Waters rais'd his Head
> To meet the Kiss, the Vulgar doubt alone;
> For sure a present Miracle was shown.
> The Gods their Shapes to Winter-Birds translate,
> But both obnoxious to their former Fate

– 'obnoxious to', namely 'exposed to', in that they are to live their new lives also as subject to the dangers of the sea. A moment later the element of wish-fulfilment is 'placed' by that sudden distancing, that playful and humane wit which, time and again and in the most unexpected places in Ovid, makes us re-adjust our expectations. We do not leave Ceyx and his wife, Alcyone, daughter of the god of the winds, on that note of pathos. There is a sort of divine mirth, a *hilaritas,* in the closing lines of their story of conjugal love:

> They bill, they tread; Alcyone compress'd,
> Sev'n Days sits brooding on her floating Nest:
> A wintry Queen: Her Sire at length is kind,
> Calms ev'ry Storm, and hushes ev'ry Wind;
> Prepares his Empire for his Daughter's Ease,
> And for his hatching Nephews smooths the Seas.

That distances, but does not destroy, both the terror and the pathos of this tale exposed to the sea of life. Now, the dream of dying together is one of the dreams that makes bearable a world of change from life to death. The gods are kind – sometimes – and commute death to metamorphosis, as here. And one sees the imaginative urgency that prompted but did not always give full force to those twelfth- and thirteenth-century versions of Ovid moralised in which metamorphosis is interpreted as being an earnest of the Christian doctrines of resurrection and immortality. The option of that interpretation is more tactfully left open by Golding's Elizabethan rendering:

All things doo chaunge. But nothing sure doth perish

and in Dryden's

All things are alter'd, nothing is destroy'd

and a few lines later in

But Death on deathless Substance has no Force.

Dryden, and his collaborators in the Garth Ovid, in transmitting the wisdom of Ovid's great vision, transmit also the undertow of that worry which accompanies the wisdom and which declares itself and yet refuses to become a feast of luxury on itself, by means of that delicate wish-fulfilment which I have mentioned. Wish-fulfilment, fantasy, 'dallying with surmise' – I do not want to give the impression that *The Metamorphoses* offers a merely Nietzschean view of art, as the illusion which makes life tolerable. What is still being asked in many of the stories – particularly in those transformations into vegetable, mineral or stone – and asked often against the grain of the story, focuses on what it is like to become an object. Even in the act of consenting to this universe of fecund change, even in the act of consenting to become (say) a tree, an intimation, a *frisson* of real death touches the imagination. One senses, sometimes momentarily, sometimes at greater length, what Eliot speaks of on the occasion of Celia Coplestone's martyrdom in *The Cocktail Party,* the 'reluctance of the body to become a *thing*'.

Given the option between tree and stone I suppose you and I would choose to become trees, would we not? In the ninth of the *Duino Elegies,* as the sequence hovers between the sufferings, the *Klage,* of the previous elegies, and the desire to praise, Rilke introduces a contemplation of the laurel, laurel perhaps that grew in the precincts of Schloss Duino. In the Leishman–Spender version it goes:

> Why, when this span of life might be fleeted away
> as laurel, a little darker than all
> the surrounding green, with tiny waves on the border
> of every leaf (like the smile of a wind): oh, why
> *have* to be human […] ?

'Warum dann / Menschliches müssen […]?' Daphne is never named
here, but, with a lovely implicitness, her transformation into laurel
hovers over the fantasy that springs up in this hesitation in the face
of destiny. Wouldn't one sooner, in certain circumstances, be a tree
than human? And the thought gathers to itself those mollifying 'tiny
waves […] like the smile of a wind', and one remembers that in *The
Sonnets to Orpheus,* in a further metamorphosing of Ovid's tale,
Daphne, now changed to a laurel tree, is still animate enough to wish
for the metamorphosis of her pursuer into the wind. As in Ovid, a
tree is endowed with lingeringly human feelings. Throughout *The
Metamorphoses* people are also changed into birds. That, conceivably,
would be an even better choice, if choice were a possibility in the
matter, or would we stick at laurels on the primitive impulse that trees
outlast birds? Springs, streams are perhaps more complicated matters.
Let's stay with the more manageable duality which ends *Finnegans
Wake* Part I, from Shem and Shaun to stem and stone, the human
voice losing its power to speak as it merges sleepily with inanimate
creation, as it becomes a thing: 'My foos won't moos. I feel as old as
yonder elm […] My ho head halls. I feel as heavy as yonder stone.'

Tree or stone? Rilke draws consciously from Ovid, choosing the
fluidity of tree and wind. Joyce refers back wittily to *The Metamorphoses*
with his two washerwomen transformed into 'yonder elm' and
'yonder stone', and he is gaily detached from the immersion he is
evoking. Wordsworth, on the other hand, surrenders himself to the
fascination of the stoniness of stone and even to the possibility of
sharing in it. Here, he is Ovid's antithesis, for this fantasy of petrification, as we shall see presently, repelled Ovid himself. The
protagonist of one of Wallace Stevens' poems, 'Le Monocle de Mon
Oncle', only goes as far as wishing himself to be 'a *thinking* stone'. The
old beggar woman in Wordsworth's early play *The Borderers* says: 'I'd
rather be / A stone than what I am', but she speaks under immeas-
urable duress. Lucy of the Lucy poems is 'Rolled round in earth's
diurnal course, / With rocks and stones and trees': there is a rightness in that, but it is the poet who speaks on her behalf and not she.

In a lesser known poem of Wordsworth's, from Sara Hutchinson's notebook, 'These chairs they have no words to utter', the poet protagonist, in a room where 'The ceiling and floor are as mute as a stone', indulges the dream that in this stone-bound stillness he can lie 'Happy as they who are dead'. However, the 'reluctance of the body to become a *thing*' forces this poet, for whom the word 'thing' was obsessive, back into the world of the sun, where

> The things which I see
> Are welcome to me.

By the end of the poem, he returns to wishing that life itself could be penetrated by this mute, as it were stone-enveloped 'quiet of death / Peace, peace, peace'. This longing for 'a repose which ever is the same', around which Wordsworth's mind circles still in a much later poem, 'Ode to Duty', elicits a swifter response from the imagination in the Lucy poem because she is not only in repose, but being 'rolled round', and also because 'rocks and stones' are tempered by the presence of 'trees', which is the rhyme word that clinches and concludes the poem, taking off from 'She neither hears nor sees' something of its full horror by calling on however momentary a response from that primitive impulse which makes us prefer to be a tree rather than a stone and which originally, no doubt, endowed trees with dryads:

> A slumber did my spirit seal;
>   I had no human fears:
> She seemed a thing that could not feel
>   The touch of earthly years.
>
> No motion has she now, no force;
>   She neither hears nor sees;
> Rolled round in earth's diurnal course,
>   With rocks and stones and trees.

Stem or stone? When Daphne, pursued by Apollo, undergoes her transformation into a laurel in Book I, the change is ultimately to be seen as beneficent. The body is willing to become a thing, but a thing which retains something of its own nature. Like all profound change the incident is touched with the pain of strangeness, the pain of initiation. But only *touched*. Daphne's wished-for metamorphosis is swift, like that in a speeded-up film of natural change:

> Gape Earth, and this unhappy Wretch intomb;
> Or change my Form, whence all my Sorrows come.

Scarce had she finish'd, when her Feet she found
Benumb'd with Cold, and fasten'd to the Ground:
A filmy Rind about her Body grows;
Her hair to Leaves, her arms extend to Boughs:
The Nymph is all into a Laurel gone;
The Smoothness of her Skin remains alone.
Yet Phoebus loves her still, and casting round
Her Bole, his Arms, some little Warmth he found.
The Tree still panted in th'unfinish'd Part:
Not wholly vegetive, and heav'd her Heart.
He fixt his Lips upon the trembling Rind;
It swerv'd aside, and his Embrace declin'd.

However, now the change is complete, Apollo declares

> because thou canst not be
> My Mistress, I espouse thee for my Tree,

and he goes on to explain that this laurel will be the Prize of Honour
and that it will crown 'The deathless Poet and the Poem'. So Ovid,
the deathless poet – and how winningly he bestows the compliment
on himself, and earns it in the act of writing the deathless poem – can
go on to speak on behalf of Daphne as Wordsworth spoke on behalf
of Lucy, and report her reaction to Apollo's words:

> The grateful Tree was pleas'd with what he said:
> And shook the shady Honours of Her Head.

If Daphne's change is only *touched* with the pain of transformation,
the arboreal change of the faithful old couple, Baucis and Philemon,
though beneficent like hers, is haunted by an image of real death. In
Dryden's version there are differences from Ovid here, his imaginative grasp of the meaning of marriage giving an added pathos to this
tale. He outdoes Ovid in a manner that makes the concluding couplet
of the following passage from Addison's 'To Mr. Dryden' – a poem
that finely sees translation as a type of metamorphosis – no mere
hyperbole:

> O may'st thou still the Noble Tale prolong,
> Nor Age, nor Sickness interrupt thy Song:
> Then may we wondring read how Human Limbs,
> Have water'd Kingdoms, and dissolv'd in Streams [...]
> How some in Feathers, or a ragged Hide
> Have liv'd a second Life, and different Natures try'd.

Then will thy *Ovid,* thus transform'd, reveal
A Nobler Change than he himself can tell.

(Examen Poeticum, 1693)

Dryden's 'Baucis and Philemon' from Book VIII is one of the great literary narratives. As translation, it certainly equals his own best work. Indeed, one finds oneself asking whether Dryden with a Shakespearian mastery of pace and tone, with a glance at the Bible here, a hint of La Fontaine there, by a deepening of the sense of the sacredness of married love, did not surpass his great Latin original by a very wide margin indeed. I cannot linger here on the couple's hospitality to the gods who call as strangers, graced as the episode is with unstinted details such as (of Baucis):

With Leaves and Bark she feeds her Infant Fire

(lightly presaging the later change to trees in 'Leaves and Bark', gently witty on 'Infant') or her kettle:

Like burnish'd Gold the little seether shone

or the old couple's attempt (and here the tenderness modulates into humour) at catching their goose as a sacrifice to the gods:

Her with malicious Zeal the Couple view'd;
She ran for Life, and limping they pursu'd.

My own concern is with the moment of wished-for change. Their continuing life is not like that continuing life of birds known to Ceyx and Alcyone. Philemon has asked of the gods

We beg one Hour of Death, that neither she
With Widow's Tears may live to bury me,
Nor weeping I, with wither'd Arms, may bear
My breathless Baucis to the Sepulcher.

The gods grant this and they further commute the 'one Hour of Death' into metamorphosis – to an oak and a linden tree. Yet the image of a death it remains – much more so than Daphne's laurel, twisting away from Apollo and finally nodding its crest:

New Roots their fasten'd Feet begin to bind,
Their Bodies stiffen in a rising Rind:
Then, ere the Bark above their Shoulders grew
They give, and take at once a last Adieu.
At once, Farewell, O faithful Spouse, they said;
At once th'incroaching Rinds their closing lips invade.

Neither the sound of that final line – the hard c's narrowing off the cavity of the throat as one speaks them – nor the line's sinister lengthening out into an alexandrine as the growth takes over, permits us to forget that this is a death stifling out the human voice. And this stifling out of the human voice, as the body becomes a thing, is a theme I shall return to shortly. Suffice it to say, 'th'incroaching Rinds' resemble less Daphne's 'filmy Rind' than another transformation – that of the nymph Perimele in Book VIII to the soil and rock of an island. Here, we realise how close pulsation can come to petrification. The speaker is Achelous the river god, who is pursuing her:

> The Nymph still swam, tho' with the Fright distrest,
> I felt her Heart leap trembling in her Breast
> But hard'ning soon, whilst I her Pulse explore,
> A crusting Earth cas'd her stiff Body o'er.

Stem or stone? The one veritable epic of petrification takes place in Book V of *The Metamorphoses* after Perseus has freed Andromeda from the sea-monster and has claimed her as his bride. These petrifications, which he brings about by brandishing the Gorgon's head at his enemies, are punishments of those who would like to prevent his marriage with the bride he has justly obtained. If one's mind balks at imagining unpleasant things as happening to oneself, the difficulty is eased by contriving a situation in which they happen to others – and to others who have deserved them. Justice, as I have said, is on Perseus' side. The imagining of these petrifications arises from such a vivid sense of the 'reluctance of the body to become a *thing*' that imagination triumphs over justice, while at the same time getting some of its gusto from the fact that justice is being done. Also, the petrification immediately threatens to stifle back human utterance into the inanimate: 'My foos won't moos […] My ho head halls', 'These chairs they have no words to utter.' Neither does a tongue that has just turned into marble:

> While yet he spoke, the dying Accents hung
> In Sounds imperfect on his Marble Tongue;
> Tho' chang'd to Stone, his Lips he seem'd to stretch
> And thro' th'insensate Rock wou'd force a speech.

This is the end of Nileus

>   who vainly said he ow'd
> His origin to Nile's prolifick Flood

– from water to marble, one of many like changes:

> Their safety in their Flight Two Hundred found,
> Two Hundred by Medusa's Head were ston'd.

The palace of King Cepheus, father of Andromeda, becomes virtually a massive cemetery cluttered with men who have turned into their
own funerary monuments. They are all there to aid Phineus, who had
formerly been promised Andromeda but who made no attempt to
rescue her from the sea-monster. He is cowardly, and when he sees
the fate of his friends, he begs Perseus for his life. Perseus 'stones'
him, too. And poor Phineus is not merely turned to stone. His stone
image, the fact of his death, embodies what essentially his life was –
that of a coward – and, self-judged, thus he stands:

> As here and there he strove to turn aside,
> The Wonder wrought, the Man was petrify'd:
> All Marble was his Frame, his humid Eyes
> Dropp'd Tears, which hung upon the Stone like Ice.
> In suppliant Posture, with uplifted Hands,
> And fearful Look, the guilty Statue stands.

Images like this strike deep – beyond any mere sense of justice done
– into the mind of a reader, and bring home with far greater finality
than arboreal change the knowledge that our death sets the seal on
all that we are, that such choices as we have made are now irrevo-
cable, that death has made an object of our past weaknesses since
nothing can now redeem or uncongeal them.

In the episode of Perseus and his assailants, Dryden has gone off
duty in the Garth edition. The translator is one Arthur Maynwaring
and very fine he is, like many of the secondary hands in this great
version – young Mr Pope, Congreve, Gay, Mr Vernon who did the
episode of the nymph turning into an island, Addison whose appearances are always to be watched for, and whose story of Phaeton and
the chariot of the sun in Book II possesses such narrative power, that
one cannot but wonder what sort of rôle Dryden played in the final
draft. Perhaps one day, someone with a preternaturally fine ear or
some energetic young scholar will solve this question in a number of
these versions, encouraged by the existence in the William Andrews
Clark Memorial Library of George Stepney's manuscript of his
version of Juvenal's '8th Satire'.[1] That same version of Stepney's, as

---

1 See George Stepney's *Translation of the 8th Satire of Juvenal*, ed. T. and E. Swedenberg
 (University of California Press, Berkeley and Los Angeles, 1948).

it appeared in Dryden's edition of Juvenal, was radically and force-fully revised. By Dryden himself? A note on the Stepney manuscript, reputedly in Pope's handwriting, believes that to be the case, and adds: 'This was what that great Man did for almost all his acquaintance.' I merely touch on the existence of this Poundian characteristic of Dryden's, prompted by wondering if Maynwaring's handling of the Perseus episode could be all his own work. It is certainly stamped with a bold use of enjambement which isn't entirely Drydenesque. But that way lies further divagation.

I began my samples of Maynwaring with, you will recall, the episode of Nileus being turned to stone, and

> the dying Accents hung
> In Sounds imperfect on his Marble Tongue.

I was using that as an example of the way the fact of metamorphosis, and the acquiescence in a world based on metamorphosis, is so often haunted by a nakedly human imagining of what death is like, and by the 'reluctance of the body to become a *thing*'. The involvement of tongue with word, and the tongue's capacity or incapacity to utter human sounds, would appear to be a theme close to a poet's most intimate sense of himself, whether he stutters it out like Hopkins in 'The Wreck of the Deutschland' – 'where, where was a, where was a place?' – and later has to wrap his tongue around that 'lush-kept, plush-capped sloe' and mouth it until he can force out heart's truth 'past telling of tongue', or whether, like Ovid, he runs the theme through a gamut of fables. That marble tongue of Nileus comes, in fact, at the dead end of a gamut which, in its upper reaches, explores that other concern of Ovid's – the frontier between human and animal, the mixture of humanity and animality in sexual adventure and violence, the question of how far the truly human can still inhere in the irrational and instinctual. Like the exploration of death – and Orpheus, venturer into Hades, is, one reminds oneself, Ovid's ideal poet as he is Rilke's – this exploration of the gamut between human and animal releases a characteristic *frisson*, often at the moment of metamorphosis – at the moment when human language, of which the poet is the supreme articulator, is becoming impossible, where mean-ings are literally 'past telling of tongue'.

In story after story, as the poet sings on, human voices plunge or falter into animality, wishfully, or sometimes because their human nature – and here one feels the Dantescan element in Ovid – has been taken over by a subhuman trait of character. Thus Lycaon (Book I)

is, so to speak, 'damned' for his inhumanity by Jove, and turned into
a wolf:

> Howling he fled, and fain he would have spoke;
> But human Voice his brutal Tongue forsook.

This same drama of utterance is recurrent throughout *The
Metamorphoses*. Io (Book I), in a story of Jove's amours, which treads
a mysterious, characteristically Ovidian frontier between the comic
and the painful, is changed to a beautiful heifer:

> She strove to speak, she spoke not, but she low'd:
> Affrighted with the noise, she look'd around,
> And seem'd t'inquire the Author of the Sound.

She happens upon her father, the river god Inachus

> And lick'd his palms, and cast a piteous Look;
> And in the Language of her Eyes, she spoke.
> She wou'd have told her Name, and ask'd Relief,
> But wanting Words, in Tears she tells her Grief
> Which, with her Foot she makes him understand;
> And prints the name of *Io* in the Sand.

Inachus, who has been searching for her, realises he has found his
daughter:

> So found, is worse than lost: with mutual Words
> Thou answer'st not, No Voice thy Tongue affords
> But Sighs are deeply drawn from out thy Breast;
> And Speech deny'd, by Lowing is expressed.
> Unknowing, I prepar'd thy Bridal Bed

and he launches off into his complaint, as into an aria begun with a
slight modulation of a repeated phrase – the modulation being that
rhyme of 'Lowing / Unknowing' with which Dryden so expertly and
so simply gathers up the echo into the now to be unfolded lament.
This story, unlike that of Lycaon, ends benignly with the return from
heifer to woman:

> She tries her Tongue; her Silence softly breaks,
> And fears her former Lowings when she speaks.

And Dryden, here, uses the resources of English to make a little more
explicit that drama of utterance which is in the Latin, yet not in the
words in the same way:

> She tries her Tongue; her Silence softly breaks,

The second half of this line can be read transitively – she breaks her silence – or intransitively – silence yields itself up as she regains intelligible speech. Once more, it's the simplicity of the effect that reinforces the accuracy of the perception: she breaks her own silence by 'trying her tongue', then – and the mid-line pause registers the anxiety (ours and hers) as to whether she'll actually speak – she both breaks her silence and hears it break:

> She tries her Tongue; her Silence softly breaks,

and, indeed, not until the close of the ensuing line is the anxiety resolved by rhyme – or rather wittily half-resolved:

> And fears her former Lowings when she speaks.

A darker episode than that of Io, and another variation on our theme, is to be found in one of Addison's splendid contributions to our English Ovid, the tale of Echo. She is cursed by Juno with a grotesque speech impediment:

> for though her voice was left
> Juno a curse did on her Tongue impose
> To sport with every Sentence in the Close.

She falls in love with Narcissus – the part of Ovid's episode that deals with him, incidentally, seems to have penetrated deeply the long, cancelled passage on Saint Narcissus in Eliot's *The Waste Land*. Finally Narcissus, hopelessly in love with his own reflection, dies and

> To the cold Shades his flitting Ghost retires,
> And in the Stygian Waves itself admires.

But before this, Echo finds her supreme fulfilment in fitting her tongue to the voice of this man she loves, but who loves himself, and she utters on her own behalf the self-involved laments he directs at his reflection:

> She answer'd sadly to the Lover's Moan,
> Sigh'd back his Sighs and groan'd to ev'ry Groan.

Ovid's *Metamorphoses* take us through the whole scale of moans and groans, sighings, lowings, howlings, hissings, ape-sounds, croakings, whinnyings, bat-talk, bear-roaring, to the voicelessness of fishes. My own conclusion comes with the voicelessness – the loss of tongue – that dominates that story of the sexual violence of Tereus and 'The change of Philomel, by the barbarous king / So rudely forced', in words from T.S. Eliot's *The Waste Land*. In Garth's Ovid (Book VI) the story is told by Mr Croxall. He's not the best translator in the world for this haunting tale, and there are one or two weak lines. All the same, the general run of the thing has energy, and moments occur when this minor writer takes fire and excels himself.

One hears nothing from Ovid about Philomela's 'inviolable voice' – Eliot's phrase – when she has become a nightingale. But one sees what it was in this tale about eloquence and also about not having a voice that drew Eliot – the poet for whom 'voices', 'words', 'silence' all vibrate meaningfully, though with meanings that threaten to elude the speaker. For an early protagonist like Prufrock, 'It is impossible to say just what I mean!' Gerontion hears the silence of 'The word within a word, unable to speak a word, / Swaddled with darkness'. 'I gotta use words when I talk to you', says Sweeney in Eliot's most original dramatic work. 'What words have we? / I should like to be in a crowd of beaks without words' runs one of the desperate cancellations from *The Waste Land* manuscript. Beaks without words – this is where we are at the end of Philomela's tale, with Philomela and Procne metamorphosed into birds of blood-spattered plumage, and Tereus with the most dangerous beak of the three:

> Fix'd on his Head the crested Plumes appear.
> Long is his Beak, and sharpen'd like a Spear.

Any summary of the tale makes it sound merely ghastly. Here is mine: Tereus goes to Athens to fetch Philomela to visit her sister Procne (his wife) in Thrace. Already in Athens he is beginning to lust after Philomela. On the way back he rapes her, cuts out her tongue and imprisons her in a hunting lodge. When the truth of the matter gets to Procne, she frees Philomela and then cannibalises Tereus' son Itys, serving him up to his father, after which Philomela appears drenched in gore and hurls Itys' severed head at him. This comes at a point when the two women have worked themselves up to a pitch of hysteria. Tereus is also a hysteric – earlier in the poem he succeeds in making himself cry at his own rhetoric where he's persuading Philomela's father how badly Procne wants to see her sister. The hurling of the severed head marks a climax of hysteria in a poem which itself refuses to be hysterical. With the hurling of the head, the attitude is not that of (say) Richard Strauss's opera *Salome,* where we are being solicited into palpitating vicariousness, where we are being asked whether we, too, wouldn't perhaps like a taste of that other severed head – John the Baptist's – Salome is busy kissing. The firm Dantescan power of Ovid lies in the way he portrays the ever-accelerating, self-injuring, self-damning impetus of this gang of hysterics – 'gang' is the word Croxall uses to describe the crowd of Bacchantes that Procne takes to free Philomela, Procne herself having donned the pelt of a stag as well as a garland of vine leaves

And with religious Yellings [filled] the Skies.

What Ovid did with this tale – and his doings compelled Eliot's imagination to make of it an objective correlative to his own wholly interior drama – was to evolve the vortex of hysterias out of his own sense of the way we unpack our hearts with words, allowing them to intensify and doubly corrupt feelings that are already suspect. A poet might well have gone for the hysteria alone. Shakespeare, or whoever wrote *Titus Andronicus,* luxuriates in a debased recollection of Philomela's cut-out tongue in the melodrama of Lavinia's even gorier mutilations in that play. In Ovid this theme of the tongue always keeps in sight the theme of words, in a kind of extended piece of wit-writing, though this is wit-writing that is never *merely* witty, but capable of the most telling of tragic ironies.

We may end among 'beaks without words', but the vortex of hysterias begins with a plethora of words – with Tereus' speech of persuasion to Philomela's father:

The Eloquence of Love his Tongue inspires
And, in his Wife's, he speaks his own Desires;
Hence all his Importunities arise,
And Tears unmanly trickle from his Eyes.

He is just as eloquent when, after the rape, he lies to his wife about her sister being dead, and his eloquence succeeds once more in squeezing out those pathic tears – Ovid's handling of the story is remarkable for the way, early on, one is made to feel words breeding on words their own insincerities. The trouble with Philomela is that she, too, talks too much – uses too many words for her own good. After the rape, she vividly and at length evokes for Tereus just what morally he has done. It's a speech of over thirty lines in Croxall's version, and, like Tereus' own efforts, only too successful as a rhetorical performance with all the stops out: it so tells on the imagination of Tereus that he's flung unresisting into his hysteric's vision of rapidly alternating contraries, and two couplets here very ably catch the lurching unpredictability of his behaviour:

> Struck with these Words, the Tyrant's guilty Breast
> With Fear, and Anger, was, by turns, possest;
> Now, with Remorse his Conscience deeply stung,
> He drew the Falchion that beside him hung,
> And [...]

He doesn't, however, impale himself because of that 'Conscience deeply stung'. He doesn't cut her throat, as she asks him, to get rid of the stain on her character. 'Struck with these Words', what he wants is their source – the tongue that made him hear what he's done and which threatens to tell 'the pitying Rocks' if she can't get free. The severed tongue – and this is the bit that pleased 'those damned Elizabethans' as Matthew Arnold called them – continues

> Murmuring with a faint imperfect Sound:
> And, as a Serpent writhes his wounded Train,
> Uneasy, panting, and possess'd with Pain.

When Philomela gets the truth of the matter to Procne by weaving the words she can't speak into a piece of tapestry, Croxall reiterates the tongue theme that he has seen at work in Ovid: Procne reads the tapestry and

> In such tumultuous Haste her Passions sprung,
> They chok'd her Voice, and quite disarm'd her Tongue.
> No room for female Tears; the Furies rise,
> Darting vindictive glances from her eyes.

English usage here results in the repetition of 'tongue'. Golding's version of 1567 has a similar turn of phrase: 'But sorrow tied hir tongue.' This is all rather more concrete than the Latin which simply says 'grief choked her utterance'. But if the English over-insists, the insistence is not merely fanciful, and its concreteness is perfectly in tune with Ovid's subsequent tragic wit as it shifts from tongue to words, from words to silence.

The last three reiterations of the motif of the tongue in Croxall's version are all derived straight from the Latin. Procne, having got her sister back, works on her and on herself to dream up the right kind of punishment for Tereus. Seeing that Philomela can only speak with her hands, 'In Procne's breast the rising Passions boil', and, as they boil over, she rushes from the idea of setting the palace on fire to

> Or, his false Tongue with racking Engines seize;
> Or, cut away the Part that injur'd you.

(This isn't quite some Freudian identification of tongue and penis, but it darts back accurately, even while charting Procne's mounting hysteria, to the manner in which, as we've noted, Tereus' sexual feelings feed his eloquence.)

> A while, thus wav'ring, stood the furious Dame.
> When Itys fondling to his Mother came.

The artistically gripping thing about what I have called the poem's vortex of hysterias is that there are sudden lulls, moments when we feel the poet's own control in the manner in which he spaces out the eruptions of feeling, moments when, for all that, the lulls are terrible for the brooding they imply. The child Itys could hardly have appeared at a worse time. Procne, as one expects, sees the father in the son, and starts

> Forming the direful Purpose in her head

– of sacrificing him, that is. But as he approaches

> And he accosts her in a prattling tone
> Then her tempestuous Anger was allay'd,
> And in its full Career her vengeance stay'd.

What leads to the child's undoing is this obsessive theme of *The Metamorphoses* that we've been exploring, exemplified in the fact that he *can* prattle. She turns from prattling child to silent sister:

> While this fond Boy (she said) can thus express
> The moving Accents of his fond Address;
> Why stands my sister of her Tongue bereft

and from now on, there is no holding back on cutting the child to pieces, or on the hysteric involvement of Philomela too – she who begins to relish the situation as she evidently relished the dressing down she gave Tereus before he silenced her.

Ovid thoroughly understands (to borrow the terms of a later culture) the psychology of damnation, yet in the very act of dramatising it he can distance the insane hysteria of his protagonists, as in the black humour of the final appearance of the tongue theme. Philomela flings the head of Itys at Tereus:

Nor ever long'd so much to use her Tongue
And with a just Reproach to vindicate her Wrong.

The tale as a whole works through a clear sense of how hysteria
involves its victims in a train of subhuman feeling and subhuman
action, and how it thrives on a diet that combines the irrational and
the calculating. Beginning in lust, the story ends in wrath. The sheer
animal violence, right up to the close when Tereus seizes his sabre to
despatch the sisters, rather than the culminating metamorphosis into
birds, is what engages Ovid's imaginings. We only know from legend
what sort of birds the sisters became and there is no question in Ovid
of the nightingale bursting into song. In all this Ovid brings fully to
mind Dante's own sense of the sullen, the violent, the wrathful, of
those who must suffer the untying of the knot of anger – 'e d'ira-
condia van solvendo il nodo'. This awareness of what people do to
themselves, of the nature of self-destruction and the tortures of the
self-enclosed ego, unexpectedly unites the poet of *The Metamorphoses*
and the poet of *The Divine Comedy*, nowhere more so – and this must
be my final example – than when Erisichthon (Book VII), having
wilfully and persistently flouted the goddess Ceres, is visited with
unappeasable hunger by Famine herself, and ends by devouring his
own flesh:

> He grows more empty, as the more supply'd,
> And endless Cramming but extends the Void [...]
> Now Riches hoarded by Paternal Care
> Were sunk, the Glutton swallowing up the Heir [...]
> At last all Means, as all Provisions, fail'd;
> For the Disease by Remedies prevail'd;
> His Muscles with a furious Bite he tore,
> Gorg'd his own tatter'd Flesh, and gulphed his Gore.
> Wounds were his Feast, his Life to Life a Prey,
> Supporting Nature by its own Decay.

(Mr Vernon)

Of the 'quattro grand'ombre', the four great shades who come
forward to greet Dante in *Inferno* IV, Ovid is third in line after Homer
and Horace – the fourth is Lucan. As Ezra Pound has it in his essay
on Arnaut Daniel: 'Dante has learned also of Ovid [...] although he
talks so much of Virgil.'

I've tried, so far, to present some aspects of the Ovidian vision as
it is brought over in a major English translation – one that ought to
be part of our literary heritage, as Pope's Homer once was. I shall next

look at Ovid in metamorphosis, at the Dantescan Ovid who influenced Eliot and at how he has been transformed and renewed in twentieth-century poetry. This also provides an exemplar of the wisdom of *The Metamorphoses* – in Dryden's words in Book XV:

> Nor dies the Spirit, but new Life repeats
> In other Forms, and only changes Seats.

2 T.S. Eliot: Meaning and Metamorphosis

In *The Metamorphoses* the story of Tereus, Philomela and the severed tongue comes as a climax to several other tales, where the drama depends on the poet's sense of having a tongue, or of feeling it turn to marble, or of hearing it lapse out into bird or beast noises or into silence. The possession of a tongue and our capacity to use it, 'the involvement of tongue with word [as I have said] would appear to be a theme close to the poet's most intimate sense of himself'. This is an awareness that draws T.S. Eliot magnetically to the Tereus–Philomela story in writing *The Waste Land*. Long before that, to be tongue-tied, to be incapable of saying just what one means, already haunted Eliot's poetry. At times he even yearns for tonguelessness, or his protagonists do. Other poets – Hopkins with his 'where, where was a, where was a place?', the Peruvian Vallejo with his 'Desde ttttales códigos' ('According tttto such codes') – other poets have *forced* the impeded tongue into speech.[1] Hopkins even forces it into a tormented lyricism. But Eliot disdains what would perhaps have seemed to him such expressionist self-advertisement. More impersonally, he does however choose a fragmented art form where psychic wholeness can yet be hinted at by the use of myth and of metamorphosis.

'I am no longer concerned with metaphors but with metamorphoses.' Thus Georges Braque in *Cahiers D'Art*. His words might stand as epigraph not only to the modernist phase in painting, fragmenting reality to reconstitute it in non-imitative forms, but also to certain aspects of the collage-poems of Pound and Eliot. Literature will go on to concern itself with metaphors, of course, though what Braque seems to mean by metaphor in painting is that by realistically imitating the appearance of an object, by letting your imitation stand in place of that object, you are denying the creative mind its full plastic power. By metamorphosis, as distinct from metaphor in Braque's sense, the mind could transform that object into a less predictable, a more variously faceted image. Music, which does not concern itself with metaphor in any exact sense of the meaning, also, in the hands

---

1 See César Vallejo, *Poemas Humanos, a bilingual edition* (Grove Press, New York, 1968), p. 26.

of Schoenberg, followed the way of fragmentation, building new wholes out of its atonalised constituents, venturing on new sound paths. In both visual and literary art, the notions of fragmentation and metamorphosis travel together, as at the climax of *The Waste Land* within sight of Babel:

> *Poi s'ascose nel foco che gli affina*
> *Quando fiam uti chelidon* – O swallow swallow
> *Le Prince d'Aquitaine à la tour abolie*
> These fragments I have shored against my ruins
> Why then Ile fit you. Hieronymo's mad againe.
> Datta. Dayadhvam. Damyata.
>   Shantih shantih shantih

Do we *hear* that any longer, or have we lost the Babelic din it makes to the rumble of a thousand commentaries? Five languages, and their differing metrical forms – or bits of them. Read aloud like this, without warning, the famous climax recalls, perhaps, our forgotten first reading, as the mind re-adjusts itself to take in and differentiate all that sheer noise, and attempts to reconstitute noise as meaning. In the reconstituting, we help to complete a metamorphosis. Literary art was always like this – to *some* degree; so that what we are reading *now* reshapes what we have read up to this point. But Eliot foreshortens the process, speeds it up, involves you in the crisis of it, and the languages are a part of that. From our first reading, scarcely possible to recall, perhaps what still remains in the memory is a sense of pleasant bewilderment, and something of that same sense returns each time we re-hear these lines and re-focus their meaning. If our act of reading is an act of metamorphosing the fragments towards a whole, metamorphosis also belongs in the passage as a directly stated theme:

> *nel foco che gli affina*

– into the fire which refines them. This Dantescan fire changes and purifies – in a word, metamorphoses; and the sliver of Dante gives place immediately to another myth of metamorphosis, that of Philomela and Procne which we have already explored:

> *Quando fiam uti chelidon*

– when shall I become like the swallow? Eliot has already used Ovid's story in Part II, the 'Game of Chess' section; in these closing lines in Part V, it is the reference to the story in the anonymous, possibly second to fourth century BC, *Pervigilium Veneris* that he fragments.

Why he uses this half line, splicing it with a snatch of Tennyson, 'O swallow, swallow', I want to go on to consider. For the moment, I offer *The Waste Land*'s climax, as an illustration of my theme that by the twentieth century, metamorphosis has become a primary component of style itself. If this is evidence for the existence of that elusive 'spirit of the age' – in montage, collage, decalcomania, in Joycean word-play – the surprising thing is the variety of uses metamorphosis has been put to. My present and necessarily limited concern, however, is with Eliot and Pound, and at this point it must be with Eliot and principally some of the early poems and *The Waste Land*. I want to extend a line of thought first pursued in Sister Bernetta Quinn's pioneering study, *The Metamorphic Tradition in Modern Poetry* (Rutgers University Press, New Brunswick, New Jersey, 1955).

Eliot and Pound both respond to the idea of metamorphosis but in startlingly different ways. Pound still shares Ovid's feeling that we belong to our world and of the essential unity of men with animal creation. If, as Pound has it, the poet's 'I' is to be confirmed and created by 'casting off [...] complete masks of the self in each poem', for him there exists an invitation to the dramatic and the creative in this process to which he actively and willingly responds. For this process, too, is grounded in a world of variety and fecundity. Ovid's own ranging along the sound scale from bellowings, lowings, sighings, hissings, croakings to speech and song bears witness to this various world. The metamorphoses which accompany these sounds may be attended by pain and distress, but they are to be wondered at. Metamorphosis may demonstrate the fragility of the self, but it also challenges the bullying autonomy of that self and it relates all selves to a single and miraculous universe.

For Eliot, on the other hand, a sense of metamorphosis often means a sense of the provisional nature of personality. If poems are 'masks of the self', Eliot's chosen masks are not Pound's Bertrans de Born with his, 'Damn it all! all this our South stinks peace' – or Sigismondo Malatesta or, as in the *Women of Trachis*, Heracles. Prufrock has seen his head 'brought in upon a platter', but he's no prophet, no John the Baptist; 'no Prince Hamlet, nor was meant to be'; he feels more like Polonius, 'Almost, at times, the Fool'. Given the imagination of metamorphosis, his thoughts would scarcely run on tree or stone, bird or beast:

I should have been a pair of ragged claws
Scuttling across the floors of silent seas.

He'll neither bellow nor hiss: he chooses silence. The young man in
'Portrait of a Lady' feels driven to become a less resourceful Proteus:

> And I must borrow every changing shape
> To find expression … dance, dance
> Like a dancing bear,
> Cry like a parrot, chatter like an ape.
> Let us take the air, in a tobacco trance –

And that passage, too, runs aground on silence in the form of a dash
and a space of white paper, having traversed the subhuman possibilities of parrot and ape with cries that resemble language yet are only
noise. Here, already in these early poems, Eliot's characteristic soundscape is taking form. It ranges from the silence that threatens to the
silence that is fecund. It takes in subhuman noises and bird-sounds.
It reminds us of the difficulty of saying just what we mean, and it
holds out the promise of meaningful speech and perhaps song. The
promise of song comes even in the legend of Philomela to which Eliot
reverts – Philomela who has no tongue and yet can sing. Silence,
speech, song, music. If this is an art that aspires to the condition of
music – and 'Love Song', 'Preludes', 'Rhapsody', *Four Quartets* would
lead one to suppose that it does – then it is a music listened for fear-
fully across chatter and troubled silences, a music mocked at by voices
inside the poet's own head.

How differently Rilke's Orpheus in *Sonnets to Orpheus* proposes to
translate the voices of the creatures of stillness – *Tiere aus Stille* – and
also the bellowing, cry, roar – *Brüllen, Schrei, Geröhr* – until he has raised
for this subworld temples in hearing – *Tempel im Gehör* – and as he
sings this world, it, too, will be forced to confess that *Gesang ist Dasein*
– song is the there-being. Well it might be, one can imagine Prufrock
glumly responding – he who never sings his love song; he who cannot
say what he means but has heard the mermaids *sing* what they mean
– for he has learned Donne's lesson, 'Teach me to hear mermaids
singing', but realises they only sing 'each to each': 'I do not think they
will sing to me.' They sing with as little concern for him, as exclud-
ingly, as the voices of the Rhine-maidens with their 'Weialala leia /
Wallala leialala' for the inhabitants of *The Waste Land*. In 'The Fire
Sermon', Section III of *The Waste Land*, this chorus keeps returning
in the wake of the words of the three Thames-daughters. On its third
recurrence it has dwindled down to 'la la', as if it had faded out to
another plane of being altogether, or as if the sordid happenings on
Margate Sands had severed the Waste Land world from that mythic

wave-length. Eliot's note points us to Wagner's *Götterdämmerung* Act III, Scene I, where the Rhine-maidens address Siegfried, speaking like the Thames-daughters 'in turn', as Eliot says. But what they in fact don't do in Act III of *Götterdämmerung* is to sing their 'Weialala leia / Wallala leialala'. They begin in Act III by lamenting that the Rhine is now dark because their gold has been stolen, just as the first Thames-daughter laments that 'The river sweats / Oil and tar'. 'Weialala' etc. is the joyful noise that *opens* the *Ring* cycle in *Das Rheingold,* before the theft of the gold – and before the pollution, that is, of the river. What is the meaning for those of us wandering in the Waste Land, of the joyful glossolalia of 'Weialala leia / Wallala leialala'? Apparently the meaning, spilling out from the Rhine-maidens' circle of exclusion, from the nursery noises of these eternal children at play is that for them, their gold safe, *Gesang ist Dasein* – song, in Rilkean parlance, is the there-being.

But the rest of us have our lives to live, such as they are, and such is Prufrock's that – is he speaking for his divided and thus plural self? – 'human voices wake us and we drown'. Silence, speech, song, music. What an ennobling hierarchy if only we could climb into it instead of always sliding back into the silence that threatens to rob speech of meaning. Prufrock drowns – 'we' drown – under a silence as deep as that in which he would choose to be a crab

Scuttling across the floors of silent seas

– a phrase which itself draws on the dehumanising threat of Tennyson's 'The stillness of the central sea'. We know what those 'human voices' already mean, or how little meaning they carry for Prufrock, in the much discussed couplet

In the room the women come and go
Talking of Michelangelo.

The women have been accused of having high-pitched voices (though Eliot does not say so) and of being culture snobs (though only literary critics could imagine the subject of Michelangelo as beyond the range of normal conversation). Accurately, Christopher Ricks has indicated the words' 'tonelessness' in this couplet.[1] And surely they are toneless because the ear receiving them – Prufrock's ear – is numbed beyond feeling; they brush against that ear as mere

1 In a talk 'Tone in Eliot's Poetry' reported in 'Commentary', *Times Literary Supplement*, 2 Nov. 1973, p. 134.

noise – not ape noise or parrot noise perhaps, but noise that excludes Prufrock as surely as the mermaids' song. In given situations, in the confusing soundscape of these poems, what is there to choose between noise and song? – in the situation, say, of the man in *The Waste Land* drafts like 'a deaf mute swimming deep below the surface' among 'concatenated words from which the sense seemed gone'. And appropriate to the desperation of this state of mind in 'Prufrock' itself is that we get the foreign sound of *Michelangelo* – 'Talking of Michelangelo' – and not the more usual 'Michaelangelo'.[1] This, again appropriately, is a poem into which we have to battle our way through an epigraph in the same language as *Michelangelo* – an epigraph in which Guido da Montefeltro offers to reveal himself to Dante because he believes his words will never get back to the human world. Prufrock speaks on the identical supposition. That same passage of Dante is preceded in *Inferno* XXVII by stanzas which evoke Guido's difficulty in finding a voice to speak *with*, and at first he can only make crackling noises out of the flame in which he is imprisoned, which he has become.[2] It would take more than Rilke's Orpheus to transmute these noises into song. From silence to song. Perhaps we may gain a little coherent speech, these poems seem to say, but can we ever sing of summer 'in full-throated ease' like Keats' nightingale? Eliot insists he is no romantic poet, yet Philomela, the nightingale, sings for him the meaningful, wordless song that transfigures the Waste Land.

However, it is all those noises that refuse to be transmuted into Rilke's Orphic song or Keats' 'full-throated ease' that make the soundscape of Eliot's poetry so distinct, when, time and again, as the changes are being rung on 'words', 'voice', 'silence', 'singing', our ear is brought up against the bird-noises of 'Twit twit twit / Jug jug jug jug jug jug', 'Tereu', 'Co co rico co co rico', 'Go go go go go', 'Quick quick quick', or foreign sounds that we have to scrutinise for meaning or the primitive radical DA, or the voice that says 'Ta ta', or the Rhine chorus snapped off to 'la la', or 'Drip drop drip drop drop drop drop', or 'Datta. Dayadhvam. Damyata.' which may mean 'Give, sympathise, control' but in the cataract of fragments at the close of *The Waste Land*, to a Western ear sounds to be running back into gibberish; or

1   In 'What Dante Means to Me' (1950) Eliot tells us that, as a young man, he read Dante via a prose crib and committed passages to memory. 'Heaven knows what it would have sounded like, had I recited it aloud', he comments. In his recorded recitation of *Prufrock*, he pronounces 'Michelangelo' 'Michaelangelo'.

2   See Michael Edwards' alert analysis in his *Eliot/Language* (Aquila, Isle of Skye, 1975), pp. 11–12.

Hoo ha ha
Hoo ha ha
Hoo
Hoo
Hoo

which – we are at the conclusion of *Sweeney Agonistes* – gets for follow-up not a stage-direction, 'A knock is heard at the door', or 'Nine distinct raps are heard at the door' but (in capital letters and measured out in verse lines):

KNOCK KNOCK KNOCK
KNOCK KNOCK KNOCK
KNOCK
KNOCK
KNOCK

This recalls an identical device earlier on in the piece: the first time the word 'coffin' ushers in the nine KNOCKs, the second time the word 'dead'. So, confronting us with intimations of mortality, and repeating the same nine-syllable cadence as in

Hoo ha ha
Hoo ha ha
Hoo
Hoo
Hoo

the nine repetitions of 'KNOCK', there on the page, recall to us the experience of gazing at one word, or of repeating it nine times over, and then realising the peculiar way in which meaning comes close to noise when it is lodged in a single and isolated syllable like this.

With this metamorphosis of meaning into noise and the reverse process, amid bird-sounds – is there any single poem of the same length with as many bird calls as *The Waste Land*? – amid da's, hoo-ha's, glossolalia, snatches of foreign quotations, the ear encounters the soundscape of a world where metamorphosis invades and shapes the fabric of the poetry itself. This metamorphosis concerns not only the significance of sounds but the significance of things seen, thought about, remembered. They acquire dangerous powers within the mind. Landscape or cityscape is as full of admonition as soundscape. As early as Prufrock, streets became 'a tedious argument / Of insidious intent', the yellow fog becomes a big cat that falls asleep curled round the house; one wears a 'necktie rich and modest, but asserted by a simple pin' and the pin becomes part of the hell that is other people –

> And when I am formulated, sprawling on a pin,
> When I am pinned and wriggling on the wall,
> Then how should I begin [etc.].

'Regard that woman / Who hesitates toward you', says a street-lamp in 'Rhapsody on a Windy Night'. You do as you are told,

> And you see the corner of her eye
> Twists like a crooked pin.

Eliot drops the uncomfortable association of pin and eye ('that ball / A prick would make no eye at all', as Hopkins put it), but he introduces on the rhyme word for eye – namely 'dry' – the contents of the memory:

> The memory throws up high and dry
> A crowd of twisted things;
> A twisted branch upon the beach […]
> A broken spring in a factory yard.

They are twisted just as the eye twists. The eye is apparently forgotten; the twisting has taken over. 'Remark the cat', says the street-lamp just as it said, 'Regard that woman', and the repeated imperative to visualise leads back to the eye, to a series of eyes: a child slips out its hand to pocket a toy, just as the cat slips out its tongue 'And devours a morsel of rancid butter':

> I could see nothing behind that child's eye.
> I have seen eyes in the street
> Trying to peer through lighted shutters,
> And a crab one afternoon in a pool
> An old crab with barnacles on his back,
> Gripped the end of a stick which I held him

The crab is groping blindly and the stress on anxious visualising seems to be fading until we get a third imperative 'Regard the moon' and the moon 'winks a feeble eye' and we have come full circle from the prostitute at the beginning to the face of the moon. In the landscape of 'Rhapsody on a Windy Night' everything turns into everything else.

If everything turns into everything else in an early poem like 'Rhapsody', what of *The Waste Land* over a decade later? Eliot, in the notes, introducing Ovid's account of Tiresias from *Metamorphoses,* Book III, says:

> Tiresias, although a mere spectator and not indeed a 'character', is yet the most important personage in the poem, uniting all the rest. Just as the one-eyed merchant, seller of currants, melts into the Phoenician Sailor, and the latter is not wholly distinct from Ferdinand Prince of Naples, so all the women are one woman, and the two sexes meet in Tiresias. What Tiresias *sees*, in fact, is the substance of the poem. The whole passage from Ovid is of great anthropological interest

and he goes on to quote it. It's a puzzle to know what Eliot means by that deadpan remark about 'of great anthropological interest' as you embark on this urbanely told incident in Ovid. It begins with Jove's argument with Juno about who gets the bigger share of pleasure from sexual intercourse, man or woman. He says woman and she, the arch-puritan, denies it. So Tiresias is called in as arbiter. He has been both man and woman, though he has never been what Eliot makes of him, an old man 'with wrinkled dugs'. He has been man and he has been woman – on separate occasions. He turned into a woman when he parted two copulating snakes with his staff. Seven years later, he (or rather she) sees them engaged in the self-same activity, and has the sensible idea that if they are parted as before, manhood may return. And so it does. As arbiter, Tiresias declares for Jove's judgement, at which Juno strikes him blind. Jove recompenses him with the gift of prophetic vision. It is this gift of prophetic vision which qualifies him for his rôle in Eliot's poem – as it qualifies him in Pound's cantos, drawn there from his Homeric context. But very differently from Pound, the business of the double sex, lingering in those vestigial wrinkled breasts, fits Eliot's whole concern with the uncertain nature of identity where nothing connects with nothing. 'Of great anthropological interest', says Eliot the note writer, apparently secure on that far side of the divide from the man who suffers, yet concluding a passage – the largest note to *The Waste Land* – where he is urging us to feel that this shape- and sex-changer actually contains within his consciousness 'the substance of the poem', that this witness to metamorphosis, 'old man with wrinkled female breasts', 'although a mere spectator [... unites] all the rest'.

Whether one feels he does so at all points in one's reading of the poem is questionable, but one senses in the urging of the note the same cast of mind that can move in the 'Rhapsody' from the image of rust clinging to a spring to that of a crab gripping a stick. For the terrible thing about metamorphosis in Eliot's earlier poetry is that, although nothing connects with nothing, everything seems to be changing into everything else, that all these things are identical, that metamorphosis is not variety and fecundity, but the phantasmagoria of a divided self, of a mind that contains and unifies and yet, in need of spiritual metamorphosis itself, depletes and dries up. The poetry seems bent on creating an appalling parody of Marvell's 'The mind, that ocean where each kind / Does straight its own resemblance find.' It is presumably Tiresias who says, in the first section of *The Waste Land*,

> Only
> There is shadow under this red rock,
> (Come in under the shadow of this red rock),
> And I will show you something different from either
> Your shadow at morning striding behind you
> Or your shadow at evening rising to meet you;
> I will show you fear in a handful of dust.

When one goes back to the drafts of the poem one realises that this is the rewriting of words (another metamorphosis) which describe the end of one more Ovidian protagonist – Narcissus, or rather the invented Saint Narcissus in Eliot's own metamorphosis of him: 'Come in under the shadow of this grey rock / And I will show you' not 'fear in a handful of dust', but (the fragment runs) 'his bloody cloth and limbs / And the grey shadow on his lips'. Self-enclosed and self-loving, 'His eyes were aware of the pointed corners of his eyes' – strange the way this line swims within reach of the line about the prostitute's eyes in 'Rhapsody on a Windy Night'. It is, one might say, the swimming within reach of other appearances, and becoming other appearances, that makes Saint Narcissus' fate more dire than that of Ovid's Narcissus. At worst, Ovid's figure simply loves his own reflection, whereas in one draft Eliot's martyred saint wishes

> that he had been a tree
> To push its branches among each other. [...]

> Then he wished that he had been a fish
> With slippery white belly held between his own fingers
> To have writhed in his own clutch, his beauty
> caught in his own beauty

Then he wished he had been a young glrl
Caught in the woods by a drunken old man
To have known at the last moment, the full
        taste of her own whiteness
The horror of her own smoothness.

In a second draft, Narcissus is sure he has *been* a tree, a fish, a girl *and* a drunken old man:

So he became a dancer to God.
Because his flesh was in love with the burning arrows
He danced on the hot sand
Until the arrows came.
As he embraced them his white skin surrendered
        itself to the redness of blood, and satisfied him.

So now we find him, martyred, 'under the shadow of this grey rock'. One takes the point in the lines about Narcissus as girl, culminating in 'The horror of her own smoothness', that self-love can also be a form of self-loathing, from which there is no escape amid the boundless lability of this protean world – a tree, a fish, a girl, but never a stable I.

Salvador Dalí, in a poem written during the thirties after the high Spanish fashion in a welter of images and entitled 'The Metamorphoses of Narcissus', also imagines his twentieth-century Narcissus as pursuing his reflections through a protean infinity. He, however, seems to find in this cultivation of delirium, this surrender to the vertigo of shapes becoming other shapes, an ideal of consciousness, overpopulating the void of interior space until it begins to resemble a film projected at eye-daunting speed. Thus one becomes interesting to oneself at the expense of never in the Socratic sense knowing oneself or wanting to. Why not give up saying what one means since meanings are so betrayingly, temptingly full of plasticity? One has reached the *reductio ad absurdum* of Wagner's patron, poor mad King Ludwig, and his declaration, 'I wish to remain an enigma even to myself.' (*His* fate was the *Waste Land* fate of death by water.)

Narcissus proved a temptation to overwriting to Eliot as well as to Dalí. The blind Tiresias, however, was a good choice for the interior vision that was to *see* all this panorama of dread: he bears the physical evidence of his dual identity, but as a prophet he points outwards from his own psychic wounds towards human history and he can stand for something in the poet without the issueless 'dancing on the hot sand' that Narcissus seems to encourage. That 'something' has to be spoken, and the wonder is that Eliot ever managed to lift the morass of it into speech (let alone song), since the hell he must have inhabited for years seems literally unspeakable.

The pain which threatens human response in the poem forces on to the poet – and us – a sense of a possible range of response forbidden to the inhabitants of the Waste Land. Within the poem, and outreaching mere psychological compulsions, are images like that of the interior of the church of Saint Magnus Martyr, with its

Inexplicable splendour of Ionian white and gold.

That that should be the interior of Saint Magnus Martyr, and not a flicker of the self-regard of Saint Narcissus Martyr, must have been meaningful to Eliot too. That inexplicable splendour resists self-absorption just as, on a different level, the variety of sounds resists the transmutation into Orphic song. It is this sense of resistances in the poem that, in the course of our reading, leaves us free from the idea in the notes that it is all going on in Tiresias' mind. The note may be partly compelled by vestiges of Eliot's 'proteanism', but it may also be the result of a nervousness that the daring fragmentation of this poem – a totally new artistic venture on Eliot's part, ratified and inten-sified by Pound's advice – might not reconstitute itself as an artistic whole in the mind of the reader. But the sound world of the poem resonates in all our minds, as it teaches us to hear according to an acoustic we did not know we possessed. Tiresias may (for Eliot) '[unite] all the rest', but his is not the only or/the most important voice in the poem. That voice says DA – give – whereas he only says he has 'foresuffered all'.

I have alluded to the soundscape of *The Waste Land*. I want to look now at the elements of that soundscape, to see how the tale of the tongueless Philomela emerges out of its gamut of sounds and coun-tersounds – of silence, speech, song, music. Speech and the failures of speech are associated with psychic pain in Eliot. 'It is impossible to say just what I mean!' Prufrock tells us. In *The Waste Land*, the theme of speech – the legend of Philomela embedded in it – reaches back to a number of anguished jottings in the drafts. We hear of people with 'dogs' eyes ... heads of birds / Beaks and no words'. 'What words have we? / I should like to be in a crowd of beaks without words.' None of this gets through into the final poem, but its traces do, spaced, measured, heard against other possibilities along the route of this journey to an empty chapel where, after various kinds of silence, the grass is singing, to the shore where finally 'the arid plain' is 'behind me'. One is very conscious in following out the steps of this journey, of silence and of words in a number of languages, of bird-noises and song, and the way these create the structure and make it a structure of meanings once the reader's mind has collaborated in putting it all together, reconstituting even noise as meaning, meta-morphosing fragments into a whole. Some of the words, like '*Frisch weht der Wind*' ('Fresh blows the wind'), belonged to song in their orig-inal context, as did 'O the moon shone bright on Mrs Porter / And on her daughter / They wash their feet in soda water', though in that original context, the ballad 'reported to me', says Eliot, 'from Sydney, Australia', it is not their feet they wash.[1] Silence in *The Waste Land* is ambivalent, multiple in meaning. At the most basic level it is the typo-graphical white spaces on which no words are written, and which are let into this poem at so many points. Thus in the first section one goes from the ecstatic moment in the Hyacinth garden

Looking into the heart of light, the silence

on to the metamorphosis of 'Desolate and empty the sea' –

Oed' und leer das Meer

then to the physical blank of white paper, before the poem cuts into the bitter comedy of Madame Sosostris, famous clairvoyante. And the physical blank of the paper images the desolation and emptiness of that sea over which Isolde's vessel fails to come into view. The German phrase, balanced on the edge of white silence, calls up those other German words, previously quoted in the poem, the song of the young sailor,

Frisch weht der Wind
Der Heimat zu

('Fresh blows the wind / Towards home') a phrase which, cutting away from – it is a filmic 'cut' I mean – 'I will show you fear in a handful of dust', has led us to the promise of the meaningful silence, which is 'the heart of light', in the Hyacinth garden episode.

Eliot's quotations are used with extraordinary accuracy. He knows *Tristan and Isolde*, not as the man who can tell you which is the best of fifteen recordings to buy, but as someone for whom certain moments

---

1 Soda water was, of course, looked upon as a contraceptive device – at any rate in 'Sydney, Australia'.

of the work say – and the same is true of his Dante and Verlaine – 'Look, you are not alone in your feeling. All this has happened before in other minds, in other times.' The song of the young sailor is a case in point: it is the one unaccompanied fragment in the opera; it occurs in the silence that follows the prelude, 'heard from a height, as if from the masthead' according to Wagner's stage-directions; it has the imper-sonal freshness of a folksong, its haunting, literally super-terrestrial[1] nostalgia is heard against silence and involves 'memory and desire' (the sailor's longing is for his girl). It is broken into by Isolde's 'Who dares to mock me?' in the opera, and by the orchestra slicing off its accompanying silence as this story of mortal sufferings begins to move – at times seems to slide will-lessly – towards death and trans-figuration. In the poem, suspended in typographical space, '*Frisch weht der Wind*' ushers in the fecund silence of the Hyacinth garden, and its universalised longing isn't really quenched until we reach '*Oed' und leer das Meer*' ('Desolate and empty the sea'), from the opera's emotional low-point, and the blank paper that follows the Hyacinth garden episode. Eliot's sources are metamorphosed in their new setting, yet metamorphosed within a continuity where longing reaches towards a possible fullness, always threatened by feelings of desolation, as in *Tristan*. Both the threat and the fullness are measured by silence: on the one hand the nightingale 'Filled all the *desert* with inviolable voice'. Yet all that another voice can say is, 'Speak to me. Why do you never speak. Speak.' and demand, 'Do you remember / Nothing?' Out of the ensuing silence of white space, the manuscript had once read, 'I remember / The hyacinth garden.'

An episode which strangely variates upon that preluded by the sailor's song 'heard from a height' is Eliot's use in Part III of Verlaine's recreation of another auditory effect 'heard from a height' in Wagner's *Parsifal* – namely the boys' voices suddenly impinging from the dome of the Chapel of the Holy Grail, 'And O these childrens' voices singing in the dome!': '*Et O ces voix d'enfants, chantant dans la coupole!*' In the opera, these voices of boys impinge on the deep masculinity of the singing of the Knights of the Grail – and Verlaine's line beautifully recreates the surprise and purity of that Wagnerian moment in his own sonnet. In *The Waste Land* '*ces voix d'enfants*' impinge on a very different song:

1 Logically this should be 'super-marine', yet in the opera house, for all the para-phernalia of a scene on board ship, the sound seems disembodied and to be coming from beyond this world. One never sees the singer, but merely hears this '*Stimme eines jungen Seemans*'.

O the moon shone bright on Mrs Porter
And on her daughter
They wash their feet in soda water
Et O ces voix d'enfants, chantant dans la coupole!

Then, after a blank space:

Twit twit twit
Jug jug jug jug jug jug
So rudely forc'd.
Tereu

Haven't we come down from the dome lower than from the mast-head? '*Oed' und leer*' is desolate but noble. What of these bird-noises after the nightingale's voice that has been called 'inviolable' and after the equally inviolable song of praise of the children for the holy grail? Eliot suggests, perhaps, that the nightingale only says 'Tereu' because it cannot get out all of the word 'Tereus' and the Elizabethan imitation of its notes – 'Jug, Jug, Jug, tereu she cries', according to John Lyly – represents for Eliot a crude deformation of that inviolable voice which has notes in common with '*ces voix d'enfants*':

       yet there the nightingale
Filled all the desert with inviolable voice
And still she cried and still the world pursues,
'Jug, jug' to dirty ears.

And the switch from 'cried' to 'still [...] pursues' in that, from past to present, turns the screw of continuing pain. Yet accompanying that pain is the memory of an inviolable voice and, within the drama of utterance which is the poem, and against that psychic wounding which brought forth the poem, presses the sense of a possible whole-ness, a desire to rise into speech and song despite that wounding, that severed tongue, and, though 'rudely forced', to sing inviolable. After all, it is the 'dirty' ears – 'the dirty ears of death; lust' according to the passage in Eliot's draft – that can only hear the single note of the nightingale's jug and not the roulade of its inviolable voice. And so the sounds oscillate, in an uneasy state of metamorphosis, between roulade and twitter, between 'inviolable voice' and the deformations of 'dirty ears', between meaning and noise.

    Still in the world of bird-sound – but moving now from noise back to meaning – it is the imitation of the hermit thrush with its 'Drip drop drip drop drop drop drop' which suggests the sound of water that could make bearable the rocky aridity. And it is the cock – Eliot's cock speaks French – that presages rain with its 'Co co rico co co rico',[1] primitive sounds that give place to that other sound and root word, DA. In certain of Eliot's bird calls – and I am thinking also of a later poem like 'Marina' with the woodthrush singing through fog – there is a hint of self-forgetfulness, a will-less surrendering up of the merely human. One recalls the composer Olivier Messiaen, to whom also *Tristan* spoke deeply, and *his* desire to go beyond western chromaticism via the language of birds, with his composition of an immense body of piano-music based on an exhaustive cataloguing of bird calls. Yet the will-lessness of *Tristan* and Messiaen's own dissolving of will by discarding the tensions of sonata form and listening to what the birds have to tell him are in many ways foreign to Eliot's discriminative listening. It is perfectly possible to hear in the song of a bird merely the song of one's own self-conceit. If ultimately Eliot is to ask

> Teach us to care and not to care
> Teach us to sit still
> Even among these rocks

the will-lessness implied there is in search neither of the ecstasy of *Tristan* nor Messiaen's subtle evasion of human tension and pain.

I have spoken of the extraordinary accuracy of Eliot's use of his sources, and nowhere is this more strikingly in evidence than in the way he reverts at the close of *The Waste Land* to the Philomela–Procne–Tereus legend in the passage with which I began

> *Poi s'ascose nel foco che gli affina*
> *Quando fiam uti chelidon* – O swallow swallow

> [Then he dived into the fire which refines them
> When shall I become like the swallow – O swallow swallow].

Now *The Waste Land* does not need to be shored up ('These fragments I have shored against my ruins') by a study of its sources, and merely to demonstrate how Eliot has metamorphosed those sources could

---

1 'Co co rico co co rico' sounds primitive and right, though, perhaps one should add, only to a non-French ear. The French poet Philippe Jaccottet tells me that there is more of 'Cockadoodledoo' – clearly Eliot couldn't use *that* sound – in 'Co co rico' than an English or American ear immediately perceives. The *coq gaulois* crows boastfully to the French ear in those sounds that for you and me and T.S. Eliot suggest in its *Waste Land* context a primal dawn cry bringing rain and a measure of release from and relationship beyond the tensions of the all-too-human.

prove a mechanical way of illustrating my theme. Yet in moving among his sources one is moving among works of art that have made our civilisation what it is – *The Divine Comedy, The Metamorphoses, Pervigilium Veneris* in its lesser way, Wagner's *The Ring, Tristan* and *Parsifal, The Tempest* (a drama of metamorphosis itself), *Fleurs du Mal.* Sooner or later, if one hasn't already done so, one is going to encounter these works, and if one looks on Eliot as an exemplary creator, one is bound to notice what he did in re-activating passages from them. One might also even go so far as to say that you cannot hear the opening of *Tristan* any longer, or the boys' voices in *Parsifal,* without thinking of Eliot's now famous translation of those moments, even though the *Parsifal* moment is 'foregrounded', as the linguists say, by isolating another man's words – Verlaine's – against the imitation bird-noise of 'Twit twit twit'. And that experience of thinking back to Eliot in the opera house pleasantly confirms his contention in 'Tradition and the Individual Talent', 'The existing monuments form an ideal order among themselves, which is modified by the introduction of the new (the really new) work of art among them … the *whole* existing order must be, if ever so slightly, altered' – a conception, one might add, of the entire history of art as one vast process of metamorphosis.

In realising the accuracy of Eliot's use of his sources, one learns something of the continuity of men's attempt to know their situation, and one grasps anew the way 'the individual talent' comes into possession of an exact knowledge of its own situation – becomes capable of uttering it, stating it – by opening itself to the great past instances, losing and finding identity through the encounter in a metamorphosis of self. What the individual talent loses is the unnerving, unnerved sense of naked homelessness and lonely complaint. What is found is that human woes, though specific to oneself in the uniqueness of one's situation, are no longer homeless or condemned to formless outcry.

When shall I become like the swallow – '*Quando fiam uti chelidon*'? I don't know what sort of literary currency *The Vigil of Venus – Pervigilium Veneris* – enjoys at the moment, if any. Yet Eliot's fragment points us back to a rich poem and so aware has one become throughout *The Waste Land* of the implications of silence, speech, song, the source which also rings these changes, must be, if ever so slightly, altered, as in the more august cases of *Tristan* and *Parsifal.* It is in the final stanza of the *Pervigilium* that Eliot recognizes a forecast of his own state of mind. This stanza opens with 'illa cantat' ('she sings') – it is a bird that sings – proceeding with 'nos tacemus' ('we are silent') and weaving a way through 'tacere', 'tacendo', 'tacerent' and ending up on the word 'silentium'. This stanza, arising out of the legend of Procne, Philomela and Tereus in the poem's preceding stanza, comes, in its poised uncertainty, as an unexpected conclusion to this poem which welcomes Venus and the spring and is winningly humorous about Cupid and the virgins. Allen Tate, who translated the *Pervigilium,* says of it, 'Up to the last two stanzas the poem is moving, it has its peculiar subtleties; but it is not brilliant. In those two last stanzas something like a first-rate lyrical imagination appears.'

Tate's own version is a little stiff in the joints. I offer, in order to relate the poem to Eliot, Thomas Stanley's sprightlier seventeenth-century translation of the apposite section.

> The warbling Birds on every tree,
> The Goddess wills not silent be.
> The vocal Swans on every lake
> With their hoarse voice a harsh sound make;
> And Tereus hapless Maid, beneath
> The Poplar shade her Song doth breath;
> Such as might well perswade thee, Love
> Doth in these trembling accents move;
> Not that the sister in those strains
> Of the inhumane spouse complains.[1]

I must interrupt the flow of all this to comment that Stanley had got it wrong, or was following a corruption in the text here, for according to Mackail's text, the bird beneath the poplar shade *does* complain. Stanley, again, is hardly up to the true harshness of the swan noises among which the mellifluousness of 'Tereus hapless maid' breaks forth, and which the original Latin stridently and forcefully mimics at this point:

> iam loquaces ore rauce stagna cycni perstrepunt.

However, he improves as he goes on in these two final stanzas – in his version, of course, they are parcelled out into octosyllabic couplets and thus unrecognisable as stanzas. But now for the part which seized on Eliot's imagination:

---

1   See Thomas Stanley, *The Poems and Translations*, ed. G.M. Crump (Clarendon Press, Oxford, 1962), pp. 215ff.

We silent are whilst she doth sing;
How long in coming is my Spring?
When will the time arrive, that I
May Swallow-like my voice untie?
[*Quando fiam uti chelidon*]
My Muse for being silent flies me,
And Phoebus will no longer prize me,
So did Amiclae once, whilst all
Silence observ'd, through silence fall.

If that strikes you as too briskly neat, this is what Allen Tate makes of it:

She sings, we are silent. When will my spring come?
Shall I find my voice when I shall be as the swallow?
Silence destroyed the Amyclae: they were dumb.
Silent, I lost the muse. Return, Apollo!

But there, again, the hortatory imperative and the rather jaunty double rhyme (swallow/Apollo) miss the tone of fearful uncertainty in 'I lost the muse through being silent, nor does Apollo consider me, look back at me':

perdidi musam tacendo, nec me Apollo respicit

where one can see how the poet's fears for the loss of voice must have spoken directly to Eliot with his own awareness of the depletion of energies endlessly coming between him and poetry, and also with that constant effect in his poems, right from 'Prufrock', of the poem doubting its own capacity to proceed, to spit out the butt-ends of its days and ways, to unravel itself, to translate 'The word within a word, unable to speak a word'.

So did Amiclae once, whilst all
Silence observ'd, through silence fall.

One needs a gloss on Amyclae. The phrase containing the word reaches back to *Aeneid*, Book X, and Virgil's 'tacitae Amyclae'. The inhabitants of Amyclae came, interestingly, from Laconia. As to why they kept silent and how this brought about their fall, the three detailed explanations already current among commentators by the fifth century are of secondary importance here.[1] That the silence was

---

1 These are: (1) They observed the Pythagorean custom of a quinquennial silence and an abstinence from slaughter of animals. Attacked by serpents, they were

ultimately self-destructive is what principally matters in our present exploration. A second gloss would also seem to be in order about a point that may already have troubled you: why does the poet in *Pervigilium Veneris* ask when he will be like the swallow and cease being silent, rather than when he will be like the nightingale? Perhaps urban and urbane Romans thought swallows sang like nightingales? At all events, Tate offers the plausible suggestion 'that the poet when he asks *Quando fiam uti chelidon ut tacere desinam?* is hoping that he may become, as the swallow, companion to the nightingale', Procne and Philomela being sisters (the *Pervigilium*, incidentally, appears to use the older legend whereby Procne is the nightingale). 'This interpretation', he adds, 'has, I think, little to recommend it; but the reader may take his choice.' So much for Allen Tate.

What T.S. Eliot supposed about all this – if anything – is an insoluble question, but what he got from this passage is clear. In splicing it together with 'swallow swallow' he links the Latin poet's gesture of longing for a significant music across the centuries with Tennyson's in 'O Swallow, swallow, if I could follow, and light / Upon her lattice I would pipe and trill.' He sends us back to the *Pervigilium Veneris*, not to worry about whether the swallow will sing as companion of the nightingale, but to experience the hesitation between silence and song, and the desire for song as against silence, overshadowed by the pain of the episode of Tereus' rape. We think back once again at '*Quando fiam uti chelidon*' to the moment in the 'Game of Chess' section and

> The change of Philomel, by the barbarous king
> So rudely forced; yet there the nightingale
> Filled all the desert with inviolable voice.

Sir James Frazer, footnoting the Loeb Apollodorus, reflects: 'The later Roman mythographers somewhat absurdly inverted the transformation of the two sisters, making Procne the swallow and the tongueless Philomela the songstress nightingale.' Although Frazer gave poets much to think about with *The Golden Bough* – *The Waste Land* and *The Cantos* depend on it – and although he translated Ovid's

---

themselves killed since forbidden to kill. (2) They suffered the attacks of their neighbours in silence and perished because of their non-resistance. (3) They had, in the early days of the city, given frequent false alarms of its being attacked. The authorities forbade such alarms, so that when a real invader finally appeared, the inhabitants perished through their silence.

Fasti (into prose), one sees from this remark why he never wrote poems himself. It is precisely the idea of the tongueless Philomela that speaks to – that sings for – the poet, once she has become the nightingale. For Eliot, inviolable song must somehow be possible despite violation, and despite the self-violation that preyed on him at the time of *The Waste Land*. Tongueless, or feeling incapable of words – 'What words have we? / I should like to be in a crowd of beaks without words' – he must persist through words to meanings and to silences that are meaningful and not merely the uneasy accompaniment of neurotic dread, as in

> Speak to me. Why do you never speak. Speak.

There is much ground to be covered after the final 'Shantih shantih shantih' of *The Waste Land* reaches out over the silence: the poem ends without punctuation and the white space now suggests, perhaps, the paradox of the emptiness that might become plenitude. But not yet. There is too much pain too close. Eliot will live for many years '*nel foco che gli affina*' before, in *Little Gidding*, Part I, he can say:

> And what the dead had no speech for, when living,
> They can tell you, being dead: the communication
> Of the dead is tongued with fire beyond the language of the living.

'Tongued with fire'. The phrase, whatever it means now in Eliot's poetry – and it means Pentecost – seems like the metamorphosis of other meanings, meanings that have been lived through and beyond, and among which there hover the antitypes – the shadow of Philomela bereft of tongue, and the tortured 'Burning burning burning burning' of 'The Fire Sermon' in *The Waste Land*. But this is to overshoot my present concern and to anticipate my next, which is to place against Eliot Ezra Pound and, among other things, *his* use of the stories of Baucis and Philemon, of Tereus, Procne and Philomela.

3 Ezra Pound: Between Myth and Life

The poet, in the act of 'making it new' (Pound's phrase) is simultaneously re-living the past. He does so variously – through the language he inherits, through the masters he follows, through the myths which often anticipate his own themes and even his own life. The unity of European culture is such that there is an infinite number of literary situations that cause us to feel we have been here before. The originality of an author often comes to precisely this: his ability to make us experience on the pulses a multitude of meanings that time, bad translations and now the disappearance of the classical curriculum are distancing from us. He does so by imaginative effort – as Chapman (say) painfully struggled to rescue Homer from the allegorizing of previous commentators. Pound, in order to make it new, reached out towards the Greeks from the – on the face of it – questionable paganism of Swinburne, though Swinburne sometimes seems to have been of more use to Pound than the commentators were to Chapman. Pound, in a curious way, re-lived *The Odyssey* – indeed, from early on, he regarded authors, their characters and the figures of history as being possibilities for reincarnation in his own person. That is one of his favourite variations on the idea of metamorphosis.

I want to look at some of the details in Pound's re-living of the Odysseus story and to consider how his literary metempsychoses – for he re-lives many stories – ray outwards to touch on the legends of Baucis and Philemon, of Tereus and Philomela. But, first, by way of prelude, a couplet I have quoted before:

> Nor dies the Spirit, but new Life repeats
> In other Forms, and only changes Seats.

That quotation comes from *The Metamorphoses,* Book XV, in Dryden's supreme translation. The poem has there reached its philosophical climax with the entrance of Pythagoras, who adds to the theme of metamorphosis that of metempsychosis.

In a novel where a kidney is being metamorphosed into a breakfast and where, smelling it burning, Leopold Bloom goes 'stepping hastily down the stairs with a flurried stork's legs', his wife Molly exclaims, 'Oh, rocks!' when he informs her that the word 'metempsychosis' means 'the transmigration of souls'. 'Tell us in plain words', she asks and patiently he explains, 'Some say they remember their past lives' – though he seems not to understand that *he* is Ulysses redivivus. More lucid than Leopold Bloom, Pythagoras, on whose behalf Ovid speaks in Book XV, is said to have recognised on view in the temple of Hera the shield he himself once carried when he was Euphorbus at the siege of Troy. W.B. Yeats, in an early poem with the unwieldy title 'He thinks of his past greatness when a part of the constellations of heaven', appropriates the claim of the Celtic wizard Mongan about a previous existence:

> I have been a hazel-tree, and they hung
> The Pilot Star and the Crooked Plough
> Among my leaves.

The idea of metempsychosis was evidently in currency once more among poets and theosophists, employed with varying degrees of seriousness and wit, or merely as a handy metaphor. Even T.S. Eliot hints at it in dedicating *The Waste Land* to Ezra Pound; '*il miglior fabbro*'.

In calling him 'the better craftsman' in this dedication, Eliot, using Dante's words of acknowledgement to Arnaut Daniel, touches feelingly but lightly on a theme which can so readily transform itself into a leading motif of metempsychosis – Arnaut Daniel redivivus as Ezra Pound! Furthermore, Dryden, Eliot and Pound stand together in so far as all of them (Dryden in his translation of the philosophic core of Ovid's fifteenth book, Eliot in *Little Gidding*, Part II, Pound in Canto LXXXI) achieve a peak in their careers by an act of literary metempsychosis, by allowing themselves, each in his different way, to be spoken through by the dead. The process is, of course, by no means a passive one: to adapt Sir John Denham's phrase on translation, 'a new spirit [is] added in the transfusion'. The passages from Eliot and Pound have received widespread attention and I shall comment on them only in passing. In the meeting with the 'familiar compound ghost / Both intimate and unidentifiable' in *Little Gidding*, Eliot begins by submitting himself to another man's metre – Dante's *terza rima* – and to the attempt to bring over an effect equivalent to that in English. His metrical concern is, you might say, almost a translator's concern, and into this translation which is also an original poem, through the metre and the phraseology, through the introduction of the familiar compound ghost, his identity wavering and changing, enter the voices of the dead – Dante, Baudelaire, Mallarmé, Yeats, Milton, Virgil. Few have written more penetratingly on this episode which so intricately combines metamorphosis and metempsychosis than Michael Edwards in his essay 'Renga, Translation, and Mr Eliot's Ghost',[1] where he asks, 'doesn't this section [...] enact the strange and partly shifting relationship of a poet to his masters in the creative moment itself – in the very act of making the verse in which those masters are met with anew?' A similar process is at work in Pound's Canto LXXXI from *The Pisan Cantos*, in an equally celebrated passage beginning 'Yet / Ere the season died a-cold' and modulating into 'Pull down thy vanity, it is not man / Made courage, or made order, or made grace'. As in the case of Eliot, the basis of the achievement is metrical, as Hugh Kenner has demonstrated in a subtle analysis of this canto, Pound running through a gamut of past metres including those of Chaucer and Dante, biblical parallelism, Cavalier song and Imagist free verse.[2] The famous 'Pull down thy vanity' passage is spoken, like the chastening words of the ghost in *Little Gidding*, by a mouth other than the poet's, though it is the poet who must give tongue to this voice. This time the voice emanates, not from a compound ghost but a compound deity – a strange mixture of Nature, Aphrodite and the Old Testament God. This last comes as an unexpected addition to the pantheon of Pound who had previously suggested that the Old Testament should be replaced by Ovid's *Metamorphoses* and told Harriet Monroe: 'Say that I consider the writings of Confucius, and Ovid's *Metamorphoses* the only safe guides in religion.'[3]

In *Little Gidding* Eliot writes (and with the appearance of the familiar compound ghost there the lines take on new meanings):

And what the dead had no speech for, when living,
They can tell you, being dead: the communication
Of the dead is tongued with fire beyond the language of the living.

These lines might serve outside of *Little Gidding* as a commentary on the rôle of the dead and the rôle of quotation in Pound's own cantos. Of course, Pound over-reaches himself with this device of quotation, but the speech of the dead as embodied in their written (sometimes spoken) words can often with Pound, in the juxtaposition of even the most fragmentary quotations, achieve results of Webernesque

---

1 *Poetry Nation Review*, Vol. 7, No. 2 (1980), p. 16.
2 See the analyses in Hugh Kenner's *The Pound Era* (University of California Press, Berkeley, 1971), pp. 489–92 and Donald Davie's Pound (Fontana/Collins, London, 1975), pp. 92–5.
3 *The Letters of Ezra Pound*, ed. D.D. Page (Faber, London, 1951), p. 250.

compression and intensity. For example, in Canto XLIX, Pound at one of the still points of the work invents a poem in the impersonal mode of Chinese landscape poetry – 'by no man these verses', he insists:

> For the seven lakes, and by no man these verses:
> Rain: empty river: a voyage,
> Fire under frozen cloud, heavy rain in twilight.
> Under the cabin roof is one lantern.
> The reeds are heavy; bent;
> And the bamboos speak as if weeping.

And so it goes on for more than a page, the passage itself a kind of quotation from one of the great past modes where the deliberate expression of one's own personality was not the poet's concern. 'And by no man these verses'. When this motif recurs in the Pisan sequence (Canto LXXIV) Pound, the broadcaster from Radio Rome, is a prisoner of the American forces and identifying himself with Odysseus in distress. At the motif's first appearance, it is metamorphosed by the briefest of quotations from Homer: namely what the imprisoned Odysseus says to the Cyclops when the Cyclops asks him his name – Oûtis, Noman. The Pound runs

> ΟΎ ΤΙΣ, ΟΎ ΤΙΣ? Odysseus
>   the name of my family.

I spoke of Webernesque compression and this is it. The snatch of Homer – Oûtis, Oûtis – Pound repeats with a question mark and then, in face of the question, re-asserts his own identity: 'Odysseus / the name of my family'. In this canto, where names are important, Pound – like Christopher Smart in the madhouse – tells over those of his fellow inmates with affection. At the next reprise, ΟΎ ΤΙΣ is preceded by the Chinese ideogram for 'there is not' and followed by the line 'a man on whom the sun has gone down'. That repeated snatch of Homer, that voice from the dead, is tongued with fire by its new context and by its reminding us of 'and by no man these verses' – no man, Odysseus–Pound is writing them now, as he re-lives the sufferings of Homer's hero.

This is Pound at sixty. But let us go back in time. The young Ezra Pound also felt that he was re-living, being taken over by literary characters or their authors. In an early poem, 'Histrion', with more than a touch of pre-Raphaelite uplift, the young poet declares:

No man hath dared to write this thing as yet,
And yet I know, how that the souls of all men great
At times pass through us,
And we are melted into them, and are not
Save reflexions of their souls.
Thus am I Dante for a space and am
One François Villon.

Such metempsychoses are momentary, admits Pound

This for an instant and the flame is gone.

And then he proceeds, with a rather Rossettian glance at the philo-sophical tone of the *dolce stil novo*, to speculate about the rôle of the self, the 'I', in all this and the way the 'I' is lent to these 'Masters of the Soul' who 'live on' in it.

If Pound had not done better with the theme of the Masters of the Soul living on, the poem need not concern us. What's interesting is that 'Histrion' – literally 'a stage-player' – with its stress on the way the soul of the player is taken over by his part – anticipates that other formulation of Pound's, the persona or player's mask, which governs his later methods and gives its title to the 1909 collection *Personae*. He speaks in his essay 'Vorticism' of 'casting off, as it were, complete masks of the self in each poem. I continued in a long series of trans-lations, which were but more elaborate masks.' So Pound in his poems and translations wears the mask not only of dead authors, but of characters from their works and from history; and Browning, Odysseus, Sigismondo Malatesta, the anonymous author of *The Seafarer* and Li Po all live again. That translations – 'which were but more elaborate masks' – should have been a vital part of this process reminds one once more of Dryden, who also found his way to a fuller and truer self by speaking for the dead, for Lucretius and Ovid among others. Pound's first wholly mature book was *Cathay* – a book of translations from the Chinese, and the principal mask there for Pound is Li Po, the conscious outsider. Translation becomes now a means of extending, of consolidating one's sense of identity. It's not merely a question of the weakly expressed neo-platonism of 'Histrion' where into the 'I' 'some form projects itself'. 'Casting off [...] complete masks of the self' implies an active rôle for the poet: what is projected into the self calls for an answering effort of the self to embody and utter its discovery. The dead must rise again in the poetry. Metempsychosis for Pound is a matter of co-operation.

So in the discarded first version of Canto I, which appeared in

Poetry for June 1917, Pound enters into an energetic colloquy with Robert Browning and, in his search for the subject of his new and 'exceeding long' poem, he asks of Browning

> what were the use
> Of setting figures up and breathing life upon them
> Were't not *our* life, your life, my life extended?

That all this is supposed to be taking place in Sirmio on Lake Garda, once inhabited by Catullus – a dead poet whom Pound also engages in spirit colloquy – and that the day is Corpus Christi, are also important. Pound goes to some pains to create the processional ebullience of the religious festival in a bustling, rather over-eager Browningesque style. And, for all the immaturity of this first draft, how accurately his intuition circles round the central mystery of this day – Corpus Christi, the feast in honour of the consecrated host, a celebrating of transubstantiation, that Christian metamorphosis of the bread and wine into flesh and blood, that ultimate confirmation of the power of the risen dead. Yet for Pound, 'a pagan fundamentalist' as Robert Duncan calls him, it is precisely the pagan elements in this festival that attract him:

> Mid-June: some old god eats the smoke, 'tis not the saints;
> And up and out to the half-ruined chapel.

Eliot's vegetation gods in *The Waste Land* stir with intimations of a metamorphosis that is the Christian resurrection; the empty chapel there – he had already, incidentally, come upon his friend's 'half-ruined chapel' before writing his own poem – yearns to be filled with Christ. Pound, on the other hand, is travelling in the opposite direction: Corpus Christi stirs with intimations of the vegetation gods and the miracles of Ovid's *Metamorphoses*. As for the half-ruined chapel, it was Pound who said that if he had the money *he* would restore the temple to Aphrodite at Terracina and the stone eyes would again look seaward. In the present poem, he writes:

> Gods float in the azure air,
> Bright gods, and Tuscan, back before dew was shed,
> It is a world like Puvis?
> > Never so pale, my friend,
> 'Tis the first light – not half light – Panisks
> And oak-girls and the Maenads
> Have all the wood. Our olive Sirmio

Lies in its burnished mirror, and the Mounts Balde and Riva
Are alive with song, and all the leaves are full of voices.
'Non è fuggito.'
                    It is not gone.' Metastasio
Is right – we have that world about us.

'All the leaves are full of voices' – 'for the leaves were full of children':
once again we track the Eliot of *Burnt Norton* in Pound's snow.[1] For
Pound 'all the leaves *are* full', not 'were full'. We need not shore fragments of past myths against our ruins, like Eliot at the conclusion of
The Waste Land: 'we have that world about us'. Pound is claiming that
the gods return as images of present experience. Eliot, so Pound
might have said, devitalises the past with his 'These fragments I have
shored against my ruins', and Canto VIII accuses, 'these fragments
you have shelved'. The gods need not be the pale gods of Puvis de
Chavannes' paintings, though, as Pound wrote in a lovely early poem,
'The Return', that is the bloodless condition the world of 1912
banished them to:

> See, they return; ah, see the tentative
> > Movements, and the slow feet,
> > The trouble in the pace and the uncertain
> > Wavering!
>
> See, they return, one, and by one,
> With fear, as half-awakened;
> As if the snow should hesitate
> And murmur in the wind,
> >   and half turn back;
> These were the 'Wing'd-with-Awe',
> >   Inviolable.
>
> Gods of the wingèd shoe!
> With them the silver hounds,
> >   sniffing the trace of air!
>
> Haie! Haie!
> > These were the swift to harry;
> > These the keen-scented;
> > These were the souls of blood.
>
> Slow on the leash,
> >   pallid the leash-men!

---

1   Kipling's story, 'They', also seems to have contributed to Eliot's phrase (see Helen
    Gardner, *The Composition of 'Four Quartets'* (Faber, London, 1978), p. 39).

We must not let ourselves be diverted from the very real subject of this poem by Pound's 'poetic' stance in 'See […] ah, see.' At one level, it is an attack on classical studies in so far as they have failed to keep the gods alive, have failed to re-incarnate them in our own culture. Lost traditions, lost awarenesses, lost energies are what Pound – 'after strange gods' in Eliot's mock—was in search of, for 'these were the souls of blood', not for shoring or shelving.

When Pound came to revise his first version of Canto I, the Corpus Christi celebrations were scrapped: the bright gods and Tuscan were reserved till later on: what was retained was the blood metaphor. The first canto was to consist almost entirely of a translation – transfusion or verbal transubstantiation, as you will. In this translation by Pound of a Renaissance-Latin translation of Homer, with Pound, as usual, addressing its dead author ('Lie quiet Divus. I mean, that is Andreas Divus'), the rite is a blood rite, to enable the dead – but particularly the prophet Tiresias – to speak with Odysseus in Hades of what is to come. Odysseus, one of Pound's principal personae, stands now in the forefront of a poem in which Pound is to go on re-living his story and speaking on his behalf:

> Dark blood flowed in the fosse,
> Souls out of Erebus, cadaverous dead, of brides
> Of youths and of the old who had borne much.

Then we hear the voice of Tiresias:

> 'A second time? why? man of ill star,
> 'Facing the sunless dead and this joyless region?
> 'Stand from the fosse, leave me my bloody bever
> 'For soothsay.'
>   And I stepped back,
> And he strong with the blood, said then 'Odysseus
> 'Shalt return through spiteful Neptune over dark seas,
> 'Lose all companions.'

This prophecy was to fulfil itself in Pound's own case with a fair amount of accuracy, in his self-identification with Odysseus in the cantos of his Pisan confinement, and in the doubtful homecoming of the later and mostly inferior cantos, *Rock-Drill* and *Thrones*. Already in his 'Hugh Selwyn Mauberley' the self-assured, insular and English voice that buries Pound at the opening sees him as an Odysseus whose literary voyagings are to be deprecated as the aberration of someone 'born / In a half-savage country, out of date'. In his prose,

Pound calls Odysseus 'the live man among the duds', but he also states that after the unprovoked sacking of the Cicones in *The Odyssey,* 'Ulysses and Co. deserved all they got' ('Hell', *Literary Essays*). In *Guide to Kulchur* he reflects on Odysseus' 'maritime adventure morals' and tells us that 'Dante's Odysseus sailed after knowledge without putting his own will in order'. And this is an uncanny – albeit unconscious – diagnosis of his own deepest fault. The man who applauded Mussolini's 'maritime adventure morals' in the invasion of Ethiopia might have been thought to know with some part of his mind that 'Mussolini and Co. deserved all they got thereafter'.

Much in the early cantos is couched in the language of heroic myth and the autobiographical cantos sometimes use this language in relating the voyaging and sufferings of Pound to those of Odysseus. To begin with, Pound seems not to suffer at all. 'The live man among the duds', he puts the duds – profiteers, bankers, armament manufacturers – into a hell (as Eliot has it) 'for other people', a hell invoked in some of the crassest writing in this very uneven poem. The Pisan sequence changes all this. The re-living of heroic myth represents an idea that Pound, like Yeats, looked for in the modern world. That is one reason why the figure of metempsychosis appealed to both their imaginations. But for Pound, in the Pisans, a myth re-lived must accommodate itself to a range of diction that Homer himself might have hesitated to put into the mouths of Odysseus' men:

> Pisa, in the 23rd year of the effort in sight of the tower
> and Till was hung yesterday
> for murder and rape with trimmings plus Cholkis
>> plus mythology, thought he was Zeus ram or another one
>>> Hey Snag wots in the bibl'?
>>> wot are the books ov the bible?
>>> Name 'em, don't bullshit ME.

Such are the voices of Odysseus–Pound's companions in adversity. And follows the Chinese character for 'there is not' and then: ΟΎ ΤΙΣ / a man on whom the sun has gone down'. 'In the 23rd year of the effort' refers, of course, to the Fascist calendar with which Pound eventually begins dating his letters. For Pound took calendars seriously – and this shows throughout the Chinese cantos – as a way of incorporating myth into time. The Italian critic Massimo Bacigalupo[1]

---

1   See his *The Formèd Trace* (Columbia University Press, New York, 1980), pp. 33–4.

has pointed to Pound's invention (half joke, half serious) of a new pagan calendar when he announced in the *Little Review*:

> The Christian era came definitely to an END at midnight of the 29–30 of October (1921) old style.
>
> There followed the Feast of ZAGREUS [that is Bacchus – Dionysus], and a Feast of PAN counted as of no era; the new year thus beginning as on the 1st November (old style), now HEPHAISTOS

And Pound goes on to detail the names of the new months and the new feasts. Interestingly enough, in the light of that discarded first canto, Epithalamium is the new name for 'ancient Corpus Domini, 15th June' and the feast is now under the auspices of Kupris – Aphrodite, that is.

Bacigalupo also reminds us that 30 October 1921, when the Christian era comes to an end, is Pound's birthday (he was thirty-six) and the day on which James Joyce's *Ulysses* was completed, a coincidence of some note for Pound. Like Eliot in *The Waste Land*, he was deeply in debt to the stylistic invention of Joyce's book, having read it chapter by chapter in Joyce's typescript. His own story of Ulysses–Pound was now decisively under way and into its splendid second canto. Here Zagreus (Bacchus–Dionysus) is introduced in a retelling of Ovid. He is the god whose feast falls on Pound's birthday and whose energies are to second those of Odysseus in Canto I:

> 'From now [...] my altars,
> Fearing no bondage,
>   Fearing no cat of the wood,
> Safe with my lynxes,
>   feeding grapes to my leopards,
> Olibanum is my incense,
>   the vines grow in my homage.'

Canto II, of course, is an exemplary work of the utmost literary tact, but the programmatic Pound, Bacigalupo insists, 'believes himself a new re-incarnation of Dionysus'. And, one might add, with some justice.

For the energies of Dionysus, the hope of renewal seemed embodied already in Pound's discovery of the principal writers of a young century, in his completion of a handful of masterpieces – *Cathay*, 'Homage to Sextus Propertius', 'Hugh Selwyn Mauberley' – and in that irreverent, intuitive exactness which was to prove capable of helping Eliot into the full possession of his powers through Pound's drastic reshaping of the *Waste Land* manuscript.

I want to move now from that hard word which troubled Molly Bloom, back to metamorphosis pure and simple. I must necessarily be selective here. I cannot notice all the varieties of it in Pound that Sister Bernetta Quinn lists in *The Metamorphic Tradition in Modern Poetry*. My concern is chiefly with two of the myths we have encountered before – Baucis and Philemon, and finally Philomela and Tereus.

I begin with something Quinn glances at – Pound's 'The Tree'. With the publication in 1979 of H.D.'s memoir, *An End to Torment*, which reprints *Hilda's Book*, the manuscript to which 'The Tree' originally belonged, one sees how that youthful poem stands in relation to Pound's early biography and the biography in relation to much later work. 'The Tree' was written for the poet and novelist H.D. – Hilda Doolittle – when Pound, a very young man, was engaged to her. It seizes on an intuition that is very precious to him, a quasi-mystical experience he seems to have undergone, and he embodies it in the Baucis and Philemon story. Despite a dash of Wardour Street in 'Nathless', it is a far better poem than 'Histrion':

> I stood still and was a tree amid the wold,
> Knowing the truth of things unseen before;
> Of Daphne and the laurel bough
> And that god-feasting couple olde
> That grew elm-oak amid the wold.
> 'Twas not until the gods had been
> Kindly entreated, and been brought within
> Unto the hearth of their heart's home
> That they might do this wonder-thing;
> Nathless I have been a tree amid the wood
> And many a new thing understood
> That was rank folly to my head before.

You will have recognised the literary paternity of that poem – Yeats' 'I have been a hazel-tree' which I quoted earlier; though, unlike Yeats, Pound is concerned with metamorphosis and not metempsychosis in this piece. This particular kind of metamorphosis, celebrating an Ovidian sense of unity with things, is one to which he will return many times – most famously in the early poem 'A Girl': 'The tree has entered my hands, / The sap has ascended my arms.' 'The Tree' was the only poem Pound ultimately retained from *Hilda's Book*, the typescript he bound for H.D. in vellum, and he placed this poem first in his selected poems. *Hilda's Book* is crammed with tree poems: Pound used to meet H.D. in the apple-orchard behind the Pounds' house at Wyncote, and they would also spend time together in the tree-house in a maple in the Doolittles' garden. She, even in old age, signed her letters to him 'Dryad', his youthful name for her.

To say Pound was a tree lover sounds insipid – aren't we all? – and to call him a dendrophil will hardly do either. But his re-living of the Baucis and Philemon myth, entwined with that of Daphne, resulted in a line of continuity within an increasingly fragmented *oeuvre*. Zagreus (Bacchus–Dionysus), the god with whom Pound identifies himself, similarly metamorphoses into tree form – into the stock that produces the vine. Thus the 'IO' of the cry 'IO ZAGREUS!' in Canto XVII is not only the cry that hails the god, but the Italian 'I' (io) that draws into a single unity the poet, the god and the experience that informs a poem like 'The Tree':

> So that the vines burst from my fingers
> And the bees weighted with pollen
> Move heavily in the vine-shoots:
>   chirr-chirr-chirr-rikk-a purring sound,
> And the birds sleepily in the branches.
>   ZAGREUS! IO ZAGREUS!

Throughout the cantos – re-emerging after all the aridities and obsessions – there is an awareness of sacred places, specifically of sacred woods, reminiscent of the haunts of the gods in Ovid's *Metamorphoses*. They are visited by maelids – nymphs of the orchard – and dryads, and you will also find bassarids there – the maenads of Bacchus–Dionysus. These groves, as they impinge on the embattled world of the cantos, counter-stressing, however fragmentarily, Pound's tendency to a willed didacticism, seem images and intuitions of a possible wholeness, an attempt to keep that wholeness alive within a poem which increasingly refuses to cohere. Amid these groves water, light and air interact and the presence of such groves can be felt even in architecture: Venice, for Pound, in the splendid Canto XVII, is 'the pleached arbour of stone'. Early commentators took this to be a sign of distrust for Venice, a marmorealising of the vital world. On the contrary, the vital, arboreal world lends a fluid life to stone.

To the question 'Tree or stone?' in my first lecture, Pound might well have said, 'Both.' In writing of our 'kinship to the vital universe, to the tree and living rock' in the early 'Psychology and the

Troubadours',[1] he seems to be thinking forward to that marble relief in the building he so much admired, the Tempio Malatestiano, where sea-swirls and tree-swirls flow on the surface of the stone, compelled by a common energy, the whole enclosed on either side by pilasters whose stone trunks flow up into capitals that break into acanthus and oak leaves.

The same intuition seems to prompt his poem 'The Tree' as that which begins the late *Rock-Drill* cantos: 'That you lean 'gainst the tree of heaven, / and know Ygdrasail', which in its reprise becomes:

'From the colour the nature
    & by the nature the sign!'
Beatific spirits welding together
    as in one ash-tree in Ygdrasail.
        Baucis, Philemon.

This is the beginning of Canto XC, the first of four remarkable cantos, that in a very mixed sequence, *Rock-Drill*, have something of the coherence and power of the Pisans. It continues the motif put into the mouth of a peasant in LXXXVIII:

Said Baccin: 'That tree, and that tree,
'Yes I planted that tree …'
                Under the olives
Some saecular, some half-saecular.

Pound's dendrophilia is hardly powerful enough to save the cantos of *Thrones* which come four years later in 1959, but it is still in evidence. His latest discovery there is the Na-khi kingdom in South West China, and one of the things that attracts him to the Na-khi is the vegetation and their respect for it – willows, junipers, spruce and fir. Amid all this enters briefly a new hero, Elzéard Bouffier, who set out to reafforest Provence with his bare hands, yet we hardly see enough of him to give the sequence the kind of coherence the mysterious groves give to some of the earlier cantos.

Again one must go back to Pound's youthful days. The relationship with Hilda Doolittle had taken place in the outer suburbs of Philadelphia, Pennsylvania. The Sylvania part of it strikes one in her memoir and it strikes one in the Hilda poems.[2] It recurs in the descrip-

1 Ezra Pound, *The Spirit of Romance* (New Directions, New York, 1952).
2 In H.D.'s autobiographical novel *HERmione* (New Directions, New York, 1981), p. 63, Hermione (H.D.) looks to George Lowndes (Ezra Pound) to define her as 'a reflection of some lost incarnation, a wood maniac, a tree demon, a neuropathic dendrophil'.

tions of the Wyncote district in Noel Stock's *Ezra Pound's Pennsyl-vania.*[1] At the most basic level, and as in so many American urbs and suburbs, the streets of Pound's Wyncote were named after trees. Even the Philadelphia mint, where his father worked, stood on the corner of Juniper and Chestnut Streets in the city itself. Pound, recalling Wyncote in 1957, remembers his father planting pear, peach and cherry, and he asks his correspondent about the oak ('purty tall in 1900') and 'THE apple tree'. When late in life he is released from Saint Elizabeth's Hospital and returns to spend a couple of days in Wyncote, he goes out in the middle of the night in search of an evergreen which he and a friend had planted behind the church years before.

In her memoir *An End to Torment* (New Directions, New York, 1979). H.D. speaks of 'the Dryad or Druid that Ezra had evoked so poignantly' in the Hilda poems; she writes about the tree-house in the maple where they embraced each other – 'no "act" afterwards though biologically fulfilled, had had the significance of the first *demivierge* embraces', she says – and in evoking the scene when her father, Professor Doolittle, showed Pound the door, she does so by recalling the motion of the treehouse from a few pages before ('We sway with the wind. There is no wind. We sway with the stars. They are not far.' One sees from this, perhaps, why in writing 'The Tree' for her Pound should have taken off from Yeats' poem where the poet recalls being a tree with the pilot star and the plough among its leaves.) Here is H.D.'s evocation – what is remarkable about it is her sense of biographic and poetic continuity from the sylvan days in her father's garden, to one of Pound's most memorable sacred groves in *The Pisan Cantos*, Canto LXXIX:

> We were curled up together in an armchair when my father found us. I was 'gone'. I wasn't there. I disentangled myself. I stood up; Ezra stood beside me. It seems we must have swayed, trembling. But I don't think we did. 'Mr Pound, I don't say there was anything wrong ...' Mr Pound it was all wrong. You turn into a Satyr,: a Lynx, and the girl in your arms (Dryad, you called her), for all her fragile, not yet lost virginity, is *Maenad, bassarid.* God keep us from Canto 79, one of the *Pisan Cantos.*
>
> Mr Pound, with your magic, your 'strange spells of old deity', why didn't you complete the metamorphosis. Pad, pad, pad, ... come along my Lynx.

1 See Noel Stock, *Ezra Pound's Pennsylvania* (The Friends of the University of Toledo, 1976).

H.D., like Pound, consciously re-lived myth. In her long poem, *Helen in Egypt* – 'my own cantos', as she says – she identifies herself with and defends Helen of Troy. In the memoir she tells us with naive intensity of Pound's Odysseus identification, 'His father's name was Homer.' In the extract I have just quoted she sees how the legends that sustained their youth in Pennsylvania are still those to which Pound returns in Canto LXXIX and in captivity. I have the impression that the lynx passage in LXXIX was more famous with English readers twenty years ago than it is today: George Dekker wrote briefly but subtly about it then in his excellent book *Sailing after Knowledge* (Routledge and Kegan Paul, London, 1963). As in so many of the sacred wood passages throughout the cantos, it begins at dawn with maelids – the fruit tree nymphs – consorting with Dionysus and the bassarids. But, now, the reverie opens out of a Christopher Smart-like naming over of myth figures and fellow captives:

> O Lynx, wake Silenus and Casey
> Shake the castagnettes of the bassarids.

Dekker writes of the lynx passage, with its references to Kore (Persephone) and her eating of the pomegranate, as containing an 'oblique and very beautiful treatment of a young girl's fascination with sex'. If this is true, the lynx chorus bears out convincingly H.D.'s sense of its association with those early days in Pennsylvania, in its trans-formation of Swinburnian paganism and the dated mode of the Hilda poems into something universal and durable. Here is an extract from this extended section of the poem:

> 'Eat of it not in the under world'
> See that the sun or the moon bless thy eating
> Κόρη Κόρη for the six seeds of an error
> or that the stars bless thy eating

> O Lynx, guard this orchard,
> Keep from Demeter's furrow

> This fruit has a fire within it,
> Pomona, Pomona
> No glass is clearer than are the globes of this flame
> what sea is clearer than the pomegranate body
> holding the flame?
> Pomona, Pomona,
> Lynx, keep watch on this orchard
> That is named Melagrana

or the Pomegranate field
> The sea is not clearer in azure
> Nor the Heliads bringing light.

Here is Pound between myth and life, drawing together the threads of a tragic existence; reaching back to the experience he had had in youth of metamorphosis, of a mystical unity with the tree-world, the world of 'THE apple tree'; recreating the vulnerable sexuality of that time which must have deepened the experience; and, before long, he is to addresss directly the girl who shared the experience with him in the words, 'Δρυάδ [Dryad] your eyes are like the clouds over Taishan / When some of the rain has fallen / and half remains yet to fall.' Here is Pound, steadied against his own wilfulness and rancour, by a vision in which youthful sex, the tree-world, the lynxes of Bacchus– Dionysus bring quiet and order to that endlessly exacerbated will of his.

It is the exacerbation of will and the will's attempts to do the work of imagination that make large areas of the cantos such tedious reading. Pound wants to solve the universe and then comes to confess in *Drafts and Fragments*, published in 1968, the last of the canto volumes,

> That I lost my center
>> fighting the world.
> The dreams clash
>> and are shattered –
> and that I tried to make a paradiso
>>> terrestre.

In this extraordinary volume of bits, Pound has abandoned both his willed didacticism and the pretence that the cantos could ever achieve an ultimate formal coherence. The poetry gains immensely: *Drafts and Fragments*, published after fifty years' work on this 'exceeding long' poem, remains one of Pound's most beautiful books. Fifty years! Perhaps Pound's tedious stretches in this extended poem come to no more than the tedious stretches of any other poet who has laboured long but at *separate* poems – say Browning, Tennyson, Victor Hugo? I doubt that. The cantos fail – if that is the right word – for two over-riding reasons: because (as Pound says of Dante's Ulysses) he has not '[put] his own will in order', and because he pursues to a quite unprecedented extreme the metamorphic style where the reader's mind is counted upon to re-shape the fragments into significance.

The wonder is that the cantos succeed as often as they do and that, over decades, Pound can still convincingly link up his fragmented motifs, as my final example will try to show.

I conclude with Pound's transformation of the story of Procne, Philomela, Itys and Tereus. He first tackled this in Canto IV of 1919, a relatively early work. Like the Baucis and Philemon story, it reaches forward over the years: it becomes intimately entwined with the story of Odysseus' homecoming, and thus with Pound's own hoped for return from the prison camp at Pisa. Writing *The Pisan Cantos* there, the wreck of Mussolini's Italy all about him, the threat of trial or possible execution always imminent, it must have seemed at times that for Ezra Pound–Oûtis–Odysseus there would be no home-coming.

Let us go back to less desperate days, to that fourth canto of 1919 – a canto whose composition actually pre-dates Canto II where, as we saw, Pound could confidently identify himself with Dionysus. In his first handling of the Philomela/ Tereus story, Pound anticipates Eliot's use of it in *The Waste Land* and the contrast with Eliot could scarcely, be greater. While Eliot is to seize on the myth to express his own alienation, responding to the suggestion of the cut-out tongue and also to the promise of song filling 'the desert with inviolable voice', Pound places the story in a montage sequence with other myths, suggesting the metamorphosis of common themes by different cultures. The most relevant of these to the cannibalising of Itys is the Provençal story of the serving to Lady Soremonda by her husband of the heart of her lover, Cabestan. Pound – once more he anticipates Eliot here – uses the device of a reiterated bird-call (Procne as swallow) to link the incidents, via name of child, cry of swallow and what the husband and wife say to each other. The Latin here is reworked from Horace's 'three times mournfully [she called] Itys':

> Ityn!
> Et ter flebiliter, Itys, Ityn!
> And she went towards the window and cast her down,
>   All the while, the while, swallows crying:
> Ityn!

The poem cuts back to the moment before Soremonda casts herself from the window and her husband says:

> 'It is Cabestan's heart in the dish.'

And Soremonda replies:

> 'It is Cabestan's heart in the dish?
> 'No other taste shall change this.'
> And she went toward the window,
>   the slim white stone bar
> Making a double arch;
> Firm even fingers held to the firm pale stone:
> Swung for a moment,
>   and the wind out of Rhodez
> Caught in the full of her sleeve.
>   … the swallows crying:
> 'Tis. 'Tis. Ytis!

There is no reprise of Ovid's story until the Pisan sequence and this time we feel not only its metamorphosis across cultures, but within one man's mind, as it attracts to itself counterpointing themes that reiterate or ironise the distress of Pound–Odysseus. For Pound, now, there is no possibility of an equivalent to the grand operatic gesture of 'No other taste shall change this': often all he can do is listen to the meshing and clashing of the contents of his own mind.

In the Pisan sequence, Canto LXXIV, an attentive reader almost expects a replay of the Itys motif via the sound of Odysseus' Oûtis, Oûtis: is this a prelude to some word-play on 'It is', 'Itys', 'Ityn'? Apparently not. Then when Pound goes on, within a matter of lines, to tell the story of the Aboriginal god, Wanjina, whose father removes his mouth for having named too many things, one similarly expects he will revert to the Tereus–Philomela story of the silenced tongue. He doesn't. At least, not yet. It is difficult, however, not to believe that all this was stirring somewhere at the bottom of his mind, for within three cantos it re-surfaces.

Now, in the early cantos, Pound has echoed and re-echoed a fragment of the chorus which immediately precedes the entry of Agamemnon in the first play of Aeschylus' *Oresteia*:

Helenaus, heleoptolis, helandros

Pound, in a context of destructive passions there, punningly refers this chorus to Helen of Troy and Eleanor of Aquitaine, both fatal women. Once again he is referring from one culture to another. The chorus itself means 'Destroyer of men, destroyer of cities, destroyer of ships'. Robert Fagles' Penguin version of *The Agamemnon* felicitously renders the puns into English as

> Helen!
> Hell at the prows, hell at the gates
> hell on the men-of-war.

In Aeschylus this chorus is preparing us for Agamemnon's home-coming – he is outside with the unheeded prophetess, Cassandra, among his baggage. We know that his wife, Clytemnestra, is Helen's sister, so we must expect the worst of her, re-alerted by those puns. In the Pisan detention camp the chorus and its context take on a renewed life in Pound's mind. For one thing, he (Oûtis–Odysseus) thinks readily of that commonplace of classical studies – the contrasted homecomings of Agamemnon and Odysseus from the Trojan war. In this new context of the end of another war, Clytemnestra appears in the Pisan sequence as the destructive twin to Helen, boasting over her husband's corpse: 'like a dog ... and a good job / [...] dead by this hand'.

In Canto LXXVII occurs a reprise of the theme of naming via one of the other prisoners and then the re-introduction of Wanjina, the mouthless god:

> and Tom wore a tin disc, a circular can-lid
>   with his name on it, solely:
> for Wanjina has lost his mouth.

There follows an Eliot-like stretch of blank paper and silence. Within a matter of lines Cassandra – she who has a mouth and a tongue and yet no one will listen to her prophecies – is on the scene:

> the wind mad as Cassandra
>   who was as sane as the lot of 'em.

A silent space and then:

> Sorella, mia sorella.

That Cassandra, silenced, unheeded in her prophecies, resembles Pound, is signalled both by the space and by 'Sorella, mia sorella', – 'Sister, my sister'. And once one has mentally translated the Italian one realises that Pound's maddening habit of quite arbitrarily making the going difficult for his reader had hidden from one, within the Italian phrase, a fragment from Swinburne's poem, 'Itylus':

> Swallow, my sister, O sister swallow.

These are the words of the tongue-bereft Philomela to Procne, Pound travelling back to the poet who, as he said, kept alive a measure of paganism 'in a papier-mâché age', whereas Eliot with *his* 'O swallow swallow' in *The Waste Land* travels back to Tennyson, the poet of impaired Christian belief.

'Sorella, mia sorella' comes towards the end of Canto LXXVII. LXXVIII has a reprise of the Itys motif from Canto IV – 'ter flebiliter, Itys' ('three times mournfully [she called] Itys', as quoted previously) – coming almost immediately after the reappearance of Cassandra:

> Cassandra, your eyes are like tigers,
>   with no word written in them
> You also have I carried to nowhere
>   to an ill house and there is
>   no end to the journey.

What is happening with moving implicitness in the Pisan sequence is that the theme of not having a tongue, the theme of Odysseus' sufferings and return, and the theme of Agamemnon's return (in Pound's case the question of any possible return is in some doubt) attract one another. In doing so, fragments of the themes are suddenly activated and, as in a work of music, come into unexpected prominence, grow out of and mirror one another. Thus there is probably another – if you like, musical – reason why Cassandra and the Tereus story confront each other in Pound's collage of motifs. For in Aeschylus' *Agamemnon*, when the captive Cassandra enters in the wake of Agamemnon, asking, 'Apollo [...] / where have you led me now, what house' (and Pound echoes that line), the chorus compares her to 'the nightingale that broods on sorrow, / mourns her son, her son'.[1] There is some justice in saying that Pound is being over-compressed, yet what is filling his mind and what brings silent eloquence to his allusion here was once, after all, the common property of all minds that had received even a modicum of classical education.

And the fragmented musical motifs continue to build up their significances as the sequence proceeds. The birds – presumably departing swallows near the camp – write out the notes of their treble scale on the telegraph wires in Canto LXXXII. This summons up the repeated cry, 'Terreus! Terreus!' Tereus, the violent man, leads now, by association, to the idea of war. War circles us back in this same canto to the beacons – 'a match on Cnidos, a glow worm on Mitylene' – that bring news of the fall of Troy at the start of *The Agamemnon*.

---

1   Aeschylus is using here the version of the tale in which Procne, mother of Itys, becomes the nightingale and her sister Philomela the swallow.

There is, of course, one disquieting thread that runs through Pound's remarkable recurrences to the House of the Atrides and the House of Tereus. He handles the resemblance between himself and Cassandra with some tact and with startling poetic energy. But the curious want of self-knowledge persists in this hell which is now no longer just 'for other people': the Troy that has fallen here is the Troy of the Axis powers, those prophecies of his that were ignored included the ranting broadcasts he made over Rome radio in time of war. Wanjina named too many things and had his mouth taken away. Pound, in his own life, was to suffer all the implications of the half-read wisdom of that image. His own loss of tongue, the aphasia – to some degree perhaps self-imposed – which overtook him in the finally acknowledged remorse of the 1960s, rhymes pathetically with the myths which had long moved through his mind and which, an Odysseus returned home at last to Italy, he must live out in chagrin and in silence.

4 Metamorphosis as Translation

I have touched already on the way metempsychosis – the word that puzzles Molly Bloom – comes, in Ovid's fifteenth book, as the crowning form of metamorphosis. The idea of reincarnation is one of the surmises, at least in the form of a metaphor for literary descent, that some of the most unlikely writers have shown themselves willing to dally with. Dryden, in his 'Discourse Concerning Satire',[1] delights in the fact that Ennius 'believ'd according to the Pithagorean Opinion that the Soul of Homer was transfus'd into him'; and – in the Preface to the *Fables* – that Spenser insinuates, 'that the Soul of Chaucer was transfus'd into his Body'; that he himself, John Dryden, has 'a Soul congenial to [Chaucer's]'.[2] And he lends his voice not only to Chaucer, in his translation of that poet, but also to Ovid, the celebrator of 'the Pithagorean Opinion' in Book XV:

> Those very Elements which we partake
> Alive, when dead some other Bodies make:
> Translated grow.

So the soul of Ovid is 'transfus'd' into the body of John Dryden. Dryden's pun on 'translated' comes as no accident in this context, where he is at work as translator and where – the implication would seem to run – a chief variety of metamorphosis embodies itself in precisely this art. So my final 'variety of metamorphosis' appears as that same act of literary metempsychosis, the translation of poetry.

In translating poetry you are either 'transfus'd' by the soul of your original or you are nowhere. In achieving this metamorphosis, our major translators recover, carry over and transform the energies of past civilisation. By translating poetry I do not mean the merely journeyman efforts, such as what passes for Sophocles (say) in the oft-reprinted Penguin of *The Theban Plays*. I mean translation at the level of artefact. It will have differing degrees of fidelity to the original, but it must be achieved art. My own measure is not Watling's Sophocles, but (among others) Gavin Douglas, Chapman, Dryden,

---

1 *Of Dramatic Poesy and Other Critical Essays*, ed. George Watson (Everyman, London, 1962), vol. II, p. 111.
2 *The Poems of John Dryden*, ed. James Kinsley (Oxford University Press, 1958), vol. IV, p. 1457.

Pope, Pound, as I have tried to show elsewhere, in my *Oxford Book of Verse in English Translation*.

For the great translation – and in what other form would one prefer to read a version of a major work? – is as rare and commanding as the great poem. To illustrate my measure one has only to place side by side, say, Dryden and Lattimore. Here is Dryden – from *Iliad*, Book I – Dryden, our greatest verse translator, as he describes the sacrifice to Apollo and the ensuing feast:

> Then turning back, the Sacrifice they sped:
> The fatted Oxen slew, and flea'd the Dead:
> Chop'd off their nervous Thighs, and next prepar'd
> T'involve the lean in Cauls, and mend with Lard.
> Sweat-bread and Collops were with Skewers prick'd
> About the Sides; imbibing what they deck'd [...]
> Now when the rage of Eating was repell'd,
> The boys with generous wine the Goblets fill'd.
> The first Libations to the Gods they pour:
> And then with Songs indulge the Genial Hour.
> Holy Debauch! Till Day to Night they bring,
> With Hymns and Paeans to the Bowyer King.
> At Sun-set to their Ship they make return,
> And snore secure on Decks, till rosy Morn.
>
> (I, lines 627–32, 643–50)

Here is Lattimore in the climax of this same passage. He certainly lays out for our inspection every word that is there in the Greek, but does he achieve metempsychosis?

> Then after they had finished the work and got the feast ready
> they feasted, nor was any man's hunger denied fair portion.
> But when they had put away their desire for eating and drinking,
> the young men filled the mixing bowls with pure wine, passing
> a portion to all, when they had offered drink in the goblets.
> All day long they propitiated the god with singing,
> chanting a splendid hymn [...]
> Afterwards when the sun went down and darkness came onward
> they lay down and slept beside the ship's stern cables.

In exploring the theme of that dialogue with former ages a poet is drawn into when he confronts a text from the past, I also want to reflect on the relation between the man and the moment and the way a translator's recovery of the past can stand alongside the central artistic effort of his time, and thus alongside his own best work. This theme will allow me to consider briefly Pound's sequence *Cathay*, his free versions of traditional Chinese poems, and its relation to Vorticism, a movement mainly of the visual arts in London in the years immediately preceding and during the First World War, with its highpoints in the paintings of Wyndham Lewis, the sculpture of Henri Gaudier Brzeska, and Pound's own *Cathay* versions. The Pound we shall meet here is a different Pound from the wrecked Odysseus of the later cantos, yet the period – that of the First World War – is already creating the disillusion whose consequence will inevitably entail that wreckage. Why, at the moment of Vorticism, a work of translation should parallel the efforts of painting and sculpture is something I shall also wish to consider. Furthermore, the phase of Vorticism was a critical moment for London as a cultural centre and there is a tragic postscript to any history of that phase, a postscript which involves both the city and the fate of Ezra Pound. So the direction of my argument will be from a general consideration of the poet as translator to a particular consideration of Pound's metamorphosis and use of Chinese poetry in the London of 1913 to 1915.

I want, to begin with, to range over the subject of the translation of poetry and its link with the major work of certain authors. A first measure of this relation is the sheer degree of imaginative scope and effort it takes to recover a past work in another tongue – or, indeed, at the practical level, a past or *present* work in another tongue. For the practical level is where the translator must start and the first experience he undergoes here in confronting his text is that it immediately falls apart, Greek or Russian polysyllables becoming English monosyllables, rhymes losing their identities, phrases going halt that a moment since (as Collins says) 'in braided dance their numbers join'd'. The first experience on the practical level of the translator – whether of long past or of present texts – is not so much one of metamorphosis as of disintegration. He might, as he grapples with his chosen work, feel that Dante's voice were addressing precisely *him*, when in the *Convivio*, the poet announces that 'nothing which hath the harmony of musical connection can be transferred from its own tongue to another without shattering all its sweetness and harmony'.[1] However, in making that imaginative effort required if the translated poem is to find its true metamorphosis – 'transfus'd', that is, into the body of an *English* poem – the translator might gain courage from

1 *The Convivio* (Temple Classics, 1943), p. 34.

another voice, that of Sir John Denham in the Preface to his translation of Virgil, *The Destruction of Troy* of 1656.[1] Denham long ago realised what scholarly opinion has been slow to grant, namely that it is not

> [the translator's] business alone to translate Language into Language, but Poesie into Poesie; and Poesie is of so subtile a spirit, that in pouring out of one Language into another, it will all evaporate; and if a new spirit be not added in the transfusion, there will remain nothing but a Caput mortuum, there being certain Graces and Happinesses peculiar to every Language, which gives life and energy to the words.

Denham knows that the imagination must find and use these 'certain Graces and Happinesses' in doing its work for the translator. In opposing the 'word for word' type of translation – what he calls Verbal Translation – he sees, with wit and clarity, what Verbal Translation must entail, whether you write as an 'expert in the field' or not: 'whosoever offers at Verbal Translation', he says, 'shall have the misfortune of that young Traveller, who lost his own language abroad, and brought home no other instead of it; for the grace of the Latine will be lost by being turned into English words; And the grace of the English by being turned into the Latine Phrase.' Our supposed translator – if he is any good – will find encouragement in Denham, because Denham grants the imagination its necessary dues when faced by that disintegrating foreign text. If he hasn't poetic imagination – if he knows in his heart that he cannot translate 'Poesie into Poesie', however deft he thought himself at translating 'Language into Language' – he may yet have the good sense to turn back before he ventures into this world of shifting shapes and changing identities. Because it will not be long before he realises that it is *his* shape and *his* identity which are being called into question. The words of T.S. Eliot, speaking of Pound's translations, might give our translator a final directive nudge one way or the other: 'Good translation', says Eliot, 'is not merely translation, for the translator is giving the original through himself, and finding himself through the original.'[2]

'Poesie into Poesie'. Denham's words seem to be an echo of George Chapman defending his own translation of *The Iliad* earlier in

---

1 In T.R. Steiner, *English Translation Theory 1650–1800* (Van Gorcum, The Netherlands, 1975), pp. 64–5.

2 'Introduction' to Ezra Pound, *Selected Poems* (Faber, London, 1948), p. 13.

the century: 'With Poesie to open Poesie'. Chapman brings me to my first example of the imaginative effort involved when a major talent undertakes to translate a major work from the past. What stood between Chapman and Homer? The short answer is centuries. The rest of the answer is other men's efforts to understand *The Iliad*. For, as soon as commentaries came to be written on Homer, it seems as if the moralists had moved in – moralists Pope was still trying to see past in the eighteenth century. The legacy of the years and of Renaissance humanism was a poem where nobility was the keynote, where Achilles before all things was noble and not – as we should now admit – massively self-misguided, and where the diction of the poem must be adjusted to these preconceptions. Chapman's *Seven Books of the Iliades* of 1598 passively followed such requirements; then, as he tells us, 'the first free light of my Author entered and embold- ened me' and we get ultimately the version of 1611, and for the first time we begin to distinguish the outlines of the Achilles we recognise today. To what degree Chapman, arrogant and wilful himself, achieved this feat through an act of self-discovery, perhaps not even a biographer could securely say. But it is difficult not to feel that Chapman's renewed assaults on the poem result in renewed inward- ness, a sense of self that so totally transforms Achilles in the later version and takes him, for all time, out of the hands of Homer's moralising commentators. The struggle with Achilles meant that once Chapman came to work on *The Odyssey* of 1614–15, he could much more readily rescue Odysseus from the moralisers and allegorisers, and dramatise through Odysseus' mistakes and final homecoming his own hard-won progress towards stoic virtue.

The imaginative effort shows at other levels in Chapman's *Iliad* than characterisation and that this effort does not everywhere meet with success, that it sounds *merely* effortful, stays with one as a frus- trating impression. What metre should one use in translating Homer? An English hexameter, insisted Matthew Arnold. A ballad metre, said Francis Newman. Alas, Chapman's fourteeners – presumably a desire to match Homer's hexameters with a longer line than in English blank verse – uncomfortably recall Newman's ballad metre and even Arnold's jest that it sounded like Yankee Doodle. One could hardly say that of the final version of 1611 which, together with *The Odyssey*, formed the climax of a truly immense labour. The fourteeners now read much more freely, though there still hovers about them the feeling that they are not the inevitable solution to the formal problem. Words must be found to block out those long lines and there are occasions when one senses a certain logorrhoea at work filling in the blanks. In the process of revision, Chapman will even extend 'Nine heralds' to 'Thrice-three vociferous heralds'. Yet, as Pope was to say, Chapman, despite 'fustian', must be granted that 'daring and fiery spirit that animates his Translation'. For at other times the diction, not wedded to a relentless ennobling, persuades one that an imaginative energy has passed into the metrical form and that Chapman's enjambements have become expressive – as when the old Trojan chiefs see Helen, and are forced to admire her beauty despite themselves:

> And as in well-growne woods, on trees, cold spinie Grasshoppers
> Sit chirping and send voices out that scarce can pierce our eares
> For softness and their weake faint sounds; so (talking on the
> > towre)
> Those Seniors of the people sate, who, when they saw the powre
> Of beautie in the Queene ascend, even those cold-spirited Peeres,
> Those wise and almost withered men, found this heate in their
> > yeares.
> > (III, lines 161–6)

Or again, when helmeted Hector is amused that 'the horsehaire plume' (as Chapman has it) frightens the child he is trying to pick up, he

> doft and laid aside
> His fearful Helme, that on the earth cast round about it light.
> Then tooke and kist his loving sonne and (ballancing his weight
> In dancing him) these loving vows to living Jove he usde
> And all the other bench of Gods.
> > (VI, lines 509–13)

And there follows his prayer that the child will be his equal as a warrior. 'All the other bench of Gods' is characteristic of Chapman's lively diction as are, elsewhere, 'belabouring / The loaded flowers' (which is what a numerous swarm of bees does); the sea 'spits everie way the fome'; and 'life puts out againe / Man's leavie issue'.

One sees why Dryden, exhausted by his Virgilian labours, should, in turning to Homer, have found new imaginative strength in Chapman's diction – for Chapman himself had shown a certain impatience with Virgil and declared of the latter's swarm of bees as against Homer's, on which it was modelled: 'Virgil hath nothing of his own, but only elocution; his invention, matter and form being all Homer's;

which laid by a man, that which he addeth is only the work of a woman, to netify and polish.'

Chapman laboured to produce an *Iliad* and an Achilles he could believe in – his aim 'with Poesie to open Poesie'. Without that effort his *Odyssey* and his Odysseus would have been very different achievements. As it stands, it is one of the most remarkable long poems of the Renaissance, its readableness generated by Chapman's finding, at last, the right formal solution – decasyllabic couplets, where, when he feels called on to tuck in more piety than is to be actually found in Homer, he can at any rate do so at a convincing pace.

When Keats looked into Chapman's Homer what he looked at were parts of both poems. I do not need to dwell on their impact— the story is well known. What is less well known is that on *two* occasions – this and a later one – the fundamental impetus towards further creation came to Keats from reading translations. The second occasion involved Keats' reading of another Chapman enthusiast – namely Dryden and *his* translations from Chaucer and Ovid. The exuberant masculinity of these was one lesson he learned and – a simultaneous lesson – the use of a more firmly articulated couplet than he had been capable of in *Endymion*. Keats serves me merely to emphasise the salutary relationship between translation and original work. My immediate concern now is Dryden himself.

I have already given an example of his Homer. It coincides with that last phase of his poetic life – perhaps his greatest – the fruit of which was the many translations in his *Fables* of 1699. If one's experience of Chapman's imaginative struggle as translator is of a man 'coming through', seeing not only his subject but himself more clearly, the same is true with whatever differences of Dryden. His versions of Ovid, for example, show his release once and for all from tawdry Restoration ideas about women and he becomes, in *Baucis and Philemon*, in *Ceyx and Alcyone*, in the story of Deucalion and Pyrrha from Ovid's first book, a great poet of the tenderness of married love. There is a sense of renewed intimacy in some of these late translations which signals Dryden's thankful break from his former rôle as public poet and theatrical entertainer. Perhaps most tantalising of all is his first book of the *Iliad*, written when he had turned aside from Virgil admitting 'the Grecian is more according to my genius than the Latin poet'. This first book promises our greatest Homer so far. Had he lived and gone on, as he intended, to complete the poem, presumably Pope's great but often Virgilian version would never have been written. The spirit of Chapman would have 'transfus'd' the body of a new Homer in the first book of which the formal rightness of the heroic couplet canalises and refines that vigour Dryden admired in Chapman's own diction. Tennyson thought Dryden's first book greater than Pope's. The passage on which he takes his stand is the moment when Achilles is on the point of attacking his chief, Agamemnon, and Athena descends, seizes Achilles by the hair, and dissuades him. Tennyson instances Pope's couplet where Achilles has ceased his reply to her:

> He said, observant of the blue-eyed Maid;
> Then in the Sheath return'd the shining Blade.

'How much more real poetic force there is in Dryden', exclaims Tennyson, putting beside that this:

> He said, with surly Faith believ'd her Word
> And, in the Sheath, reluctant, plung'd the Sword.[1]

The energy, which Tennyson admired, runs all through this first book of Dryden's *Iliad* and it goes together with an energy of mind which, as in his first book of Ovid's *Metamorphoses*, can view the actions of Jove for what they so deviously are, and yet balance against Jove's amoralism a sense of his awful majesty. Yet this majesty stays immitigably pagan. It refuses to take on that weight of Christianised nobility which baulked the Renaissance attempt to see Homer whole and which still hampered Pope. Dryden's first book of *The Iliad* remains one of the great might-have-beens of literature – for once, in dealings with Homer, the imagination has thrust Virgil from the forefront of things, and has not yet capitulated before Milton's coldly noble divinity. The quarrels in the poem, both human and divine, drew their energy from all Dryden had experienced of kings and politicians, and the unmoralising drive carries with it the disabused clearness of mind that had seen through its own world without running aground on mere cynicism.

Another example of this same powerful trend – a disabusal with the public and a re-energising of the personal world – had already revealed itself in *Sylvae* of 1685, and once more the new element showed in Dryden's dealings with past literature—with the renovation of Horace: particularly in his recreation of the personal, convivial and amicable Horace of the Second Epode and some of the Odes. This renovation of Horace was, of course, a trend of the age, and

---

1   *Alfred Lord 'Tennyson: A Memoir By His Son* (1897), vol. II, p. 287.

Dryden made of that trend – the thrust of a civil war and political disappointments behind it – a sharply defined means of self-expression. I cannot linger on this aspect of Dryden, because I want to place beside his break-through via translation to a new level of meaningful discourse that of another poet and near contemporary whose example was important for Dryden – Abraham Cowley.

In the far off days when I was at Cambridge, no one told us to read Cowley. We were put on to Dr Johnson's *Life* of him in order to study 'Johnson on metaphysical poetry', and one gathered that Cowley was a second-rate metaphysical who had failed at heroic poetry but had done rather better in his elegy 'On the Death of Mr Hervey'. Some years later, I picked up a Victorian edition of his essays, and realised that, of the poems with which they were liberally sprinkled, all the best were translations – from Seneca, Martial, Virgil, Horace, Claudian. These centred on the private life and the withdrawal from the court-world. As in the later case of Dryden, Cowley's disillusionment permitted him to listen to himself and, once again, he did so not in self-absorbed lament, but by realising that other men in other ages had experienced these feelings and that in making current their words he was finding his own. This wasn't the Cowley of *The Mistress* or of the *Davideis*. Looking around for more translations by Cowley, one saw why not only the convivial Horace should have appealed to him, but the Anacreontea, where we find the image of the poet as un-public figure, dancing or drinking with his friends, his mind on the present:

> Crown me with Roses whilest I Live,
> Now your Wines and Oyntments give.
> After Death I nothing crave,
> Let me Alive my pleasures have,
> All are Stoicks in the Grave.

One should, of course, have taken to heart what Dr Johnson said in that *Life*. He rates highly the Anacreon versions and says of Cowley: 'his power seems to have been greatest in the familiar and the festive' and: 'The Anacreontiques [...] of Cowley give now all the pleasure which they ever gave.' Clearly, Cowley was on the wrong track with poems like the unfinished and unfinishable 'Davideis' and its epic pretensions: perhaps he is even guying himself when he says with Anacreon:

> I'll sing of Heroes, and of Kings;
> In mighty Numbers, mighty things,

Begin, my Muse; but lo the strings
To my great Song rebellious prove.

One of the songs that comes forth instead is the Anacreontic called
'Drinking'. Cowley does not convert this charming poem into a
Restoration toper's song, in the vein of Rochester. With something
prophetic of Dryden's cosmic imagination when the latter warms to
Ovid's vision of a teeming and miraculous universe in *Metamorphoses*,
Book I, Cowley brings to the familiar and the festive a brimming
freshness, an eager imaginative generosity. In the translation Cowley
attains a cosmic grandeur which eludes him in the theatrical heavenly
vistas of the *Davideis*:

> The thirsty Earth soaks up the Rain,
> And drinks, and gapes for drink again.
> The Plants suck in the Earth, and are
> With constant drinking fresh and fair,
> The Sea it self, which one would think
> Should have but little need of Drink,
> Drinks ten thousand Rivers up,
> So fill'd that they o'erflow the Cup.
> The busie Sun (and one would guess
> By's drunken fiery face no less)
> Drinks up the Sea, and when h'as done,
> The Moon and Stars drink up the Sun.
> They drink and dance by their own light,
> They drink and revel all the night.
> Nothing in Nature's Sober found,
> But an Eternal Health goes round.
> Fill up the Bowl then, fill it high,
> Fill all the Glasses there, for why
> Should every Creature drink but I,
> Why, Man of Morals, tell me why?

It's surely right that the translator of these lines should have produced
as his masterstroke an imitation of Horace's tale of the town and
country mouse – a poem, that is to say, which is light in tone and yet
whose lightness does not obscure the theme of being true to oneself
in accepting the common luxuries of life:

> Fitches and Beans, Peason, and Oats, and Wheat,
> And a large Chestnut, the delicious Meat
> Which Jove himself, were he a Mouse, would eat

– this being set against the restless urging of the town mouse:

Let savage Beasts lodge in a Country Den,
You should see Towns, and Manners know, and Men;
And taste the gen'rous Luxury of the Court,
Where all the Mice of Quality resort.

'The Country Mouse' seems to me Cowley's finest single poem. It is translation but with a good deal of latitude. The tale is told at far greater length than Horace's tale, yet it is the perfect example of the translation of Horace's manner into English. One might almost say this is a Horatian poem that Horace never wrote, yet one in which his spirit transfused that of an English poet and saved him from pretension and from the dispersal of his genuine self and energies. This is a major example of (in Eliot's words) 'the translator [...] giving the original through himself, and finding himself through the original'.

Civilisations tend to become ingrown and cease to hear the voices of previous eras except in their own reduced vocal range. This has been – often unjustly, I think – one of the complaints against Pope's Homer. The *Times Literary Supplement* reviewer in welcoming Lattimore's Homer – 'as crystal clear', he writes 'as a mountain stream; yet [... with] its sources in no English hills' – pauses to say of Pope's Homer that it 'was produced for educated *cognoscenti*, and merely reflected the poetic fashions of the day'. One can challenge this inane demotion of Pope by turning to a characteristic passage – say the attack on Achilles by the River Scamander, with all those kinetic verbs, all those hurryings forward across the couplets that so energetically fulfil Pope's stated aim: 'to keep alive that spirit and fire which makes [Homer's] chief character':

Now bursting on his Head with thund'ring Sound,
The falling Deluge whelms the Hero round:
His loaded Shield bends to the rushing Tide;
His Feet, upborn, scarce the strong Flood divide,
Slidd'ring, and stagg'ring. On the Border stood
A spreading Elm, that overhung the Flood;
He seiz'd a bending Bough, his Steps to stay;
The Plant uprooted to his Weight gave way,
Heaving the Bank, and undermining all;
Loud flash the Waters to the rushing Fall
Of the thick Foliage. The large Trunk display'd
Bridg'd the rough Flood across: The Hero stay'd

On this his Weight, and rais'd upon his Hand,
Leap'd from the Chanel, and regain'd the Land.
Then blacken'd the wild Waves; the Murmur rose,
The God pursues, a huger Billow throws,
And bursts the Bank, ambitious to destroy
The Man whose Fury is the Fate of Troy.
He, like the warlike Eagle speeds his Pace,
(Swiftest and strongest of th' aerial Race)
Far as a Spear can fly, Achilles springs
At every Bound; His clanging Armour rings:
Now here, now there, he turns on ev'ry side,
And winds his Course before the following Tide.

(XXI, lines 263–86)

When a recent theorist of translation, L.G. Kelly in his book *The True Interpreter* (Basil Blackwell, Oxford, 1979), turns for once to look at a major example of the art, all he can summon up faced with Pope's *Iliad* is: 'This is Homer in a powdered wig declaiming in a baroque theatre.' Pope, one must begin by admitting, had trouble with the simplicities of Homer and some of the 'lower' vocabulary, since his own diction is often extremely elevated and not easy to descend from. The kind of difficulty shows in a letter from one of his collaborators, Fenton, to his other collaborator, Broome – the *Odyssey*, unlike the *Iliad* which was all Pope's work, being shared out among the three of them. Fenton is worried at the prospect of Book XX of the *Odyssey*, where all sorts of low words occur. He writes despondently: 'How shall I get over the bitch and her puppies, the roasting of the black puddings […] and the cowheel that was thrown at Ulysses' head, I know not.' In the event, Fenton made the bitch into a 'mother-mastiff', the black puddings into 'sav'ry cates' and the cow-heel became 'That sinewy fragment […] / Where to the pastern-bone by nerves combin'd / The well-horn'd foot indissolubly join'd.' But Fenton was not the happiest of Pope's collaborators, being capable of couplets like:

Rolling convulsive on the floor is seen
The piteous object of a prostrate Queen.

Pope works at a different level from that. His *Iliad* is one of the great translations and so, more fragmentarily, is the *Odyssey*. We are still being told, this time by a contemporary English poet, Norman Nicholson, in his selection of Cowper's poems, that Pope reduces

Homer to porcelain and cameos.[1] When Pope in part fails, as in a
sometimes unwieldy diction or his creation of a Jupiter who stands
too close to Milton's God in *Paradise Lost* for comfort, his failure is
on a more august level than that of producing cameos. His successes
are magnificent and unparalleled – among them at times (and this
surprisingly) an unexpected fidelity, which resembles Pound's, to the
irreducibly foreign and distant. Unlike Pound, Pope did not always
find it easy to allow this to show through, and one of the incidental
dramas of his Homer occurs in the way his notes are often at vari-
ance with his text. Frequently the notes register something which is
palpably there in Homer, yet has to be smoothed over, made a little
more abstract in Pope's poem in order to satisfy Augustan and
Virgilian notions of high seriousness. Yet this is not always so. And
sometimes Pope succeeds where you might least expect it – in his
awareness of Greek barbarity, an awareness that over a century later
seems to have eluded Matthew Arnold in his 'On Translating Homer'.
What eluded Arnold and what Pope could see had to be recovered;
and it was recovered, not by nineteenth-century British Hellenism,
but in Germany and by Nietzsche. Pope perhaps would have recognised what Nietzsche meant when he spoke of 'the contradictions
inherent in the Homeric world, so marvellous on the one hand, so
ghastly and brutal on the other'. For Pope has a footnote of his own
– these notes are another brilliant aspect of his translation – in which
he mocks the idealising of the Greeks by Madame D'Acier, an earlier
French translator and commentator. The Greeks, Pope points out,
were in the habit of slaughtering all enemy males and transporting
their females into slavery. An example I want to quote from Pope
comes not in the *Iliad* but from Book XXII of the *Odyssey*, one of the
books where Pope himself was in sole charge. This passage describes
the punishment of Penelope's faithless women-servants and of
Melanthius, who had previously insulted the disguised Ulysses. The
relentless march of the couplets here – and on other occasions Pope
can attune his couplets to tenderness or to a biblical nobility of phrase
– the snap of the rhymes, the refusal to be diverted into moralising
comment, that favourite device of the Renaissance and Augustan
translator, all these result in a verse that catches the unfeeling
barbarity of the episode, verse at a far remove from those Ovidian
graces with which Pope sometimes softens Homer's style. The
speaker in this passage is Ulysses' son, Telemachus. He reflects on

1   *A Choice of William Cowper's Verse* (Faber, London, 1975).

how the women-servants, who have lain with Penelope's suitors,
should be executed:

> Then thus the Prince. To these shall we afford
> A fate so pure, as by the martial sword?
> To these, the nightly prostitutes to shame,
> And base revilers of our house and name?
>   Thus speaking, on the circling wall he strung
> A ship's tough cable, from a column hung;
> Near the high top he strain'd it strongly round,
> Whence no contending foot could reach the ground.
> Their heads above, connected in a row,
> They beat the air with quiv'ring feet below;
> Thus on some tree hung struggling in the snare,
> The doves or thrushes flap their wings in air.
> Soon fled the soul impure, and left behind
> The empty corse to waver with the wind.
>   Then forth they led Melanthius, and began
> Their bloody work: They lopp'd away the man,
> Morsel for dogs! then trimm'd with brazen shears
> The wretch, and shorten'd of his nose and ears;
> His hands and feet last felt the cruel steel:
> He roar'd, and torments gave his soul to hell –
>   They wash, and to Ulysses take their way;
> So ends the bloody business of the day

(XXII, lines 495–516)

William Cowper, tackling that same passage some sixty years later, in
a version of the *Odyssey* which is often powerfully translated, allows
the edge to be taken off the blatant barbarity there by giving the
episode a kind of Miltonic lift, the gust of his cadence carrying with
it a movement that is half righteous indignation, half shocked sensibility, quite foreign to Homer and to Pope's hold there on the ghastly
and the brutal.

One does not, of course, undertake translation merely to show how
different other cultures are, or to give barbarism an airing. The eighteenth century found Horace so appealing because of the degree of
poetic civilisation he represented – a fineness of balance, insight and
wit that they felt to be recoverable and necessary in a civilisation like
that of eighteenth-century England with its own daily barbarities
which needed tempering. This desire to transmit the strengths of
another literary civilisation is something one experiences right

through the history of translation. It shows the historic instinct of translators as they operate in a given civilisation and at a given time.

Translation requires, then, basically two things – the man and the moment: a man like Ezra Pound, for example, and a moment like the year 1913 when the widow of Ernest Fenollosa sent Pound her deceased husband's notebooks, containing very literal translations from Chinese and Japanese. What translation has too often implied, instead of the marvellously right choice of the intelligent Mary Fenollosa, who herself spotted Pound because of a group of his poems in *Poetry* magazine, is that someone is commissioned by Penguin Books to translate (say) Sophocles, someone who has never written a line of verse in his life. The verse of Pound's *Cathay*, published in 1915, translates 'Poesie into Poesie' and in a way in which Chinese poetry had never before been rendered into English. As in Pound's 'Lament of the Frontier Guard':

> By the North Gate, the wind blows full of sand,
> Lonely from the beginning of time until now!
> Trees fall, the grass goes yellow with autumn.
> I climb the towers and towers
>   to watch out the barbarous land:
> Desolate castle, the sky, the wide desert.
> There is no wall left to this village.
> Bones white with a thousand frosts
> High heaps, covered with trees and grass;
> Who brought this to pass?
> Who has brought the flaming imperial anger?
> Who has brought the army with drums and kettle-drums?
> Barbarous kings.
> A gracious spring, turned to blood-ravenous autumn,
> A turmoil of wars-men, spread over the middle kingdom,
> Three hundred and sixty thousand,
> And sorrow, sorrow like rain.
> Sorrow to go, and sorrow, sorrow returning.
> Desolate, desolate fields,
> And no children of warfare upon them,
>   No longer the men of offence and defence.
> Ah, how shall you know the dreary sorrow at the North Gate,
> With Rihaku's name forgotten,
> And we guardsmen fed to the tigers.

One measures that as poetry and not for its suitability as a crib to the works of Li Po. For that purpose it is hardly usable, though Arthur Waley, who also translated Li Po and rather disapproved of Pound's attempt, was not above stealing a line here and there to grace his supposedly more literal rendering. What Waley lacks is the finesse of that ear which, with Pound, was 'so close to the mind it [*was*] the mind's, that it [had] the mind's speed', in Charles Olson's phrase.[1]

In his study *Ezra Pound's Cathay*,[2] Wai-lim Yip tellingly places side by side with Waley the poignant line from Pound's version of Li Po's 'The River Merchant's Wife': 'Called to a thousand times, I never looked back'. Waley dents that, so to speak, to make it look like all his own work; he writes:

Called to, a thousand times, I did not turn.

The same poem, in Pound, opens with the woman saying: 'While my hair was still cut straight across my forehead'. Wai-lim Yip shows us Waley muffing this clear line about the girl's fringe with: 'Soon after I wore my hair covering my forehead'.

The surprising thing about Pound is that, at the stage of *Cathay*, knowing no Chinese, prompted only by the notes of Ernest Fenollosa, faced by a poetry without articles before its nouns, without cases, genders, tenses, he should have intuited so much about the nature of Chinese and primarily its use of the single line placed dramatically against the next single line, an effect that Waley's translations with their busy syntax sometimes tend to cancel out. It is Pound's sense of the effect of the line unit that puts him, with *Cathay*, into that select band of translator-poets whose work – and here I revert to a theme I have already glanced at – re-incorporates a past civilisation into the central artistic effort of their time. Let me illustrate, with one of the briefer *Cathay* poems, this *paratactic* – one thing placed *beside* another – as distinct from *syntactic* drama – one thing fluently *linked* to another. There is the tiny poem, Li Po's 'The Jewel Stair's Grievance', one of those many traditional poems of disappointed love:

The jewelled steps are already wet with dew,
It is so late that the dew soaks my gauze stockings,
And I let down the crystal curtain
And I watch the moon through the clear autumn.

1 Charles Olson, *Projective Verse* (Totem Press, 1959), p. 5.
2 Wai-lim Yip, *Ezra Pound's Cathay* (Princeton University Press, New Jersey, 1969), p. 89.

How often, in *Cathay*, as in poems like this, one feels that Pound's mastery comes from the way he handles the single line unit (as Waley rarely could) and the inevitability of cadence he can bring to it: there is 'Lament of the Frontier Guard' with its:

A gracious spring, turned to blood-ravenous autumn

or (in the same poem):

I climb the towers and towers
   to watch out the barbarous land

or in 'South-Folk in Cold Country', where the single line is broken down into montage:

Surprised. Desert turmoil. Sea sun.

Or again in the same poem, the montage of the two neighbouring lines:

Flying snow bewilders the barbarian heaven.
Lice swarm like ants over our accoutrements.

Donald Davie, in *Ezra Pound, Poet as Sculptor* (Routledge and Kegan Paul, London, 1964), was surely the first critic to see what was at work in instances like these when he writes:

The poem establishes a convention by which the gauge of a poetic line is not the number of syllables or of stressed syllables or of metrical feet, but the fulfilment of the simple grammatical unit, the sentence.

I began by referring to the man and the moment. Here we have the man *making* the moment, the moment and also the future. For, from Pound's moment of discovery, the writer's attention is to continue to rest on the line as poetic unit – as in William Carlos Williams, in George Oppen and in the Black Mountain poets. As Davie proceeds to say: 'It was only when the line was considered as the unit of composition, as it was by Pound in *Cathay*, that there emerged the possibility of "breaking" the line, of disrupting it from within, by throwing weight upon the smaller units within the line.' One of the examples he gives is from the poem 'The Bowmen of Shu' – that superbly fractured line:

Horses, his horses even, are tired. They were strong.

In the rhythmical pauses of that line, any mere purposes of

translation as crib have been surpassed: that line contains the rhythmic direction of much later poetry – by Pound and by others. Davie points us back to as early as 1913 where, in 'Provincia Deserta', Pound was already fracturing the line into an architecture of rhythmic pauses:

> At Rochecoart,
> Where the hills part
>   in three ways,
> And three valleys, full of winding roads,
> Fork out to south and north
> There is a place of trees … grey with lichen.

That is Pound in 1913. Here is Williams thirty years later in the poem that came to be called 'The Descent', building on discoveries Pound had made available earlier in the century:

> The descent beckons
>   as the ascent beckoned.
>   Memory is a kind
> of accomplishment,
>   a sort of renewal
>   even
> an initiation.

Now W.C. Williams, like his friend Pound, had learned much that he could convert to poetic usage from the Vorticist group in which Pound was active. Although Williams was not in London at the time, he read the Vorticist periodical *Blast*. In the second issue, the sculptor Gaudier Brzeska wrote a manifesto in which he spoke of deriving his emotions as sculptor from the arrangement of surfaces, from the lines and planes defining surfaces. In a fascinating unpublished essay of 1915 called 'Vortex – W.C.W.' Williams translates the terms of Gaudier's manifesto into the terms of a poetry where the word 'plane' is used to reinforce Williams' idea of a poetry of line pulling against line, a poetry where the sense of physical resistance is paramount, where words and groups of words make up the resistant facets of a poem – a terminology obviously opposed to the impressionistic drift of contemporary free verse in writers like Amy Lowell.

By 1913, Pound, in fragmenting the line into rhythmic components, was beginning that shift of emphasis to the weight and duration of each syllable, what Davie speaks of as 'the reconstituting of the verse line as the poetic unit, slowing down the surge from one line into the next in such a way that smaller components within the line (down to the very syllables) can recover weight and value'.

When, in 1913, Mrs Fenollosa sent Pound her husband's notes, what time and again must have sprung to Pound's attention was the way Chinese poetry is a poetry where the line unit is the unit of attention – line on line, with clear components but seldom enjambing with the next line. So translation in *Cathay* became for Pound an exploration into the possibilities of extending his *own* poetry: he was not just doing a job (like the Penguin translator of Sophocles' *Theban Plays*); he was growing as a poet, he was extending that emotional concentration he was already seeking for in heaving against the Edwardian idiom, against the fluent slackness of much then-contemporary verse.

Pound had, in fact, begun this redirection before Mary Fenollosa sent him her husband's notebooks. He had begun it with Oriental models in mind. Like Fenollosa, he came to Chinese via Japanese. What had initially interested him was the compactness of Japanese haiku – those little three-line poems. Already by 1913, he had condensed (after six months' work) a much longer poem into the haiku-like brevity of the famous 'In a Station of the Metro':

> The apparition   of these faces   in the crowd:
> Petals   on a wet, black bough.

He had noted there the way in haiku the insight often presents itself as an isolated image, not just a simile introduced by the word 'like', but by the paratactic alignment with the initial experience of the poem: one thing held over against another, divided and yet united by the electric spark which flies between them.

This basic insight is what distinguishes Pound's orientalising from that of sinologists like H.A. Giles or from a lot of Arthur Waley: it is what allies the man and the moment. As I have pointed out earlier, the moment of Pound's *Cathay* was the moment of the Vorticist movement, the moment when, in England, the machine, cubism and (among other things) the Japanese print had produced unexpected consequences. Japan was in the air from Gilbert and Sullivan's *Mikado* of 1884 to Puccini's *Madame Butterfly* of 1904, from the *japonerie* of Whistler's paintings to the prints painted in the background of a dozen Van Goghs. The Japanese, in fact, were also opening themselves to the west: hence Fenollosa's presence in Tokyo, an American from Harvard who went as Professor of Philosophy in 1878 and stayed on to become Imperial Commissioner of Fine Arts. Pound, speaking of the new insights he had gained via Vorticist art in *The Egoist* in June 1914, wrote:

> I trust the gentle reader is accustomed to take pleasure in 'Whistler and the Japanese'.
>
> From Whistler and the Japanese, or Chinese, the 'world', that is to say, the fragment of the English-speaking world which spreads itself in print, learned to enjoy 'arrangements' of colours and masses.

So much for Pound.

Europe's greatest debt to the Japanese print – cheap, and long collected by artists – was this lesson of formal disposition, this tendency to abstract forms, the arrangement (as Pound says) of colours and masses. One sees why Pound should have considered himself a Vorticist, for there is surely a parallel between Pound's poetry, drawing attention to its own linearity, and to its segmenting of that linearity into lengths meant to be *clearly heard*, and a visual art of colours and masses in arrangement, reacting (like Pound) against vagueness, and using sharp line, facet and plane meant to be *clearly seen* and not dissolved away into *sfumato*, into the mists and twilights of *symbolisme*. 'These new men', says Pound in his book on Gaudier,

> have made me see form, have made me more conscious of the appearance of the sky where it juts down between houses, of the bright pattern of sunlight which the bath water throws upon the ceiling, of the great 'V's' of light that dart through the chinks over the curtain rings, all these are new chords, new keys of design.

Vorticism itself, having learned from the very faceted, very planar art of Cézanne, was (like early cubism) a movement of translation – translation from Oriental art and from so-called primitive art. Somewhat like Pound in *Cathay*, the artists translated 'without knowing the language' – they wanted the simplified, dynamic forms for their own purposes, regardless of the *tribal* meanings or functions of (say) African fetishes. The pre-war years, in London and Paris, were, like the Renaissance, one of the great phases of cultural translation, of metamorphosis in the widest sense. The artists of the Renaissance wanted to live with the forms of classical antiquity. The artists of 1912 wanted to live with the forms of China, Japan, Africa and the South Sea Islands. As Gaudier Brzeska headily writes in *Blast* for June 1914:

The knowledge of our civilisation embraces the world [...] We have been influenced by what we liked most, each according to his own individuality, we have crystallised the sphere into the cube, we have made a combination of all the possible shaped masses.

Anyone who visited the Vorticist show in London in the spring and summer of 1974 at the Hayward Gallery must have realised that, as Pound saw it, London *was*, for a phase, a vortex, drawing energies into itself, and re-using them – hence Pound's label for the movement. A vortex for Pound meant a cone of energy, a whirling force attracting outside energies to itself. London, thought Pound, could be another Rome, 'a vortex drawing strength from the peripheries'. Wyndham Lewis wrote: 'We will convert the king if possible. A VORTICIST KING! WHY NOT?' Here in London existed the most far-reaching single art movement that, with the exception of pre-Raphaelitism, Britain has ever known, but it was to be tragically foreshortened by the war. Its members were scattered. Gaudier was killed, Lewis went away to the front and his principal Vorticist canvases – fifteen or more very large paintings – were lost or destroyed. No London dealer took up the Vorticists as Vollard and Kahnweiler took up the cubists in Paris. By the 1920s the movement was forgotten and the Bloomsbury set, in the shape of Roger Fry and Clive Bell, prevailed as arbiters of taste. In 1937 Lewis characterised himself and his contemporaries as 'the men of 1914', 'the men of a Future that has not materialised'.

The wave of energy throughout Europe and England, which made men like Pound believe they were living in a new Renaissance, was spent in England by the First World War. It had its renewals in Paris. It reached Russia (until group antagonisms and political suppression ended it there) in the work of Malevitch, Popova, Kliun, Tatlin and the constructivists: El Lissitsky, another masterly artist, was inspired by the typography and illustrations of Lewis' magazine, *Blast*. The Revolution extended for a while in Russia what the war and Bloomsbury sapped in England. Gaudier dead; Lewis impoverished; forgotten as a painter, since, for ten years, from 1921 onwards, he never exhibited; Pound demoralised and, like D.H. Lawrence, abandoning the England on which he had centred his hopes for a new age; Pound in Italy swallowing Mussolini whole. These were the sad facts of the twenties.

Cathay already had preluded a tragic atmosphere beyond and above the exciting rhetoric of the Vorticist manifestos. The man was a great translator. The moment was of an era of cultural translation – from Japanese, Chinese and from Easter Island forms. It was also the moment of the assassination of the Austrian archduke at Sarajevo. These *Cathay* poems of departures and battles were being worked on in 1914, the first year of the war. When Gaudier received the book in 1915 he was in the trenches. He wrote back to Mrs Shakespear:

> I use [the book] to put courage into my fellows. I speak now of the 'Bowmen' and [... 'Lament of the Frontier Guard'] which are so appropriate to our case.
> (Ezra Pound, *Gaudier Brzeska* (New Directions, 1970) p. 68)

Pound admired the implicitness of Chinese poetry – as he shows in his note to 'The Jewel Stairs' – and there is an implicit relation between these translations and the war itself. Hugh Kenner in his book *The Pound Era* (p. 202) has brilliantly pointed out the way in which this admiration of implicitness is made over into the implicitness of the translation. Kenner praises *Cathay* for bringing the past abreast of the present – the present being the First World War:

> *Cathay* is largely a war-book using Fenollosa's [cribs] much as Pope used Horace or Johnson Juvenal, to supply a system of parallels and a structure of discourse [...] Perfectly vital after half a century, they are among the most durable of all poetic responses to World War I.

Kenner's apposite and moving sentences celebrate a moment when poems from a remote age were suddenly metamorphosed into poems of present consequence, when the recoverable past renewed itself at a time of tragedy and of European chaos. It is an old story – and takes us back by way of epilogue to one of Pound's acknowledged forebears, also the witness of a disordered time – Gavin Douglas and his Virgil. Greater than the original, according to Pound. Certainly a translation capturing, as none other does, that sense of instability and threat to civilised values that gives an undertow to Virgil's cadences. Again, it is a story of the man and the moment – a time of imminent disorders and daily insecurities culminating in the battle of Flodden in 1513 and the destruction of Scotland's youth. It was in that very year, 1513, that Douglas completed his *Aeneid* – a year whose train of disasters involved not only the spirit of that undertaking, but his ultimate exile and death. The story is too long to be told here, but once again it is one where the tensions and energies of an age found expres-

sion in an effort of poetic recovery – a literary metempsychosis of
Virgil in Renaissance Scotland – and where a translation stood in the
forefront of the creative works of its era, much as Pound's *Cathay* to
the twentieth century, and Dryden's major translations and Pope's to
their respective ages.

Sources

'The Presence of Translation: a View of English Poetry', published in Rosanna Warren (ed.), *The Art of Translation: voices from the field* (Boston: North Eastern University Press), 1989

'The Poet as Translator', introduction to *The Oxford Book of Verse in English Translation* (Oxford: Oxford University Press),1980

'Classical Verse Translated', a review of Adrian Poole and Jeremy Maule (eds), *The Oxford Book of Classical Verse in Translation*, in *Arion* (third series, 4:2), Fall 1996

'The New Oxford Book of Sixteenth-Century Verse', a review formerly entitled (though not by me) 'Doggerel and Mushrumps' of Emrys Jones (ed.), *The New Oxford Book of Sixteenth-Century Verse*, in *The Independent*, 29 June 1999

'Some Aspects of Horace in the Twentieth Century', in Charles Martindale and David Hopkins (eds), *Horace Made New* (Cambridge: Cambridge University Press), 1993

'Martial in English', a review of D.R. Shackleton Bailey (trans. and ed.), *Martial Epigrams*, in *The New Criterion* (13:3), November 1994

'Why Dryden's Translations Matter', in Stuart Gillespie (ed.), *John Dryden, Classicist and Translator, Translation and Literature* (10, part 1), 2001

'Shelley and Translation', a review formerly entitled 'The Poet as Translator' of Timothy Webb, *The Violet in the Crucible: Shelley and Translation*, in the *Times Literary Supplement*, 22 April 1977

Poetry and Metamorphosis (Cambridge: Cambridge University Press), 1983

Index